What Matters Most

Selected pieces

by

Chris Woodhead

What Matters Most

Selected pieces

by

Chris Woodhead

Edited by

Christine Woodhead

The University of Buckingham Press

Published in 2017 by

The University of Buckingham Press

Yeomanry House

Hunter Street

Buckingham MK18 1EG

A CIP catalogue record for this book is available at the British Library

ISBN 978-1-908684-82-0

Printed and bound in Great Britain by
Marston Book Services Ltd, Oxfordshire

Acknowledgements

I am grateful to Judy Corbett and Peter Welford for encouraging me to produce this book and for their ever helpful comments, and to John Clare for his guidance and editorial suggestions. I would also like to thank my publisher at the University of Buckingham, Christopher Woodhead (no relation), who got to know Chris during his time at the university as they good-humouredly unravelled the inevitable mix-ups over post and emails.

Contents

Foreword

Blessed with a powerful intellect and bracingly contemptuous of orthodoxies, Chris Woodhead was exhilarating company. Emperors, in his view, were usually naked and the boat always needed rocking, nowhere more vigorously than in the world of education.

His wider world view was essentially mystical. 'The meaning and significance of literature, art, music, religion and the murkiness of one's existence eludes us' he once wrote, 'and that is the fascination of our existence.'

Underpinning that fascination was a strong aesthetic sense that drew him to the beauty of landscapes, of paintings (invariably landscapes shading into abstraction) and of his elegantly furnished homes. 'The love of beauty,' he said, 'makes life for many of us worth living.' 'Too easy' was always his most damning criticism; difficulty was what mattered, whether in art, literature or an apparently unclimbable rock face. 'Patience and hard work are essential if we are to engage with and understand the richness of the world in which we live,' he insisted.

Unsurprisingly then, the cardinal virtues for Chris were courage and fortitude, and he had them both in spades: the courage of his convictions in the often fanatically hostile world of education politics, and the fortitude to bear the onslaught of Motor Neurone Disease. As his audience knew, Chris didn't 'do' self-pity. Lost on none of them, however, was the truly cruel irony of a man who had always prided himself on his physical fitness, a cross-country runner and lifelong rock climber, being struck down by a disease that left his mind clear but his body wasted. 'MND,' he noted, 'is not much fun.' His fearlessness in dealing with it, illustrated in some of the pieces here, makes for harrowing reading; the more harrowing when one realises that they were dictated to his wife, Christine, in lucid, immaculately punctuated sentences, as he lay inert in a wheelchair.

As Chris always acknowledged, his last ten years would not have been possible without Christine, who has compiled this book. In a tribute to her astonishing devotion, he wrote in one of his blogs: 'There are saints in this world, and I am lucky enough to be married to one.'

Much, but not all, of *What Matters Most* is about schools, a subject on which some would say Chris was out of joint with his times. If so, it was an affliction shared by very many of his readers in *The Sunday Times* (and by very many of mine in *The Daily Telegraph*). He was unconvinced by comprehensive education, firmly believed in a system tailored to children's differing abilities and aptitudes (as envisaged by the 1944 Education Act) and wholly committed to academic selection, recalling time and again his own grammar schooling in the late 1950s and early 1960s. 'Children', he observed trenchantly, 'are not equally intelligent and some are not very intelligent at all; why pretend otherwise?'

The drive by politicians and education bureaucrats to blur, and even deny, those differing abilities and aptitudes had, he increasingly believed, corrupted education from the mid-1960s onwards, leading to debased standards, pseudo subjects, dubious qualifications and, worst of all, a 'child-centred' ideology that glorified 'relevance' and 'accessibility' and required teachers to become 'facilitators of learning' instead of authoritative dispensers of knowledge.

Supposedly egalitarian policies had betrayed generations of children by failing to stimulate the most academically able or meet the needs of the vocationally inclined; the introduction of comprehensive education had damaged the life chances of the very children it was meant to help. The challenge now was not grammar schools for all, a fantasy first peddled by Harold Wilson in the early 1960s, but the reinvention of secondary modern schools, the post-war alternative for the less academically able, as centres of vocational excellence.

Chris's disillusion set in during the late 1990s while he was Her Majesty's Chief Inspector of Schools. Having spent, he said, 30 years trying to improve state education, he could see from his ringside seat no real progress, only 'the gap between human hope and the intransigent reality of the world in which we live.' After resigning as head of Ofsted in 2000, he set about describing the causes of his despair in two angry books, *Class War* (2002) and *A Desolation of Learning* (2009).

But he had not abandoned his commitment to reform. He became chairman of Cognita, responsible for running a chain of private schools, from which vantage point, as befitted a radical libertarian, he proposed a complete freeing of the system. 'Politicians and bureaucrats', he said, 'should keep out of education and allow market forces and parental choice to flourish in the state sector as they do in the world of private education.' The mechanism would be vouchers, each worth the cost of educating a child in a state school. Parents would be free to spend theirs in either a state or private school; if the latter, they would be allowed to top it up with their own money.

Although these things were the bread and butter of my relationship with Chris over many years, they were not what mattered most. It was his lifetime's reading, the coherence of his literary tastes, his familiarity with the entire canon of the English literary tradition ranged along his shelves; that was what made him who he was. He traced the beginnings of it to a summer's day in 1963, when, not quite 17, he found in *Wuthering Heights* 'a world of volcanic passion in which human beings were caught in the inescapable hand of fate'. Books, he realised, 'furnished not just a room but a life'. The following year he came across John Cowper Powys's *Wolf Solent*, a seminal discovery movingly celebrated in this book. Later highlights included D H Lawrence, Iris Murdoch and the poet Geoffrey Hill.

In his last essay, published posthumously, Chris described the exaltation of finally, at the third attempt, reaching the top of Ladhar Bheinn, a mountain on the Knoydart peninsula that looks across the Sound of Sleat to Skye. He wrote: 'Then, one day, everything went right, and I shall never forget walking along the summit ridge to the trig point'. I was with him that beautiful day in September 2004, as I had been on the two previous occasions, and I shall never forget it or him.

John Clare

Chris walking in the Cuillins in 2004 on one of his trips to north-west Scotland with John Clare.

Introduction

Chris Woodhead is best known as the 'controversial' Chief Inspector of Schools from 1994 to 2000. At one time a regular contributor to Radio 4's *Today* programme, his warm, calm and intelligent voice was as familiar to his listeners then as his forthright but clearly argued views were later to those who read his newspaper articles. People who were naturally suspicious of the progressive ideas of the education establishment were relieved to hear someone articulating what they felt was just common sense. From when he resigned as Chief Inspector in 2000 until his death in June 2015 at the age of 68 from cancer, exacerbated by the Motor Neurone Disease that had afflicted his last ten years, he continued to attract a loyal readership through his weekly question and answer column for *The Sunday Times*. He also wrote an education blog for that newspaper, many examples of which are included in this volume. Although his published writings are almost exclusively on the topic of education, there are also pieces here that relate to one of his other passions, literature.

I first met Chris in 1993 when he came to London as Chief Executive of the School Curriculum and Assessment Authority, and worked with him throughout his time as head of Ofsted. We married in 2006, at Gwydir Castle in the Conwy valley, a fortified manor house dating from Tudor times with wonderful gardens, lovingly restored over the last twenty years by Peter Welford and Judy Corbett, who have been close friends ever since. We, at that time, were living in north Wales in an old farmhouse, reached by a track across two fields. The diagnosis of MND came in the same year, almost same month. Eventually, when our house in Snowdonia became too difficult for a life which would continue to involve regular trips to London, we looked for somewhere a bit less remote, though we continued to get to Snowdonia whenever we could. By 2009, we had found a derelict Georgian house in Ludlow, which we restored; then when stairlifts also became impractical we moved to a converted barn in (still rural) Herefordshire, close to the Welsh border. In a radio interview a year before his death, Chris was asked whether he chose these rather remote and inaccessible places as some kind of protest against his disability. No, he was not trying to prove anything, he said, but he had never been comfortable in towns, and even as a boy growing up in south London he would escape to the countryside on his bicycle whenever he could. It was not just the countryside that was important to him; he also loved old houses and beautiful things; creating an attractive living environment was one of his pleasures. Even in the months before he died he was still buying antique furniture, still looking at property websites and still trying to persuade me that we should buy a house in France.

His other passions were music, paintings and, unsurprisingly for one who began his career as an English teacher, literature. He counted himself incredibly fortunate to have met one of his heroes, Sir Geoffrey Hill, in around 2008 ('one of the greatest blessings', as he says in the article here, 'I have been lucky enough to receive'), who became a close friend and would visit us often in Snowdonia, Ludlow and Herefordshire. Their shared characteristics and enthusiasms, for literature in particular, meant that conversations with Geoffrey enriched his life hugely. One of the lasting memorials to this friendship is that our 'stone house with the slate shimmer' in Snowdonia appears in *Oraclau* (*Broken Hierarchies*, OUP, 2013) and the 'half-Welsh hill' behind us in Herefordshire appears in a recent, as yet unpublished, poem. Sadly, since I wrote these words, Geoffrey has died, exactly one week after the anniversary of Chris's death. I last spoke to him two weeks earlier, the day before his 84th birthday. Geoffrey was a huge comfort to me after Chris died, and I shall miss him enormously.

One of their shared interests was the writer, John Cowper Powys. Neither of them had much time for Powys's poetry, but both admired *A Glastonbury Romance* and Chris had a special personal allegiance to *Wolf Solent*, which he was invited to explain to the Powys Society in 2002 where he gave the paper included here. The books he liked most he read and re-read over the years: *War and Peace* and *Anna Karenina*, *Middlemarch*, *The Portrait of a Lady*, some Iris Murdoch and John Fowles, Shakespeare's plays, T S Eliot. Browsing in second-hand bookshops was one of the many pleasures which was to be quickly lost to him once Motor Neurone, from about the autumn of 2009, forced him to use a wheelchair.

Before his illness, Chris was a fit, quick, agile and energetic man. He would wake early and leap out of bed in his drive to get on with things. As he told his radio interviewer in May 2014, 'my impatience was legendary'. So it is hard to imagine just how painful the gradual loss of mobility was, and with what stoicism and dignity he dealt with increasing dependency. Being a natural protector of those close to him, it wasn't only self-sufficiency he had to relinquish, but a deeply felt sense of responsibility.

He spoke about fortitude as 'a neglected virtue in the 21st century', but said that he had always believed that to be alive, to be a human being, is necessarily to suffer, and that Shakespeare probably had it about right in *King Lear* when he wrote 'As flies to wanton boys are we to the gods;/They kill us for their sport'. He refused to dwell on life not being 'fair', as in any case futile, but more fundamentally because he was suspicious of the sentimental obsession with 'fairness' as a symptom of our refusal to accept that some things are beyond our control. He had always wanted to believe, he said, that he had real stoicism. That he did have was reflected in the degree of resignation he showed in the face of the further illnesses, which were certainly aggravated, if not caused, by his enforced immobility. What he knew intellectually was now, in his personal situation, something that he had to practise: that continuing to focus on our feelings is not going to get us anywhere. And it is these lines of poetry that he asked to be read at his memorial service:

> *If it is without*
> *Consequence when we vaunt and suffer, or*
> *If it is not, all echoes are the same*
> *In such eternity. Then tell me, love,*
> *How that should comfort us—or anyone*
> *Dragged half-unnerved out of this worldly place,*
> *Crying to the end 'I have not finished'.*

(from *Funeral Music, King Log,* Geoffrey Hill, 1968)

This rational, unsentimental view characterised Chris's approach to education, and this brought him into conflict with the mainstream of education thinking, where the leading figures had very different ideologies, believing that education should be built around the child's instincts and interests. Michael Gove, looking back on Chris's achievements, described the heart of his mission as being to cast light on genius, to enable us to see what minds far greater than ours have to tell us about our shared humanity. This was a precious inheritance, and it was one in which most of us could share if properly taught. A giftedly charismatic speaker, he could be very persuasive in explaining his ideas to teacher and headteacher audiences, and there would usually be a large measure of agreement about what he suggested as constituting good teaching and why subject knowledge continued to matter for its own sake when the world was talking only about skills and relevance. His speaking, just as his writing, was remarkable for its precision and clarity of expression. He loathed cliché, not just for stylistic reasons, but because it militates against original thinking and, therefore, authenticity. As Al Alvarez puts it in *The Writer's Voice*, 'The language of insincerity is cliché – the debased phrases and dead metaphors that come automatically, without thinking, without any personal input from the writer'. Education jargon had had similar consequences, with too many ideas being absorbed by the profession as pre-digested thinking.

The pieces here on education are from a collection of articles and blogs written over the last twenty years. A pervading theme of the blogs was grammar schools, and he based many of them on his own experience at Wallington Boys' Grammar School, which he attended from 1957 to 1964. It was not a matter of having been 'happy' at school, though I don't mean to imply that he was miserable, but that looking back he could see that here he had an example of the kind of school that developed resilience, that valued knowledge, that taught you that anything worthwhile had to be worked for. These are themes that recur in his book, *A Desolation of Learning*, published in 2009. We worked together on the research for that book, using some of our own GCE O and A level papers, covering between us 1962 to 1974, for the chapter *Dumbing Down: The Proof.*

For a couple of years in the late 1990s, Chris reviewed books for *The Sunday Telegraph*, work which he very much enjoyed and would have continued if his new contract with *The Sunday Times* had not precluded it. I have included the Kathleen Raine piece because he was intrigued by her story, and by the captivating account of it in her *Autobiographies*. He met her once, when she must have been almost 90. Later, during one of our trips to the Lakes, we sought out the house in Martindale where she had lived for a time during the war years, and we also went to Sandaig in north-west Scotland, the scene of her doomed relationship with Gavin Maxwell.

He was drawn to books by a natural intellectual curiosity, and, as comes through many of the articles here, an early interest in the power of words. He did not assume that everyone would have that interest or that education would necessarily engender it. What education could and should do is help us understand our talents and life's possibilities. And introduce us to great literature, which, as he says in his review of the Howard Bloom, *How to Read and Why,* 'can, if we read wisely, help us to know ourselves better and teach us how things are'.

Because of his well-known love of climbing and mountains, many of the books he was asked to review were about climbing or outdoor adventure. We did go one year to the Kendal mountain literature festival, but, with some exceptions, he was of the view that, whilst there is clearly a great deal of enthusiasm for reading and writing about climbing, there was not enough really good writing in this genre to justify an annual award. That said, he certainly admired Stephen Venables's writing, one of whose books is among the reviews included here.

The pieces on assisted dying were the hardest section for me to compile. I no longer want to think of his illness and, indeed, he didn't want me to think of him in that way after he died. But his views on the right of people in his predicament to have some options and to know that they have those options are important. MND, as someone wrote to me, and it is an image Chris himself used, is a terrible cage which gradually suffocates those with it. We were lucky enough to have one or two very loyal and supportive friends who had offered to go to Dignitas with him if it ever came to that. But in the end, I could not have let him go without me.

One thing I didn't know until after Chris's death was quite how much his strong leadership and willingness to take on challenges had helped, even rescued people during his career. I received some incredibly moving letters. He had told me a little about those posts he had held before I met him, but only to the extent that he had walked into some organisations where things clearly had to be changed and that that meant battles had to be fought. He never talked up the impact he made on people's lives. But there they were, telling me what a hero he was. Many tried to articulate why he had inspired such loyalty and why it was such a privilege to work for him.

John Clare, former education correspondent for The *Telegraph* and close personal friend, has written that Chris was 'a tough-minded Romantic'. The philosopher Anthony O'Hear has said that he was a 'truly great man'. I know that Chris himself, if asked what qualities he most admired in others, would have singled out courage; in his life, many people said they agreed with him who would not have found it easy to stand up and be counted. So he would have been proud of the *Daily Mail*'s 'Goodbye Mr Courage' on the day after his death. I think he might also have said an untiring capacity for original thought and an instinct for assumptions that need to be questioned. But above all, perhaps, it would have been judgement; judgement not just of what to think and of what to say, but judgement of character, of who one could rely on, and for what. Even when I couldn't see it at the time, he always turned out to be right in the end. It is probably not possible to sum up what constitutes greatness, but those, perhaps, are at least some of its elements.

Christine Woodhead

Our wedding at Gwydir Castle, October 2006.

Literature

Chris began collecting books as a teenager, mostly from second-hand bookshops.

Geoffrey Hill

First published in *Standpoint*, 2009

Outside, a waterfall from a blocked gutter flowed down the kitchen window. Three sodden and rather stately sheep trooped by in single file. Geoffrey looked at me across the table and nodded with satisfaction. 'I love weather like this', he said, 'Don't you?'

I nodded back. You don't, after all, buy a farmhouse half way up a Welsh hillside for the joys of perpetual sunshine. He finished his coffee and picked up one of the black notebooks in which he writes his poetry. 'I am', he sighed, 'very, very tired.'

Geoffrey Hill, England's greatest living poet, published his first pamphlet of poems in 1952 while an undergraduate at Oxford University. Now, in his old age, he is writing with intense urgency and concentration. His *Collected Critical Writings* (2008) recently won the prestigious Truman Capote Award for Literary Criticism. The news last month that he had won the election to the Chair of Poetry at Oxford was greeted with almost unanimous acclaim throughout the English-speaking literary world.

'If you sit up half the night writing, you're bound to be tired', I replied, unsympathetically. 'Why do you do it?'

He did not, he replied, have any option. 'At my age, you know you haven't got that long and I am trying, I suppose, to make up for those long periods of time when I was unable to write'.

Those blank periods are a matter of public record: serious health problems, severe depression, a move from Leeds, where he had taught for 26 years, to Cambridge. In 1988 he was invited to join the University Professors Programme at Boston University. He published just one book of poetry, *The Mystery of the Charity of Charles Péguy,* between 1978 and 1997. Finally, in 2006, he retired. 'Fifty-two years of university teaching', he once said to me, rather ruefully, 'It must be some kind of record'.

Make up for it he most certainly has. In the last three years, Hill has completed four unpublished books of poems and is currently working on a fifth. Could he, I asked, say something about the genesis and nature of these late poems?

'The first of the four books began as a result of my coming face to face with Donatello's *Habakkuk* in Florence in May 2007. The second derives from a rediscovery of the power and beauty of one of Sir Philip Sidney's lyrics in *Arcadia*, a demanding technical exercise in English "sapphics". The third is a book about my "discovery" of Wales, dedicated to the memory of my Welsh great grandfather. The fourth is again an exercise in handling rhyme, metre, rhythm – in short, "stress" – within the constraints of compact metrics and complex rhyme-patterns. The fifth, I don't feel able to talk about, as it's unfinished'.

I like to think that my wife and I contributed something to the Welsh book, *Oraclau*. Driving last May with Geoffrey from Cambridge to Wales, we stopped at Llanllwchaiarn near Newtown, where his great grandfather was baptised in 1826. The church was, predictably, locked, so we wandered round the graveyard. 'Who is that strange figure with the long white beard who kept walking in front of the camera?' Geoffrey asked when we showed him the printed photos.

En route to Llanllwchaiarn, we had driven past Bromsgrove County High School, where Hill had been a pupil from 1942 to 1950. 'We were', he said, '95 per cent working class, and I am very proud of what the majority of my classmates achieved in later life. The boy who was my closest friend in the "L" (for Latin) stream and who, having done very well at School Cert, left to work in an office, retired a few years ago as Professor of Chemical Engineering at Zurich with a DSc and numerous patents to his name. That is what I call genius. In terms of success, recognition, stability and personal happiness, I come a long way down the list of ex-pupils of BCHS in those years. As to my being a poet: at 78 (almost) I have to grit my teeth and get on with it. I would rather have been a Professor of Engineering and a more generous and loving son'.

This, I thought to myself, is the man of whom Archbishop Rowan Williams wrote: 'Geoffrey Hill remains for me the supreme voice of the last few decades … …the recent work, telegraphic, angry and unconsoled, at once assertive and self-dispossessing, is extraordinary'. So, too, is the gap between the strength of the public recognition and the bleakness of the personal judgement.

'Say that I am gifted –', one of the poems in *Scenes from Comus* (2005) declares, 'and I'll touch you/for ordinary uncommon happiness. What/a weirdo, you think. Well, yes, I was wired weird'. Were you, Geoffrey, I ask, 'wired weird'?

'Were Whitman, Yeats, Hardy? Yes, of course they were. They were also tremendously sane. Their poetry kept them sane, fulfilled their sanity, spoke of and for their sanity. I do not claim equality with them, but neither do I affect a false modesty. I think I was discerned as being 'wired weird' by my Bromsgrove schoolmates, and was to some extent ostracised for that reason. Rightly so, I think. At the same time I would claim a sanity, at once basic and overarching, for myself in terms of my craft. I may not be, but my poetry is, profoundly sane, and I believe that it will be more and more recognised to be so as time goes on. Of course', he added, 'I'll be gone by then'.

We stopped for another cup of coffee. The rain if anything was heavier. The sheep trooped back in the opposite direction, still in single file.

If the test of the 'sanity' is the ability to engage with what matters most to us, individually and collectively and, in so doing, to remain, over 60 years, scrupulously alert to the weight of both the world and the word, then Geoffrey's poetry is indeed profoundly sane. Does this mean that, as time goes by, his poems will secure a wider readership?

No, sadly, it does not. We live in an age which expects its poetry to be immediately accessible. Geoffrey does not share this populist belief. 'Accessible', he once said to me, is a perfectly good word if applied to supermarket aisles, art galleries, polling stations and public lavatories, but it has no place in discussion of poetry and poetics.

His critics allege that his poems are impenetrably difficult. The truth is that a first reading is likely to yield lines of heartbreaking beauty ('the may-tree filling/with visionary silent laughter'; or 'The marvellous webs are rimed with eternity') and wry humour ('I wish I understood myself/more clearly or less well'). Most readers will find his range of reference (from, for example, Dame Helen Mirren to Thomas Bradwardine) challenging, but a good search engine helps pretty quickly to fill in the gaps in your knowledge.

In an interview given to the *Paris Review* in 2000, Hill's response to the charge that his poetry is excessively intellectual was that life is difficult. 'Human beings are difficult. We're difficult to ourselves, we're difficult to each other and we are mysteries to ourselves, we are mysteries to each other. One encounters in any ordinary day far more real difficulty than one confronts in the most "intellectual" piece of work. Why is it believed that poetry, prose, painting, music should be less than we are? Why does music, why does poetry have to address us in simplified terms, when, if such simplifications were applied to our own inner selves, we would find it demeaning?'

Art, he believes, has 'a right to be difficult' if it so wishes. 'Cogent difficulty, that yields up its meaning slowly, that submits its integrity to the perplexed persistence of readers of goodwill, is one of the best safeguards that democracy can have'. Why? Because 'tyranny requires simplification.... Propaganda requires that the minds of the collective respond primitively to slogans of incitement. And any complexity of language, any ambiguity, any ambivalence implies intelligence. Maybe an intelligence under threat, maybe an intelligence that is afraid of consequence, but nonetheless an intelligence working in qualification and revelation .... resisting, therefore, tyrannical simplification'.

'But', he once again sighed, 'poetry is dismissed as an eccentric pursuit. If it were not so, John Humphrys would put as much effort and preparation towards harassing some cultural charlatan as he does toward making a political double dealer squirm'.

I laughed. The thought of the *Today* programme giving poetry the serious attention it dedicates to the clichés of leading politicians is frankly absurd. It is also, however, as Hill implies, deeply depressing.

If there is an answer it lies, of course, in our schools. We returned to Hill's childhood. 'At the time that county high school seemed a very ordinary school, but what seemed "ordinary" then appears extraordinary now. Its loss', he said slowly and sadly, 'has been a dreadful national deprivation and degradation'.

'I know', I said, 'I have spent the last 20 years trying to do something about it and got nowhere.' We looked at each other and laughed. The absurdity of us sitting in the middle of Noah's flood pontificating about

11

education when fine teachers across the country are forced to conform to the doctrine of 'Relevance and Accessibility' must have hit us simultaneously.

For a while, we sat in silence. I had no idea what Geoffrey was thinking. I was lost in a vivid memory of a sunny June afternoon in 1968. I should have been revising for my finals, but, bored, I'd taken a few hours off and was wandering round Bath. By chance I went into a bookshop and picked up a copy of Geoffrey's magnificent second book of poems, *King Log*.

Maybe I am 'wired weird' too, but I can only compare the experience to falling in love. There was the same sense of wonder and excitement and mystery, the sense, as Geoffrey himself has put it, of being 'brushed past, or aside, by an alien being'. I bought the book and over the intervening years have bought every subsequent book Geoffrey has written. I count his poetry and now, towards the end of our lives, his friendship, as one of the greatest blessings I have been lucky enough to receive.

He looked up. 'Could you bear', he asked, 'to watch another episode of *Prime Suspect*?' 'Of course', I replied. Politics, education and poetry might be in a mess, but 'H Mirren', as Geoffrey once put it in a poem, 'is super'.

Chris with Geoffrey Hill in our garden in north Wales, 2009.

Collected Poems by Kathleen Raine

First published in *The Sunday Telegraph,* October 2000

Towards the end of her third volume of autobiography, *The Lion's Mouth,* Kathleen Raine writes of 'the ragged pain of the longing to be reconciled'. The specific reference is to her feelings during 'the long years of separation' from Gavin Maxwell, the writer and naturalist who had such a profound impact on her life, but the phrase captures a truth which has both a general significance to us all and a fundamental importance to her poetry. To be reconciled: to those, yes, we have loved and still love whatever the current circumstances of our lives; to the lost world of childhood, when we may, like Miss Raine, have experienced, 'a place of perfect happiness, filled with the bright sun of Easter, pure living light and warmth', to, above all else, a belief in that archetypal order which, if properly understood, will transform the spiritual poverty of our materialistic times.

These are the themes Kathleen Raine was exploring in her first volume of poetry, *Stone and Flower.* They are the themes which preoccupy her still, sixty years later.

She states in this new edition of her *Collected Poems* that she has omitted 'love poems of a personal nature', and she has. There is nothing here for those who want to ponder the chapter and verse of particular relationships. The poems are, nevertheless, deeply personal and many of the most moving stem clearly enough from the pain love can bring. This is particularly true of the wonderful sequence, *On a Deserted Shore.* 'Sorrow', she writes, 'Is its own place, a glass/Of memories and dreams; a pool/Of tears'. Or, again, 'Home is the sum of all/The days that sheltered us;/The place of no return'. The sorrow is absolute, the desolation palpable.

Kathleen Raine once remarked that 'at his best Edwin Muir achieved a poetic language at once powerfully mythological, yet concrete; symbolic, yet poignant with a particular joy or anguish'. I can think of no better description of her own poetry. As in Muir's verse, 'the personal gives immediacy to the universal, which in turn gives meaning and stature to the personal'.

Take, for example, the beautiful poem 'On an Ancient Isle'. The poet comes to 'an unvisited shore' where 'limpet shells are strewn among the celandine/And driftwood from the surf'. The sight reminds her of what she as a child and her mother and grandmother before her knew: that there is but 'one paradise/Earth, sea and sky patterned with the one dream'. 'Memory', as she says, 'pours through the womb and lives in the air'.

Are such poems ever going to achieve the recognition they deserve? I can only hope that at some future time they will. The publication of Kathleen Raine's *Collected Poems* may alert readers to a poet who has been neglected by both the general public and the literary establishment for too long.

The fact is, however, that few now believe, as Miss Raine believes, that 'poetry and religion are the same thing'. She once observed that 'the word beauty and the idea of beauty has ceased to count for anything'. She is right. Talk of eternity embarrasses us. To find in the 'solitudes, desolations, steeps and distances' of mountains protection from the 'invading night and the unbroken silence of the dead' is, for example, to invite the contemptuous sneer that one has succumbed to the threadbare charms of, God forbid, nature mysticism.

We look to poets to illuminate the personal and perhaps social realities of our time. We have no inkling of any other reality. We have no concept of the sacred and little understanding of that 'great symbolic language of tradition' upon which Dante and Milton, Coleridge, Shelley, Blake, Yeats and, now, Kathleen Raine have drawn.

As a consequence, her poems are unlikely to attract wide readership. The loss, of course, is ours. Kathleen Raine's *Collected Poems* stand alongside her *Autobiographies* and her scholarly studies of Blake, Thomas Taylor the Platonist and Yeats as texts that could, if we were willing to suspend our positivist disbelief, help us to rediscover our humanity.

The 'Ring of Bright Water' at Sandaig, north-west Scotland, one of Chris's favourite places. It was home to Gavin Maxwell when Kathleen Raine knew him.

How to Read and Why, by Harold Bloom

First published in *The Sunday Telegraph,* July 2000

'Simple fictions', Sir Frank Kermode once wrote, 'are the opium of the people'. It is a politically incorrect observation in these relativist and anti-elitist days, but it is true. Most readers read to kill the time; to lose themselves in the excitement of the story; to forget, if only for an hour or two, the dissatisfactions and vicissitudes of their own waking lives. What, though, of complex fictions? Why is it that some readers are drawn to texts which challenge their habitual perspective on the world so as to force a re-evaluation of their experience and aspirations? And, if this re-evaluation is a goal worth pursuing, how can we read better so as to learn more?

These are questions which have pre-occupied Harold Bloom for the best part now of fifty years. His latest book, *How to Read and Why,* comes to the conclusion that we read 'in order to strengthen the self, to learn its authentic interests'. For Bloom, 'the pleasures of reading are selfish rather than social'. He is sceptical of the 'traditional social hope that care for others may be stimulated by the growth of the individual imagination' and 'wary of any arguments whatsoever that connect the pleasures of solitary reading to the public good'. Reluctantly, I agree. I tried for years as a teacher of English to sustain my Leavisite belief that the study of literature has social benefits. I have come now to think that Bloom is right. Literature can, if we read wisely, help us to know ourselves better and teach us how things are. It is the source of what Bloom calls 'a difficult pleasure' that is the 'only secular transcendence we can ever attain'. But, sadly, it will not make the world a better place.

Echoing his hero Dr Johnson, Bloom argues that the first thing we must do if we want to read well is clear our minds of cant. His definition of cant as 'speech overflowing with pious platitudes, the peculiar vocabulary of a sect or coven' will resonate with anyone who listens to the news or reads the papers. It is because great writers use language honestly and precisely that they are great. But we as readers need, Bloom reminds us, to play our part. We must recover our sense of the ironic, our ability to attend to 'antithetical ideas, even when they collide with one another'. Too often our tendency is to reduce the text to our own ideological concerns.

The challenge if we want to read better is to 'clear our minds of the cant of the ideologues' so as to read 'humanly' with as much of ourselves as we can muster.

Bloom is himself the most humane of readers and the analysis he offers in *How to Read and Why* of a wide range of literary texts and authors is, ultimately, the reason why anyone should read this book.

Almost always he has something new and valuable to say. Take, for example, Hamlet's famous 'To be, or not to be' soliloquy. This is not, Bloom argues, a meditation on suicide. Hamlet is, primarily brooding, he suggests, upon the will. 'Does one have the will to act, or does one only sicken into action, and what are the limits of the will?' That, indeed, is the question: a question that is central to any serious reading of the play, and, indeed, to any examined life.

He is particularly interesting on the 'radical originality' of Faulkner's *As I Lay Dying*, West's *Miss Lonelyhearts*, Pynchon's *The Crying of Lot 49*, and Cormac McCarthy's apocalyptic masterpiece, *Blood Meridian*. The latter, Bloom judges to be the strongest, most memorable novel written by any living American novelist. Some readers, as Bloom admits, will find its 'overwhelming carnage' off-putting, but anyone who has not yet tried to endure its dark mysteries ought to ponder the sublime sentence Bloom identifies as the book's 'visionary centre':

> They rode out on the north road as would parties bound for El Paso but before they were even quite out of sight of the city they had turned their tragic mounts to the west and they rode infatuate and half fond toward the red demise of that day, toward the evening lands and the distant pandemonium of the sun.

The 'morally ambiguous greatness' of this sentence is for Bloom the greatness of *Blood Meridian*. It is a measure of his own greatness as a critic that he responds so passionately and persuasively to this and the other texts he discusses.

Hans Christian Anderson, by Jackie Wullschlager

First published in *The Mail on Sunday,* October 2000

On 15 July 1856 Charles Dickens stood on the platform at Maidstone station, jumping, metaphorically at least, for joy. The cause of his glee? Hans Christian Anderson, who had been staying with him for five weeks, was finally on his way home. Kate, Dickens's daughter, described Anderson as 'a bony bore, who stayed on and on'. Her father appears to have shared her views. On returning home from the station, he pinned a note on the wall of the guest bedroom. It read: 'Hans Anderson slept in this room for five weeks – which seemed to the family ages'.

The five hours I have spent reading Jackie Wullschlager's biography, *Hans Christian Anderson*, have dragged equally badly.

Like everyone else, I have treasured Anderson's fairy stories since I first had them read to me as a child. Wullschlager's judgement that he is 'one of the greatest and most original of European writers' is over the top. Anderson was, however, the first person to treat the traditional fairy tale as a literary genre and the stories he invented have certainly, as she says, 'entered the collective unconscious with the same mythic power as the ancient anonymous ones'. The problem, as Dickens found to his cost, is the man.

Anderson's life ought to have been a biographer's dream. His mother was an illiterate washerwoman who, after his father's death, became addicted to gin. He was a dreamy and eccentric boy, whose 'greatest delight', as he tells us in one of his several autobiographies, was making clothes for his dolls, weaving garlands and dressing up. He nevertheless felt that he was different from those about him and that he must escape from what he called his roots as a 'swamp plant'.

Escape he did, saving every penny that came his way so that a few months after his fourteenth birthday he could travel to Copenhagen to make his name and his future in the theatre. Amazingly, he survived. He had real talent as a singer and he exploited it to the full, knocking on every door that might open to him until one did.

These early years in Copenhagen were desperately hard. He was often cold and hungry, his feet froze as icy water penetrated the holes of his worn boots, he was forced to stuff paper underneath the cast-off coats people gave him so that they did not seem too big for his lean body. His 'burning ambition' and 'implacable self-belief', as Wullschlager puts it, nevertheless carried him through. Gauche, overgrown, ill-educated and ridiculous: he was the classic ugly duckling who triumphed over every adversity and over the years turned into a writer who was very much the noble swan.

His courage and determination were admirable and these early pages of the biography make interesting reading. Boredom for me set in as Anderson became the success he so desperately wanted. Wullschlager does not help. She is determined to ground her hero firmly within his cultural context. No detail is ignored. We are told a great deal about everywhere he goes, everyone he meets, more, often, than I wanted to know.

What really grates, however, is Anderson's personality. He is, in the words of Mary Russell Mitford, a popular Victorian dramatist and novelist, 'essentially a toad-eater, a hanger-on in great houses … a man who values his acquaintances for their rank and their riches and their importance in the world'. This may seem hard but it is a fair judgement. The story of Hans Anderson's life is the story of a lonely, insecure and totally self-absorbed man desperate for material security and public recognition. He broods on every slight and responds ecstatically to every show of aristocratic interest. Given the poverty of his childhood, I can understand. But I cannot sympathise, and I cannot pretend that it amounts to a life that is either edifying or intriguing.

In letter after letter he pours out his loneliness and angst, but psychologically he never makes a jot of progress. He convinces himself now and again that he is in love with a woman and teeters nervously towards various homosexual relationships. Nothing, it seems, ever happened. He draws back, unable to commit himself, and wallows in the pain of his isolation. In the end it is boring.

Wullschlager does her best to convince the reader that Anderson is a man of 'wild imagination, inner rage, and tormenting anxieties'. She failed to hold my attention, but, psychologically, she is no doubt right. We have, after all, the stories he wrote. His life may not have added up to much, but they do, and they grew obviously enough out of his emptiness and pain. His misery may be as tedious as everyone else's, but the Snow Queen and the Little Mermaid will continue, for adults and children alike, to evoke profoundly important and perennially fascinating emotions.

Harry Potter and the Goblet of Fire, by J K Rowling

First published in *The Sunday Telegraph,* July 2000

The Lord of the Rings meets *A Catcher in the Rye: Harry Potter and the Goblet of Fire* is a potent mix of the two books that dominated my post-Biggles pre-pubescent reading. It is an unlikely combination, but, miraculously, it works. This is a very funny, and, at times, pretty scary book which will be bought for children and read, when they can get their hands on it, with equal enthusiasm by adults. The story is compelling, the humour satisfyingly anarchic, the moral stance reassuringly strong. For once the hype proves to be justified: J K Rowling has delivered.

Her quirky imagination is as fertile as ever. The chapters, for example, describing Harry's trip to the Quidditch world games are a triumph. Typically, his tent looks like any other tent, but, once inside, it becomes 'an old-fashioned, three-roomed flat, complete with bathroom and kitchen', and, a typical Rowling touch, 'a strong smell of cats'. Her technique, as always, is to ground the magical in the mundane Muggle reality we all know too well. A wizard baby prods a slug with his dad's wand. It grows to the size of a salami. Mum rushes out of the tent and promptly treads on it. To her disgust and her baby's fury it 'bursts'. It is a domestic scenario with which we can all identify.

So, too, with the characterisation. Rowling remembers what it is to be a child, and, in *The Goblet of Fire*, an adolescent. She is unsentimental, often very amusing, and always unerringly accurate in the success of her emotional touch. 'Why do they have to move in packs?' Harry asks Ron as they contemplate a gang of a dozen or so girls 'sniggering and staring' at them. How do you 'get one on their own', overcome your embarrassment, and ask them to accompany you to the ball? As Harry says, facing a Hungarian horntail dragon is a comparative cinch.

The Goblet of Fire is, however, more *Lord of the Rings* than *Catcher in the Rye*. It is a more sombre book than its predecessors. The battle between good and evil has become more pressing, and, in its consequences for Harry and others, more serious. The horror that is Lord Voldemort is described in detail that younger children will prefer to confront in daylight hours: 'The thing inside the bundle of robes ... was stirring more persistently, as though trying to free itself … It was hornless and scaly-looking …'.

As everyone now knows, one character dies. Harry himself suffers, physically and emotionally. In the run-up to the Triwizard competition, he faces the world alone. His best friend, Ron, refuses to speak to him. Even Hedwig, the owl, turns against him. 'First Ron', Harry says, in an angry, uncomprehending outburst that children across the world will appreciate, 'then you. This isn't my fault.'

How many times have we all felt this, as children, and, for that matter, adults? The world conspires against us. Most of the time, it is **not** Harry's fault. He is a decent kid, caught up, like his readers, in a world that a lot of the time is pretty difficult to understand, doing his best, as they are, to make sense of things. It is not surprising that children identify so strongly with his predicament and adventures and ultimate triumphs.

There are other, less archetypal satisfactions. As Harry grows older, Rowling's subject matter grows more sophisticated. Hermione wrestles painfully with the fact that her friends are not falling over themselves to join the Society for the Promotion of Elfish Welfare (SPEW) and, what is worse, the painful realisation that Winky, the House Elf, does not want to be liberated from her life of domestic servitude. The liberal conscience can, it seems, be as heavy a cross to bear at Hogwarts as it is in our own unreconstructed world.

It appears from interviews that J K Rowling's own cross grows heavier as her fame escalates. This, perhaps, explains the appearance of the 'attractive blonde, Rita Skeeter, forty-three', the investigative journalist 'whose savage quill has punctured many inflated reputations'. Speaking as one whose reputation has been punctured all too often, I can only say that her problems are set to multiply. *The Goblet of Fire* is her best book yet. It will win her millions more readers, who, having devoured the latest 636 pages, will be waiting with bated breath for the next instalment. I will be waiting with them.

After Progress, by Anthony O'Hear

First published in *The Sunday Telegraph,* October 1999

Is life better than it was fifty, a hundred, a thousand years ago? In the Western world at least, most of us are better housed, fed and clothed than any previous generation. We live longer, enjoy more leisure, travel more widely. But are we any happier? Why, given our material affluence, do so many of us wallow in personal unhappiness, desperate for the solace of new age therapies? Could it be, as Anthony O'Hear speculates in his new book, *After Progress,* that our 'material and political progress' is actually the cause of our 'spiritual and aesthetic decline'?

He concludes that it is. 'Scientific reason, whose technological and political applications have brought us in the main both prosperity and peace, has destroyed the visions which once inspired man'. We have come, he argues, to believe that man is or soon will be the absolute master of his own destiny. We see ourselves as purely natural, material objects, driven by the struggle of our genes to survive and reproduce. We think of happiness solely in terms of our psychological satisfaction. And, as a consequence, our lives have inevitably become degraded. We have forgotten what it is to be human.

It is, O'Hear reminds us, 'one of the great illusions of progressivist thought that there is a solution to every problem that faces us, that we can discover that solution by reason, and that the solution consists in doing something either politically or individually'. Many problems can, of course, be solved. The basic realities of death, sickness, disappointment, inequality, misfortune in love and personal inadequacy cannot. 'Only if we live in such a way as to face these realities without illusion can we call ourselves happy'. Nietzsche knew this. We, hypnotised by the achievements of scientific materialism and the rhetoric of progressivist politics, have forgotten. We have joined, O'Hear believes, Plato's prisoners in the cave, have sunk to the level of de Tocqueville's infantilised citizens.

I suspect that some of us will resent the charge. O'Hear's is not a comfortable argument, and it runs directly counter to the spirit of our modernising age. He has the courage to tackle many of the great issues of the time: animal rights arguments, the modernisation of sexual morality, the holy grail of equality ('ideals of inclusivity reign … depressing and compromising performance and ambition in a million and one ways'), and he cuts in each case through the pap of politically correct evasion to a conclusion that is as hard and challenging as it is important to our future as a nation.

This is the one reason why *After Progress* deserves the widest possible readership. The other is that, if we are to cope with the present and to have any hope of shaping the future, we must understand the ideas which have helped define our current values and assumptions. O'Hear's range of reference is extraordinarily wide and he has a rare ability to explain complex ideas in a straightforward fashion.

He begins with Francis Bacon, and, having discussed the impact of the Enlightenment and Counter-Enlightenment thinkers, shows how Kant, Darwin, Marx and Freud contributed to the inexorable rise of science and the (supposed) liberation of man from the intellectual and political stagnation of his past. The analysis is coolly logical, but the depth of his personal engagement, his anger and sorrow at the extent to which Enlightenment optimism has stripped the world of its magic and wonder and meaning is obvious in every phrase.

Echoing Eliot, the only wisdom, O'Hear concludes, is the wisdom of humility. 'We should cultivate a realisation of what has been lost in getting to where we are today, a realisation of the paradoxes of our situation, humanly and spiritually'. He is right. We do not 'have a clue' how to combine a sense of human dignity and the sacredness of life with the technologies we now have available. 'Our politics and our mass media' do tend all too often to 'pander to the satisfaction of desire at the lowest and grossest level, and to nurture the lying discourses of equality'. Are our lives better? The material gains are obvious, but so, too, is the profundity of the loss. Perhaps, as Eliot, whose ghost looms over this remarkable book, knew, it is a matter neither of gain nor loss:

There is only the fight to recover what has been lost
And found and lost again and again: and now, under conditions
That seem unpropitious.

The New Oxford Book of English Prose, by John Gross

First published in *The Sunday Telegraph,* September 1998

A great anthology will both surprise and confirm. The individual sensibility of the anthologist ought, slowly and unostentatiously, to emerge as the pages are turned, but the book as a whole will be marked by a generosity of spirit: a determination to include as rich and as varied a selection of works as space allows and thus to demonstrate the infinite possibilities of the particular medium. Above all, each of the chosen passages will be worthy of inclusion on its own terms. Each will speak to us with exceptional urgency and real precision. On these criteria, John Gross's *New Oxford Book of English Prose* is a great anthology.

We will all, inevitably, have our particular disappointments and complaints. To focus solely on the twentieth century, I would have liked to have seen something from one at least of the Powys brothers, an extract from Kathleen Raine's *Autobiography*, a paragraph or two from Simon Jenkins to set alongside the excellent Matthew Parris. I would have liked a little more Iris Murdoch and rather fewer, perhaps, minor writers.

But such reactions are silly. No anthologist can ever satisfy the whims of every potential reader. As it is, the book is a thousand pages long. It includes work from Australia and Nigeria, India and Canada, South Africa and New Zealand, Trinidad and Egypt. It begins with Malory and ends with Kazuo Ishiguro. There are extracts from memoirs, sermons, letters, essays on a range of disparate subjects, and, rightly the biggest category, many passages from novels. It is hard to imagine a more representative selection from the work of the major prose writers in the English language. Gross is to be congratulated both on the range of material he has managed to include and the intelligence of the balance he has struck between prose from different genres, periods and nations.

He has, moreover, exceptional powers of discrimination. The anthologist faces obvious problems in capturing the essence of a novel, or, even, a sustained argument, in a passage short enough to be quoted in a book of this kind. Time and time again, I found myself coming to the conclusion that Gross had chosen exactly the right passage to illustrate a particular writer. The extract from *Voss* is, for example, quintessential

Patrick White. That from Christopher Burney's *The Dungeon Democracy* will, I hope, lead many people to read a writer they may not yet have explored. The whole character of Oxford linguistic philosophy is exemplified in the two paragraphs Gross has selected from J L Austin.

But the book is more than a selection from the work of a huge range of prose writers. It is, as Gross intended, 'an anthology not just of prose, but of prose styles'. It illustrates 'the resources and achievement of English prose as an artistic medium and an instrument of expression'. In so doing, it raises interesting and disturbing issues.

Why is it, for example, that we are so keen to slap stylistic labels on writers and why are we so suspicious of anything that smacks of eloquence and rhetoric? Gross rightly points out that it is difficult, if not impossible, to categorise major writers such as Bunyan and Dickens. 'Labels', he argues, 'are inadequate: the expressive powers of prose are too varied for them to be neatly grouped and stacked'. Indeed, great authors are great precisely because of their ability to command an exceptionally wide range of the stylistic possibilities open to them. The moral here is that if individually, and as a nation, we are to articulate and therefore understand our late twentieth century experience we simply cannot afford to pigeonhole and dismiss. We need to seize each and every opportunity that English prose offers.

In particular, we need to ask ourselves why it is, as George Steiner once put it, that 'pleasure in style, in the wroughtness of expressive forms, is a mandarin, nearly suspect posture'? We need certainly to distinguish between true and false eloquence. But 'if', as Gross puts it, 'we allow our fear of pretentious or precious 'fine writing' to frighten us off the real thing, the loss will be ours; and it will be a large one'.

There are those, like Steiner, who believe that it is already too late in that 'the ideals of literate speech' have decayed to the point where it is hard to see how they can ever again achieve anything approaching common currency. In some moods, I share Steiner's pessimism. To contemplate the impenetrable inanity of the latest bureaucratic circular, to sift through misspelt and grammatically incorrect statements written by highly qualified job applicants, to ponder the mediocrity of the drivel which fills page after newspaper page is to wonder whether we live now in a culture which has no interest in the pursuit of clarity and common sense, let alone stylistic perfection.

If this is the case, those of us who work in education and who compile anthologies are engaged alike in a futile endeavour. But the pages of *The New Oxford Book of English Prose* suggest otherwise. The times may not be propitious, but prose of imaginative and intellectual excellence continues nevertheless to be written. The original *Oxford Book of English Prose* sold more than a million copies.

The interest was and perhaps is there. I simply hope that similar numbers of the new edition will be sold: this is an anthology which cannot fail both to return its readers to their favourite authors and to introduce them to new literary delights.

Classic Novels

November 1998

Chris knew from an early age that 'books furnished not just a room but a life'.

A classic novel is a novel that has stood the test of time – by which I mean, if we are to be certain, at least fifty, and probably a hundred or more years. I have no difficulty with the concept of a 'classic'. Some novels are better than others. Classics are simply the best. A classic novel sets the individual life within the wider context of a society and its history. This is the essential test and, as Iris Murdoch once pointed out in what has become a classic essay, most twentieth-century novels are either 'crystalline or journalistic'. They do not pass the essential test.

I did not feel that I was forced to read classic texts at school. As a young child, I progressed from fairy tales to Biggles with a great deal of pleasure. There were times at secondary school when the detailed textual analysis of novels which struck me as irrelevant and over-valued left me cold. But then, in my O level year, I read, initially with some reluctance, *Wuthering Heights*, and realised the impact great literature could have.

Nineteenth-century novels like *Anna Karenina, War and Peace, The Brothers Karamasov, Emma, Middlemarch* and *Our Mutual Friend* are classic classics and will (or ought to be) on everybody's lists. If we take the inclusion of such novels for granted and focus on more recent and, therefore, more controversial and interesting possibilities, my list would certainly include:

- *The Rainbow* and *Women in Love* because, in Frank Kermode's words: 'Decadence and renovation, death and rebirth, in the last days, are hard to tell apart, being caught up in the terrors'.

- *A Dance to the Music of Time* because no twentieth-century novel more obviously passes Iris Murdoch's test: this is our history, our society.

- *The Spire* because, whilst it was written only 34 years ago and is obviously very much a crystalline fable, it speaks powerfully and eloquently and movingly to anyone who is driven to achieve anything.

- *Wolf Solent* because, 'comic King Lear' that he is, Wolf's sexual, domestic and metaphysical dilemmas resonate all too strongly.

- *The Tree of Man* because in drawing us into the lives of its characters it captures a moment in Australian history, and has, like *Voss*, an extraordinary mythic quality.

- *Portrait of a Lady* because of chapter 42.

- *A Word Child* because Hilary Burde, travelling the Circle Line, is so much a figure of our egotistic times that I am prepared to break, once again, my chronological rule.

- *A Burnt Out Case* because no twentieth-century novelist has written more movingly of the search for meaning in a world without faith.

- *The Heart of Darkness* because it exposes the danger of idealism.

- *The Untouchable* because this is the greatest work so far by the best and most intelligent contemporary novelist writing today.

I am not prepared to list books that I think should never have been given classic status. There are books I have struggled with (such as *Ulysses, Mrs Dalloway* and *Remembrance of Things Past*), but I am hopeful that at some point I will grow up sufficiently to appreciate their (to me, thus far) mysterious charms.

Wolf Solent: The Enduring Appeal

A paper delivered by Chris Woodhead to the Powys Society in August 2002 – edited from the original lecture notes.

Entrance to a Lane, *1939, Graham Sutherland OM (1903-1980)* [purchased 1953 © Tate, London 2016], *the painting on the cover of the Penguin Modern Classic edition of* Wolf Solent *that first drew Chris to the novel.*

Youthful 'literary infatuation', as Al Alvarez puts it in his latest book, *The Writer's Voice*, 'doesn't last and it's hard to be friends afterwards'. But some does. It was, I think, 1964. I should have been revising for my A levels, but, bored, I had scootered into Croydon on my Vespa 150cc Sportique and was browsing in what was Roffey and Clarke's bookshop. My eye was drawn to a new Penguin Modern Classic: *Wolf Solent*. It was the cover that appealed – Graham Sutherland's *Entrance to a Lane* (the mysterious juxtaposition of forms, the muted browns, the competing splash of yellow). Not much revision got done that night, or for four or five after. I was hooked. A lifetime's passion for the novels of John Cowper Powys, and *Wolf Solent* in particular, had begun.

Why? What was it? What forty years on is it? They are unanswerable questions, of course, but nevertheless the most important we can ask of any work of literature. Why is it that one author appeals to us more than another; one book more than another written by the same author? We can focus on aspects – stylistic, thematic, whatever – of the text. We can argue that one book or writer is 'better' than another, and this is certainly part of it. Keats is 'better', a richer, more humane poet than Dylan, much as I remain an unreconstructed fan of the latter. But, such justifications do not take us very far. We have, and pretty quickly, to recognise that we come into the equation as well. Our personalities, peculiarities, strengths, weaknesses, obsessions and fantasies explain the enduring significance of a particular text.

Or, they would, if only we could see ourselves in a sufficiently detached way. Does literature help us to understand ourselves? I used to think so, and, when I taught English and taught students to teach English it was one of my main personal and professional justifications for the subject. Now, I am not so sure. I have come to believe that repeated readings help to make us who we are. We don't necessarily 'see' the book more clearly, though if we attend hard enough we may do; we do not understand ourselves any better because the impact of the text (like that of a person with whom one has lived for a long period) has, over the years, made you the individual you are. The distinction between the reader and the text becomes hopelessly, impenetrably blurred.

Here is a trivial example of what I mean. Wolf, having quarrelled with Gerda over Urquhart's cheque, is on his way to, he thinks, give the cheque back to Urquhart. As he walks down Chequers Street he observes:

> p.479 ... that a small single leaf still lay on the pavement. His consciousness of this leaf worried his mind after he had taken only a few steps. He endowed it – thinking to himself, 'I believe it's a myrtle leaf' – with nerves like his own. He thought of it as being separated from its companions and doomed to be trodden underfoot alone. 'Damn my superstition!' he muttered, and forced himself to walk on. But then he thought, 'They'll be treading on it just at the time I'm talking to Urquhart!' This brought him to a stand-still, while indecision took him by the throat. He slipped his fingers into his waistcoat pocket. There was Urquhart's cheque! After that unthinkable scene with Gerda he *had* taken it from under the stomach of Mukalog.

'How can I expect the gods to give me luck,' he said to himself' 'when I leave living things to be trodden underfoot?' He stood quite still now, paralysed by as much hesitation over this leaf as if the leaf had been Gerda herself.

'If I go back and pick up that leaf', he said to himself, 'I shall be picking up leaves from these Blacksod pavements till next autumn, when there'll be so many that it will be impossible!' He began to suffer serious misery from the struggle in his mind.

'If I force myself to leave it there … with the idea that I *ought* to conquer such superstitions … won't it really be that I'm getting out of rescuing it from mere laziness and making this 'ought' just my excuse to avoid trouble and bother? I'll pick it up now', he concluded, 'and think out the principles of the affair later on!' Having made this decision, he hurried back, picked up the leaf, and flung it over the railings after its parent twig.

But he had forgotten the east wind. That unsympathetic power caught up the leaf, and, whirling it high over Wolf's head, flung it down upon the rear of a butcher's cart that was dashing by.

'*That* wouldn't have happened', he thought, 'if I'd left it where it was'.

I have to confess that I identify absolutely. Was I prone to such acts of manic indecision prior to 1964 when I first read *Wolf Solent*? I don't know, but I'm pretty convinced that Powys is at least partly to blame.

There has, I suppose, to be something in our own psyche, but given that propensity, whatever it may be, the books that stay with us over the years stay because something in the mental make-up of the author connects, for reasons it is impossible to articulate, with our sense of ourselves and the world. The questions that pre-occupy Wolf, and behind Wolf in this profoundly personal novel, Powys, are questions that mattered to me when I was 17, and, if anything, matter more forty years on.

The most important concerns the emotion of pity. One Sunday morning Jason Otter takes Wolf to visit Lenty Pond:

p.119 They reached the willows and poplars at last; and Wolf stared in astonishment at what he saw. He found himself standing on the brink of an expanse of water that was nearly as large as a small lake. The opposite side of it was entirely covered with a bed of thick reeds, among which he could see the little red-and-black shapes of several moor-hens moving; but from where he stood, under these willows, right away to the pond's centre, the water was deep and dark, and even on that placid Sunday a little menacing.

'He could have done it easily if he'd wanted to, couldn't he? said Jason, gazing at the water. 'The truth is he *didn't* want to! Darnley's a sentimental fool. Redfern *didn't* want to drown himself. Not a bit of it. What did he come here for, then? He came to rouse pity, to make people's minds go crazy with pity'.

'The man must have been thinking of saying just this to me all the way across the field', thought Wolf. But Jason jerked out now a much more disturbing sentence.

'The boy did upset *one* person's mind. He made one person's mind feel like a weed in this water! And you'd be surprised to hear who that person was'.

But Wolf just then felt it very hard to give him his complete attention. For although the mystical ecstasy he had just experienced had faded, everything about the day had become momentous in his hidden secretive life; and he felt detached, remote, disembodied, for all his Sunday clothes. He could hear the cawing of a couple of rooks high up in the sky; and even when they ceased cawing, the creaking of their wings seemed like the indolence of the very day itself. 'A weed in the water', he echoed mechanically; while his mind, voyaging over those hushed West-country pastures, followed the creaking wings.

'Who was it, Mr Otter, who was so upset by Redfern?'

The appeal in Jason's miserable eyes grew still more disturbing. The man's soul seemed to come waveringly forward, like a grey vapour, out of its eye-sockets, till it formed itself into a shadowy double of the person who stood by Wolf's side.

'Can't you guess?' murmured Jason Otter. 'It was I … I … I … You're surprised. Well, anyone *would* be. You wouldn't have thought of that, though you *are* Mr Urquhart's secretary and *have* come from a college! But you needn't look like that; for it's true! Darnley sentimentalizes about his death, which was unfortunate, of course, but perfectly natural

– he died of pneumonia, as any of us might! – but what drove me to distraction was this playing upon a person's pity. He always did it – from the very first day. Darnley yielded to it at once, though he never liked the boy. I resisted it. I am of iron in these things. I know too much. But by degrees, can't you understand, though I didn't yield to it, it began to bother my mind. Pity's the most cruel trap ever invented. You can see that, I suppose? Take it that there were only one unhappy person left, why, it might spoil all the delight in the world! That is why I'd like to kill pity – why I'd like to make people see what madness it is'.

Pity is ever present in the background of the novel just as it is always in the background of Wolf's mind. First, the face of the man on the Waterloo steps is never far away. He associates the worried, anxious eyes of Darnley with that look. And it is there again in the waiter from the Lovelace Hotel. Later, he asks himself if pity is what he feels for Christie. He seems surrounded in Dorset by characters with sadness or harassment or anxiety in their eyes, and agitated restlessness in their demeanours. Even the inanimate objects, Gerda's tear, the leaf, all pull against the relaxed world he is looking for, against the 'enjoyment through sensation' which he says is his purpose. It is Jason who puts the inevitability of this into words. But Wolf struggles with the question:

> p. 153 He looked closely at the manner in which the alder-root dipped so adroitly and yet so naturally into the river. Yes! It was a kind of ecstasy he aimed at; the kind that loses itself, that merges itself; the kind that demands nothing in return!

> How could this ecstasy be called love? It was more than love. It was the coming to the surface of something unutterable.

> And then, like an automatic wheel that revolved in his brain, a wheel from one of whose spokes hung a bodiless human head, his thoughts brought him back to that Living Despair on the Waterloo steps. And he recalled what Jason Otter had said about pity: how if you had pity and there was one miserable consciousness left in the universe, you had no right to be happy. Oh, that was a wicked thought! You had, on the contrary, a desperately punctilious reason to be happy.

> That face upon the Waterloo steps *gave* you your happiness. It was the only gift it could give. Between your happiness and that face there was an umbilical cord. All suffering was a martyr's suffering, all happiness was a martyr's happiness, when once you got a glimpse of that cord! It

was the existence in the world of those two gross, vulgar parodies of life, *ennui* and *pleasure*, that confused the issues, that blighted the distinctions.

Wolf is summoning up his consciousness to counter Jason's counsel of despair. He pits his psychological absorption against the 'world of commonplace tedium' which he is trying to escape from. But we are surely not meant to be convinced that Jason's 'wicked thought' can be dismissed so easily. The face on the Waterloo steps doesn't, after all, seem to give him happiness.

This links to my second example. Wolf is, of course, a supremely egotistic man. His justification for this egotism is that, in that nothing else exists, it is inevitable:

p.489 As he shuffled along, he began a deadly interior survey of his mental state. Like a black fly crawling upon walls and ceiling, his consciousness set off to explore its own boundaries. 'I have no certainty', he thought. 'I don't believe in any reality. I don't believe that this road and sky are real. I don't believe that the invisible worlds behind this road and sky are any more real than they are! Dreams within dreams! Everything *is* as I myself create it. I am the wretched demiurge of the whole spectacle ... Alone ... alone ... alone! If I create loveliness, there *is* loveliness. If I create monstrosity, there *is* monstrosity! I've got to move this creaking machinery of my mind into the right position; and then all follows. Then I can stop that old man from persecuting Christie. *Then* I can make Gerda happy without the two hundred!'

A bleak, saturnine disgust with the primary conditions of all human life took possession of him. The insane fancy took possession of him that he knew something at this moment of what the guilty lonely Power behind Life knew, as it drove towards its purpose. Was he himself, then, in league with this merciless thing, that from his deepest heart he cursed? Did he know what It felt, confronted by all these shadow worlds, dream within dream, each of them unstable as smoke and reflecting only *thought* ... nothing but circles of *thought*?

Just as when his 'mythology' was upon him he felt life surging with magical streams of sweet, green sap, so now it seemed as if he could sink through world after world and find them all blighted, all poisoned, all corroded by some perverse defect. The only comfort was that they were all equally phantasmal! Nothing was real except thoughts in conscious minds; and all thoughts were corrupted.

There is a sense in which I agree. Our thoughts and feelings and sensations are what matter most: they are who we are, where we live. We might not want to admit it, but it is true. Or at least *I* think it is – and it is why I suppose *Wolf Solent* has appealed to me so profoundly for so long. I know, however, and Powys knew, that these are words in the wind, that the mental resolve Wolf describes here, however strong, will not give him the wherewithal to deal with the real world, to negotiate the relationships in which he has become embroiled. His inadequacy in this real world has already been demonstrated countless times. The misery of his indecision, and more importantly the misery that indecision brings to others (Gerda's 'It's too late'); his mother's disappointment in him. And all this juxtaposed with the decisive, worldly and efficient Carfax. Even the smug man with the white cat at least knows how to survive in the world. And Powys is not afraid to puncture the egotism. Both Gerda and Christie tell Wolf he is a fool. And Christie is right: Wolf's interminable meditations are an evasion of reality, of his moral responsibilities.

> p. 597 He was interrupted in the middle of his speech. The daughter of Mr Malakite sprang erect upon her feet and uttered a piercing scream. Then she beat the air with her clenched hands.
>
> 'Damn you!' she cried. 'Damn you! You talking fool! You great, stupid, talking fool! What do *you* know of me or my father? What do *you* know of my real life?'
>
> Wolf drew away from her, his body bent forwards, his hands pressed against the pit of his stomach, his eyes blinking.
>
> For a second he saw himself and his useless words exactly as she described them. He saw all his explanations as if they had been one prolonged windy bellow, covering the impervious grazing of a complacent ox!
>
> But grim terror swallowed up this spasm of personal humiliation. What if this tragedy were to unsettle Christie's wits?

We are close here to the greatness of the book: the intense evocation of Wolf's consciousness, but the constant placing of that consciousness morally; the psychological absorption and ethical detachment.

We often talk about why John Cowper Powys is not valued as he should be valued. It seems to me that an appreciation of *Wolf Solent* depends on the reader first of all identifying with the feeling of disillusionment with the '… world of commonplace tedium, full of the same flat, conventional ambitions, the same sickening clevernesses?' – the world, of course, that most novelists explore. Then, we may not quite be able to share his 'mythology' – his 'staring into his soul', but we at least need to be able to understand it. And we need finally to understand why Powys/Wolf feels so ambivalent about the human consequences. How are we to weigh the miseries of indecision and their effects, the love affairs – the most agitating, as Powys points out, of all the topics in the book – against the struggle to keep hold of and eventual loss of his mythology and his defeat in the world ('Dorsetshire had eaten him up' p.575)? How are we to view the Malakite philosophy of psychological survival (who dies 'shrieking' the word 'Forget') which Wolf seems to find impossible as he battles with the pain of his experience? And the talisman he adopts at the end, 'endure or escape'? Is it all a grandiose exaggeration? A concert? In short, do I care more for Carfax and Barge?

But then again, maybe all this is to complicate what is essentially simple. There is, for example, the straightforward appeal of the characterisation, often comic:

Selena Gault: 'a crafty drayhorse edging into a field of clover'.

Mrs Torp at the school treat: 'her face rigid, yet festive, bearing an expression like a waxen murderer in Madame Tussaud's while from the top of her bonnet a big purple feather nodded with a diabolical gaiety all of its own'.

And nature – the intensely evocative descriptions of landscape that are, certainly for me, part of the novel's appeal. 'A book of Nostalgia, written in a foreign country with the pen of a traveller and the ink-blood of his home', as Powys describes it in the Preface. Well, surely no one writes better about place:

p.33 The atmosphere was cooler when they came out of the church. Its taste was the taste of an air that has been blown over leagues and leagues of green stalks full of chilly sap. It made Solent think of water-buttercups in windy ponds, and the splash of moor-hens over dark gurgling weirs.

p.85 It was quite dark now; and the north wind, whistling through the blackthorn-hedges, sighing through the tops of the trees, whimpering in the telegraph-wires, had begun to acquire that peculiar burden of impersonal sadness which seems to combine the natural sorrows of the human generations with some strange planetary grief whose character is unrevealed.

p.106 The immense Somersetshire plain, with patches of olive-green marsh-land and patches of moss-green meadowland, lost itself in a pale, sad horizon, where, like a king's sepulchre, rose the hill-ruin of Glastonbury.

In conclusion, for all that we need to engage with Wolf's mental struggles and empathise with the loss of his mythology, it is not a pessimistic book. For one thing, the love of beauty which is so pervasive is also disinterested and contemplative. It makes life for Wolf – for many of us – worth living and has no end or good beyond itself. It suggests to us that despite all the horrors of existence the world may not, ultimately, be alien and as human beings we may not, necessarily, be alienated. And we know that he will continue to derive strength from those stored up memories:

p.107 – They had to do with wild rain-drenched escapes beneath banks of sombre clouds…along melancholy quarry-pools and by quagmires of livid moss. Indescribable! Indescribable! But memories of this kind were – and he had long known it! – the very essence of his life. They were more important to him than any outward event. They were more sacred to him than any living person. They were his friends, his gods, his secret religion. Like a mad botanist, like a crazed butterfly-collector, he hunted these filmy growths, these wild wanderers, and stored them up in his mind. For what purpose did he store them up? For *no* purpose! And yet these things were connected in some mysterious way with that mythopoeic fatality which drove him on and on and on'.

Memories that are no more likely to be expunged than that narrative memory in the ink-blood of his creator has been washed away by three thousand miles of Atlantic. And then, the wisdom of the ending is worth something. Wolf has to accept the accident of timing and the mounting obstacles which mean he can never have the relationship he wants with Christie, but the truth that he discovers through their relationship is perhaps the most important truth of the book:

p.221 – 'Why not take us as we are', he said slowly, apparently addressing the missel thrush's nest, 'as two hunted, harassed consciousnesses, meeting by pure chance in endless blue space and finding out that they have the same kind of mind?'

And if those are not consolations enough, there is always that cup of tea.

Facing Up, by Bear Grylls, and A Slender Thread, by Stephen Venables

First published in *The Sunday Telegraph,* March 2000

I can understand why people risk their lives climbing in the Himalayas. I understand, too, why, driven by the need to make sense of the intensity of their experience, or, more prosaically, to fund their next expedition, so many mountaineers write books describing their adventures. What baffles me is why so many of us read these books so avidly when so often they are clichéd, formulaic and banal in their psychological insight.

Facing Up, Bear Grylls' account of his successful ascent of Everest, did almost defeat me. 'At first sight', he tells us, 'Everest is awe inspiring beyond belief, and holds a certain magic over the entire Himalaya'. I have tried for ten minutes and I have failed to write a limper piece of description. The sentence which follows is worse. 'For some reason, human nature through the decades is still irresistibly drawn to Everest, and I suppose always will be'. Indeed, Bear, but I have to say that we armchair mountaineers find it hard to survive in such rarefied intellectual air.

It is, however, worth gritting your teeth and struggling on. *Boys' Own* inanities continue to intrude ('I knew that I had to stretch myself further, and reach beyond my grasp'), but there is a basic honesty in the way Grylls tells his story that just about kept me going. His 'brash certainty' collapses instantaneously, for example, when he falls into a crevasse. Pulled out, he lay with his 'face pressed into the snow, eyes closed, and shook with fear'. Sitting comfortably in my armchair, I shook with him. He is good, too, on the sheer squalor of the experience. If you have ever wondered what it is like to have your 'pee-bottle' slip through your fingers in the middle of the night at twenty-something thousand feet, reducing your sleeping bag to a 'soggy, stinking mess', then you should read *Facing Up*.

A Slender Thread is a very different book. Bear Grylls was only 23 when he climbed Everest. Stephen Venables has been climbing since the early seventies. Having made it to the top of Everest in 1988 without using supplementary oxygen, he has nothing in mountaineering terms to prove.

He recognises that those who 'make up the mountaineering community' are 'strangely driven oddballs and misfits'. Recently married, with young children, he worries about the risk. Why, he asks, does he have 'to lead this schizophrenic existence?' Why is he driven to leave 'two faces watching bravely and smiling' as he departs once again on a trip from which he knows he may not return?

There is, as he says, something 'perverse' about this 'self-exile'. But if he is sensitive to the absurdity and honest about the selfishness, he is, more than most mountaineers, eloquent in describing the satisfactions climbing can bring. Forget the Himalayas. Anyone who has scrambled in Snowdonia will understand the 'feeling of total belonging, of oneness with the mountain', which the twelve-year-old Venables experienced lying in the sun 'intoxicated by the hot peaty smell of heather' on the summit of Rhinog Fawr. Men climb because of the intensity of 'moments when one lives utterly, totally in the present' and which give meaning to life as the years slip by.

Such moments are not, of course, at the time always pleasant. 'It was a damp arthritic sort of cold that seeped insidiously', Venables writes, 'into weary bones'. All he wanted, as he descended from the summit of Panch Chuli on the expedition described in this book, was for the 'long, long night to be over'. Then, suddenly, as he slid on the rope down the seventy degree slope, he heard 'the trivial, jocular ping of a steel peg ripping from the rock' above him. He 'felt the sudden, awful, backwards lurch into space' as he fell to what he thought was his death.

It is powerful, dramatic writing. *A Slender Thread* is neither clichéd nor formulaic and Venables is too intelligent and thoughtful a man ever to be anything other than interesting in his description of what happened to him and his analysis of how emotionally he reacted. This is one of the best mountaineering books to have been published for a long while. We armchair mountaineers are lucky that by some miracle our author survived.

Chris was often asked to review books on climbing and mountains. Here he is on Bosigran in west Cornwall, one of his favourite climbing cliffs.

On Thin Ice, by Mick Fowler, and _The Hike,_ by Don Shaw

First published in _The Sunday Times,_ August 2005

You would think, reading Mick Fowler's second volume of climbing memoirs, that he was the ultimate bumbling incompetent. He works, a bespectacled pen-pusher, for the Inland Revenue. He is, he tells us in _On Thin Ice,_ painfully unfit. He can't carry heavy loads. He struggles to acclimatise at altitude and he is hopeless in the heat. If something can go wrong, it invariably does. He has managed, nonetheless, to pack more mountaineering success into his annual hols than virtually any full-time mountaineer in the history of the sport.

Fowler's speciality is the lightweight Himalayan ascent. A couple of decades back, the expedition was the norm. A large team of climbers, assisted by an army of sherpas, would engineer the route to the summit. Ropes would be fixed and camps organised at stages up the mountain. Fowler climbs, typically, in a team of two. He sets off into the unknown, finds, if he is lucky, a crevasse to crawl into for the night, survives the inevitable avalanches and storms, and days later makes it to the top.

The margin for error is minimal; the commitment required total. This is mountaineering at its purest and most demanding. Descending from a mountain called Changabang, Fowler's companion, Steve Sustad, slips and pulls him down a snow slope towards a 1,000m drop. Miraculously, Fowler survives with only minor injuries. Sustad breaks four ribs in several places. They meet up with two other climbers and struggle on. One of these climbers is swept to his death in an avalanche. The nightmare descent continues. 'At one point', writes Fowler, 'we all ended up hanging free from a peg and a wire in the middle of a blank 100-metre wall'. On day 13 of the climb he catches himself falling asleep draped over his ice axes as, in a state of terminal exhaustion, he fights his way up the col which leads to safety.

Was it worth it? 'In bald terms', Fowler comments, 'the answer has to be no; nothing is worth the life of a friend'. But, he continues, his friend died doing what he loved. He admits that the risks he took on this climb were too high for a family man with two children, but his 'love of the mountains is such that giving up was never an option'.

Fowler is not the sort of man to analyse that love. He refers to it several times as an 'urge' that simply cannot be ignored, and in terms of introspective insight, that is that. What matters is 'maximum holiday pleasure', which means 'new places, adventure, challenges, uncertainty, interest, ethnic action and wild, preferably mountainous, terrain'. Readers with a taste for self-deprecating irony who share Fowler's enthusiasms should buy *On Thin Ice* tomorrow. It is the funniest and most gripping mountaineering book to be published for years.

The Hike chronicles the adventures of three grumpy old men who escape from family ties on weekly walks in the Derbyshire Peak District. No avalanches threaten their progress. Vertical ice walls are few and far between; forced bivouacs rare. That said, everything is relative. Hypothermia strikes, one February day, with potentially disastrous consequences, and, on more than one occasion, weary geriatric limbs stumble to complete the last half mile.

Phil 'Gruppenfuhrer' Stevens, a pill-popping, pre-pubescent 64-year-old Rommel lookalike, dedicated to the pursuit of eternal youth, drives the party out in the foulest of weathers. Freddy, who spent his working days toiling in a glue factory, ponders the meaning of life and whinges at the first drop of rain, desperate for the solace of a warm pint of beer in the nearest country pub. Don Shaw observes their constant manoeuvrings with gentle malice.

He has produced a minor classic which would make an excellent television series. Most of us who have retired or who are nearing retirement can identify with the angst of both Phil and Freddy. Minor characters, such as the infamous naked rambler on his ground-breaking jaunt from Land's End to John O'Groats, a millionaire businessman holidaying as a tramp, and the world president of the Trabant Association who appears out of the gloom, dressed as an East German soldier driving (of course) a Trabant, to rescue a frozen Freddy, enliven the plot.

The Peak District is evoked in its perennial glory. The implicit message, get off your backside and enjoy yourself in the great outdoors, is worth heeding. You should buy this one, too.

Education

As Her Majesty's Chief Inspector of Schools from 1994 to 2000, Chris spoke out forcefully against prevailing ideologies and the erosion of standards.

Foundations

Extracts from *A Desolation of Learning: Is This the Education our Children Deserve*, Chris Woodhead, 2009

My own school years – a traditional grammar school education

In that discussions about education are always personal, it is worth, perhaps, saying a little about how these disagreements have been influenced by my own experience as a child in what was a very typical 1950s south London primary school and later at Wallington Grammar School. My teachers at primary school taught me to read and write. I learnt a few facts about history and geography and natural history, enough, certainly, to send me to the library to find out more. I took the 11+ a year early and suffered, as far as I am aware, no long-term trauma.

Wallington was pretty characteristic of the period, too. The uniform included a cap which was meant to be worn to and from school. There were prefects. The cane, as I discovered twice, was the punishment of last resort. We were allocated to different houses and competition between the houses was a major aspect of school life. That competition fed through into classroom life. We were streamed according to academic ability and lists were published each week giving our position in the form. I had done well in primary school, but soon found myself struggling, which might be why I spent a fair amount of time playing the fool and ended up in the Headmaster's study with my bottom in the air. The dinners were foul and we had two or three hours of homework a night. I can remember standing in the rain waiting for a bus one November night after a detention thinking that I had one advantage over the teachers who were persecuting me: I was younger than they were, and the odds were they would die first.

So, when I say that the seven years I spent at that school opened my eyes to a world I did not know existed, I am not romanticising a period of my life that was in some ways very difficult. Visiting the school some years ago to give the prizes, I stood in the classroom where on Tuesday mornings we were tested orally on our grasp of the previous night's Latin homework. The old terror flooded back. That said, as I wandered round, poking my nose into the showers to see if there was still mould on the walls (there was, I am glad to say), I knew that this school had given me opportunities I want children today to have if they can benefit from them.

Chris took the 11+ a year early and won a place at Wallington Grammar School.

It was, first, a school which functioned as a community. We were expected to contribute to the life of our houses, represent the school in sporting and cultural activities, take responsibility for ourselves and others. Time was not wasted on citizenship and personal, social, health education (PSHE) lessons. The understandings and values these pseudo-subjects now struggle to make explicit were embedded in the everyday fabric of the school, and were transmitted all the more effectively because of that. The focus was unambiguously on the academic. There was no nonsense, to quote from the Government's Children's Plan, about 'successful learners, confident individuals and responsible citizens'. If asked, I am sure the Headmaster would have agreed that these were not unreasonable aims, but he would also have pointed out that they were aims that depended as much upon the abilities and personalities of his pupils as the magic wands of his staff, and he would have added, no doubt, that he rather hoped that his pupils might end up knowing a little more science and Latin than they did when they arrived at school.

The grammar school system – a real meritocracy

In 1979 the sociologist Frank Musgrove wrote in his beautifully astringent book, *School and the Social Order*: 'The English working class has been betrayed twice in my lifetime: first in the General Strike of 1926 and then forty years later when the grammar schools 'went comprehensive'.' He continued: 'The Labour Party did not abolish the great Public Schools, the obvious strongholds of upper-class privilege; with unbelievable perversity they extinguished the only serious hope of working class parity …the upper classes kept their Public Schools, the working class lost theirs'.

…

The political decision in 1965 to introduce comprehensive education was driven by three arguments: that clever working class children found it difficult, if not impossible, to win places in grammar schools; that if they did get in they failed academically; and that selective education had done nothing for social mobility. Frank Musgrove's chapter on selective education systematically demolishes each of these assertions.

Grammar schools may now be colonised by the middle classes. In the 1940s and 50s they were working class institutions. Musgrove examines historical data, studies of particular grammar schools in south-west Hertfordshire, Middlesborough and Manchester, and national surveys, to show that by 1953, 'using a very stringent definition of working class as manual workers', 'two-thirds of grammar school pupils were working class'. His analysis of A level examination results for 1960-1 school leavers challenges the conclusion of the Robbins Committee that 'working class children are progressively less successful than children of the same 11+ grading in other social groups'. The figures are as follows: 65% of the children of skilled manual workers got at least two A level passes, 64% of the children of clerical workers, and 67% of the children of professional and managerial workers. The children of unskilled workers did do less well, with only 56% achieving two A levels, but this statistic says more, as he suggests, about the relative intelligence of these children than it does about the failure of the grammar school as an institution – relative, that is, to a social class, which I argue is a factor that cannot be denied in any assessment of the goals of the educational enterprise. It is hard, reading Musgrove, to understand why the 'potent and mischievous myth' of the failure of working class children in grammar schools took such hold. Then, as now, I suppose, there were academic careers to build and anti-elitist prejudices to justify.

It is quite clear, moreover, that grammar schools made a very impressive contribution to social mobility. Anthony Sampson points out in *The New Anatomy of Britain* that four out of twenty-one heads of major civil service departments in the early 1970s went to 'Clarendon' schools (Eton, Harrow, Charterhouse and St Paul's). Seventeen were ex-grammar school pupils. The Head of the Civil Service, Sir William Armstrong, whose father was an officer in the Salvation Army, went to Bec School; Sir Douglas Allen, Head of the Treasury, whose father had been killed in the First World War and who had been brought up in some poverty, went to my own school, Wallington Grammar; and Sir Philip Allen, Head of the Home Office, went to the King Edward VII school in Sheffield. But, as Musgrove says, the impact of grammar schools on social mobility is perhaps most evident when we look at men in mid-career. In 1967, for example, only 7% of admirals had been educated in grammar schools, but when we move down the ranks to lieutenants nearly 60% were grammar school educated as opposed to 30% at public schools.

Sampson thought that the public schools would only survive if they became more like grammar schools. Michael McCrum, then head of Eton, agreed with him. Public schools had become less dominant and their influence, he thought, was set to decline still further. It has not, of course, happened. The majority of grammar schools were closed down, and, at a stroke, the competition was removed.

The failed attempt to make education more democratic

Fifty years ago the novelist and philosopher Iris Murdoch asked whether 'we (can) maintain educational standards while making education more "democratic"?' The experience of the last twelve years has taught us that we cannot. We can abandon our responsibility to initiate the young into the best that has been thought and written. We can impose a skills-based, socially relevant, politicised curriculum on teachers and their pupils. We can reduce the intellectual demand of public examinations so that more students appear to succeed. We can force successful schools and universities to abandon their supposed elitism and accept more students from disadvantaged homes. We can and we have done all these things. We have neither maintained educational standards, nor, if by 'democratic' we mean that every child has an opportunity to fulfil their potential, have we made education any more 'democratic'.

A little earlier in the same essay Murdoch wrote: 'Education is no longer seen as the road to freedom; it is seen as the road to a higher salary'. She thought that education in art and ideas and knowledge was that road to freedom. She knew it from her own life, just as I know it is from mine. By freedom I mean: an appreciation of what the greatest human beings have achieved; a sense of what other people in other ages knew to be important and possible; a liberation from the tyranny of the majority view; a release from the monotony of the quotidian. I want every child, every 'disadvantaged' child in particular, to walk as far as they can down that road to freedom.

...

This freedom depends, paradoxically, on the child's willingness to submit. To submit to the authority of a teacher who knows what the child does not know and to the body of knowledge, wisdom and values it is that teacher's duty to transmit. Education cannot be democratic in the sense that the child is an equal partner in the activities of the classroom. The child does not and cannot judge the importance of what he is taught, and should have no say, therefore, in the content of his lessons. So much for 'personalisation' and what is now known in the jargon as 'student voice'. So much, too, for the Government's drive to render the curriculum 'relevant' to the immediate 'needs' and experiences of the child and to dumb the demand of examinations down to an egalitarian minimum.

This obsession with process is tediously introverted

What is meant when we are told children need 'to know how to learn'? Human beings learn by listening to people who know more about the subject they are learning than they do about themselves. They learn by reading and by exploring the limits of their understanding in writing. They learn by talking to other people who are at a similar stage in their understanding. They learn, if it is a practical subject, by doing. Do children need to be taught these obvious truths? And, if the retort is, as it will be, that this misses the point completely, and that the challenge is to help children become 'autonomous' in their learning skills so that 'they can make the transition from shallow to deep learning', then what, precisely, are the metacognitive strategies which need to be taught? Is it really sensible to encourage them to 'continually question methods and processes' and, presumably, facts, before they have the faintest understanding of what these methods and processes and facts involve and mean? Is the demand that they are taught when to work as a team anything more than a genuflexion to the demands of employers for more effective team players? Do they need 'to explain the process of learning to others'? It does help on occasion to try to explain a new idea to other people, but this preoccupation with the process rather than the substance of learning is, to use John White's[1] word, tediously introverted.

Learning how to learn is, after all, not very exciting. What is exciting is learning. By which I mean having your eyes opened to the mystery and magic of a world which as a child you know nothing about. That is what good teachers do. This is what schools are for. Or were, in the days before educationalists and politicians decided that children were being fed information to 'replicate' when they should, all on, of course, their autonomous own, be engaged in a process of 'deep learning' which enabled them 'to justify, explain, exemplify, apply, compare and contrast, contextualise and generalise'. Functional skills stem, like so much else that is noxious in the world of modern education, from the cavalier dismissal of didactic teaching as a Gradgrindian anachronism. Some of my teachers at Wallington Grammar School in the 1950s and 60s fed me gobbets of information to regurgitate at appropriate moments. They were the inadequate and incompetent ones. The majority told me things I did not know and at the time often did not want to hear. They made me attend to, engage with, a world of learning which pushed back the limitations of my personal horizons and led to a sixth form in which our thoughts and arguments were very much part of the everyday fabric of every lesson.

---

[1] Professor John White of the Institute of Education, University of London, referred to 'the introverted aims of most of the school subjects' in his paper *Towards an aims-led curriculum* for the Qualifications and Curriculum Authority in 2008. This paper is discussed earlier in the chapter from which this extract is taken.

Why I resigned as Chief Inspector of Schools

This brings me back to why I resigned as Chief Inspector of Schools and, having resigned, made such a fuss. In part, it is because I have spent much of my life thinking about words. I believe that 'we should mean something by our words, and know what we mean'. I have never been able to live with the rhetoric of policy pronouncement: by which I mean the failure ever to argue the case, the unexamined assumptions, the assumption that no examination is necessary. Why, I ask myself, should ministers and the officials who draft the gobbledegook they spout get away with it? Their slipshod prose betrays either a mind that cannot think or a patronising arrogance that does not care.

Neither, to my mind, is acceptable.

The Quality of Teaching: what matters most

In 1995, after his first year as Her Majesty's Chief Inspector of Schools, Chris Woodhead wrote a paper to launch a Politeia debate on educational standards. In the chapter printed here he focused on the quality of teaching, which, as he never stopped saying, is what matters most in schools. He drew on inspection evidence, on his conversations with headteachers and teachers and on his personal experience to identify the key issues which he saw as needing continuing attention at that time.

From *A Question of Standards: Finding the Balance,* by Chris Woodhead, Politeia, 1995

The Limits of Legislation

Government action can and indeed has made a difference. The main elements within the Education Reform Act cohere to create a context in which schools are already functioning more effectively and purposefully than they did prior to 1988. But Government cannot legislate to raise educational standards; it is, though some of us who work outside schools too often forget this, only teachers in classrooms who can really make the difference.

The one response to this truism will be to argue that if teachers were better paid and better resourced, if they had smaller classes, then they would be able to do the job they are expected to do. The other is to argue that the problem is rather that they have been hedged in by too much government bureaucracy, subjected to too many highly dubious policy initiatives and submerged by too much paperwork. There is an element of truth in each of these responses. On the latter, the Government should certainly continue to review and where necessary eliminate legislative constraints. We have the National Curriculum. We have performance tables and inspection reports. Teachers and schools must be left free to deliver as they see best. On the former, no one would want to pretend that resources do not matter. It is, though, clear that schools in different parts of the country receive significantly different funds to teach the same National Curriculum. Different authorities devolve different percentages of the Potential Schools Budget to their schools. It is, at the very least, arguable that primary schools do not receive their fair share of the cake. Each of these possible anomalies needs investigation. In particular, the case for and against a national funding formula must be explored as a matter of urgency. We can make significantly better use of the resources currently allocated to education. Would, however, a decision to find, say, an extra billion for education necessarily cause standards to rise? The answer is, of course, that it would not. Good teachers may be able to teach even better when they have twenty children rather than thirty in their class; but there is absolutely no reason to believe it is the size of the class which makes a bad teacher bad. Effective teaching depends, critically, upon the teacher knowing enough and caring enough about his subject, having high expectations of his children, and being willing and able to employ a range of different teaching strategies as he pursues different curricular objectives. It has at its heart, as all of us who are or have been teachers know, a sense of intellectual challenge in which the student is led to push back the frontiers of his knowledge, understanding and skill. That challenge can occur in a one-to-one tutorial or in a lecture hall with two or three hundred students in the audience. It must, equally, be the touchstone of success when we are talking about the teaching of younger children, though here, as Ofsted's recently published report into class size suggests, the size of the class is, for obvious reasons, more significant.

The question, therefore, of what can be done to improve the quality of teaching is critical to the issue of raising educational standards. There is some truth in the complaint often made by heads and teachers that the glass is always portrayed as half empty, but we cannot tolerate a situation where between a fifth and a third of lessons are judged by inspectors to be unsatisfactory or poor.

Unsatisfactory lessons are lessons where the teacher does not have a secure personal understanding of the material to be taught, where expectations of children are far too low, and where an appropriate range of teaching methods is not employed. The answer is not whole class teaching and only whole class teaching. There is, however, cause for concern when Professor Galton tells us that for 77% of the day primary school children are working on their own. Whole class teaching, as Galton argues, means that teachers are likely to ask more challenging questions of their pupils and pupils to pay more attention and concentrate more on their work. Why is it, therefore, that only 15% of teaching time across the nation's primary schools is spent on the class being taught as a whole? Why is it that some primary schools whose children come to school not speaking a word of English ensure that the national expectations of reading for seven year olds are met by the time their children are six? The answer is that they have the highest expectations and an absolute determination to teach reading in a planned and structured way. If other schools raised their sights and thought harder about their methodology then they, too, could achieve similar results.

The drive to raise standards must focus on the quality of teaching. What, though, does this mean? What can be done? The evidence from the school inspections undertaken so far suggests that there may be some 15,000 incompetent teachers currently working in our schools. Such teachers have an influence disproportionate to their numbers. Heads, governors and teacher unions alike agree that it is in nobody's interests for an incompetent teacher to remain in post. Despite this, action is rarely taken. The competence procedures are perceived to be impossibly complex; the disruptive impact on the staff as a whole too great. These are real and understandable concerns. They do not, however, justify inaction, and the first move towards raising standards must be for governing bodies, supported by local education authorities, to make more vigorous efforts to remove incompetent teachers from the profession.

Second, standards of teaching generally need to be raised. This means recognising that many primary teachers do not have a secure enough personal understanding of the academic knowledge, understanding and skills they are now required to teach. It means that every effort has to be made to promote a national debate (involving, crucially, parents and employers alongside the professionals) in which orthodoxies are questioned and expectations heightened. We have to move beyond simplistic dichotomies of the kind posited by Caroline Gipps (on the one hand, 'the transmission model' of teaching; on the other, 'active cooperative forms of learning'); we have to restore a belief in the teacher as an authority who knows more than his pupils and has a responsibility to teach; we have to be very clear about the repertoire of pedagogic skills in which all our teachers need to be expert. Simultaneously, in its inspections of individual schools, Ofsted must concentrate above all else on the effectiveness of the teaching observed, taking scrupulous care to avoid the imposition of particular beliefs about what constitutes good practice, but challenging the ill-considered orthodoxy or the over reliance on any particular approach. We need, too, to identify where and how pupils are making the greatest progress so as to establish centres of excellence to which less successful schools and teachers can be directed.

In addition, we must continue the drive to reform teacher education so that proper emphasis is placed upon the academic knowledge which the National Curriculum requires and full recognition given to the fact that a student is most likely to learn how to teach effectively if he has the opportunity to work for a sustained period of time alongside an experienced and successful classroom teacher.

Those who argue that it is the provision of information to parents about the relative performance of different schools which is the real catalyst for change will respond sceptically to this agenda. It is true that publication of performance tables which show the extraordinarily wide range of pupil achievement across similar secondary schools (the most successful schools do around six times better than the least successful) has certainly concentrated minds and is proving, no doubt, to be of considerable interest to at least some parents. We need similar data about the performance of primary schools and it is to be hoped that the National Curriculum tests can in the near future be rendered sufficiently secure for such school by school data to be publicly available in a useful and intelligible form to parents and all other interested parties. It need not, and should not, however, be an either/or. Standards of teaching will rise (and rise most quickly) if we can involve parents, raise their expectations, and offer them more choice. We cannot, though, afford to rely solely on the exercise of that choice. Deliberate and explicit efforts to improve teacher performance need to continue.

***

A policy announcement on incompetent teachers

First published in *The Sunday Times,* July 2009

'Sack the incompetent teachers'. It is 15 years now since newspaper headlines reported the fact that inspections by the Office for Standards in Education had identified 15,000 teachers who were not up to the job. I was Chief Inspector at the time. I knew that publicising this data would not endear me to the teacher unions. It did not. From then on I became a figure of hate. I still am in some quarters.

I can only say that if I were Chief Inspector today I would want to do even more to publicise the problem. Last week Ed Balls, the Schools Secretary, announced in a White Paper that he was finally going to do something about this continuing national scandal. However, if you talk to any teacher in private they will tell you that the figure of 15,000, which was 4.8% of the teaching profession in the mid-1990s, is, if anything, an understatement now.

What is more, they will go on to say that despite Balls's claims, nobody is prepared to tackle the problem. Most headteachers are extremely reluctant to confront teachers who cannot or will not cope. Politicians do not want to upset the unions. The General Teaching Council, which was set up to monitor professional standards, has dismissed just ten teachers for incompetence since it took overall responsibility for sacking state school teachers in June 2001.

Today, incompetent teachers continue to survive, moving up the salary scale while they damage the life chances of the children they fail each time they walk through the classroom door.

As an inspector I saw many brilliant lessons. I also observed teaching that I would not have wished any child of my own to have to endure. In one lesson I watched a boy fall asleep and slide quietly off his chair. Sitting at the back of the classroom, fighting to keep my own eyes open, I had every sympathy. There but for the grace of God, I thought, go I.

The lesson, which was on Ted Hughes's poem *Pike*, should have been riveting. There was not, in fact, a spark of excitement. The teacher had read the poem in a spectacularly monotonous voice and then reduced it to something resembling a tedious crossword puzzle. At the point where the boy gave up the ghost the teacher was dictating notes he had dug out of a moth-eaten folder. He seemed to be bored stiff; everyone else in the classroom, including me, certainly was. I can still remember the joy I felt when the bell rang and our collective misery ended.

You, no doubt, have similar memories from your own days at school. You will certainly have been taught by teachers who, however hard they tried, simply could not keep control. This inability to impose discipline on the class is the most common, and dramatic, form of incompetence.

Inspectors are meant to sit passively observing what happens in the classroom. Sometimes, when discipline breaks down and low-level disruption and disobedience seem set to escalate into a major altercation between the pupils and the teacher, they have to take over. In my experience, the signs are obvious from the moment the children barge noisily into the classroom. Good teachers greet the next class at the door and usher them to their desks with smooth efficiency. Incompetent teachers preside over an immediate chaos. They will ask the children, quietly at first, to settle down. When nobody takes the slightest notice they will repeat the request, raising their voices until they are red in the face and bellowing.

Ten minutes into the lesson the disorder will of its own accord typically subside into relative quiet. The teacher seizes the opportunity and makes, perhaps, a little progress. Then somebody will take it into their head to crack a joke or knock somebody else's bag onto the floor and the class is back to square one. The children who want to learn sit in patient despair, knowing that the whole fiasco is a waste of time.

Now Balls has announced that teachers will in future need a 'licence' before they are allowed to teach and that they will be subjected to five-year 'MoT' tests. Should we applaud? Has a government minister at last understood a fundamental problem that is blighting our children's education? Sadly, the answer to both these questions is no. This latest policy announcement will change nothing.

The truth is that teachers must already be licensed before they can teach. They have to pass a teacher training qualification and have then to be judged competent in the classroom. The MoT test is apparently to be conducted by the very headteachers who should have been monitoring the performance of their staff over these past 15 years. Last week's ministerial announcement was one more government gimmick, designed to grab a few headlines and persuade the electorate that public service reform is still high on the political agenda. Teachers who know that they are failing their children can continue to sleep easy in their beds. Good teachers can reflect on a new bureaucratic absurdity that is about to deflect them from the job they love.

There is nothing in last week's policy announcements to applaud. On the one hand, we have old initiatives such as academies and specialist schools rehashed yet again; on the other there are new ideas that are simply batty. Having, for example, invested billions in the teaching of phonics and only last year insisted that phonics was the key to all progress, Balls now says that it is up to every teacher to do what they think best. He promises one-to-one tuition when he knows it cannot be afforded, and, incidentally, should not be needed if children had been taught to read properly in the first place. Oh, and all will be well, because parents can sue if they do not like the education their children are receiving.

It would be a joke if it were not for the fact that children's lives are at stake.

***

A report from the Prince of Wales's summer school

First published in *The Sunday Times*, July 2004

What is the likelihood that your child will come home from school one day and say: 'Mum, Dad, I had a great lesson today. I read an extract from a newspaper on traffic congestion and then analysed a poster from the Government on why teaching is a great profession'?

Pretty unlikely, don't you think? The question was posed last week by Stephen Miles, an English teacher from Somerset, at the third annual Prince of Wales summer school for teachers of English and history in state schools, which was held in Buxton, Derbyshire. Miles then went on to remind delegates that there had been no poetry or imaginative prose in this year's English tests for 14-year-olds.

He and most of the delegates at the conference found this regrettable. Nor were they convinced that teaching is the profession it once was. 'Strange, isn't it,' one said to me in the bar, 'the Government spends millions of pounds on adverts selling teaching as the most important job in the world and does everything it can to eliminate every jot of professional joy.

'The National Curriculum is a fragmented, over-prescriptive, banal nightmare. The assessment criteria that dominate every moment of our professional lives grow more and more Byzantine. Day after day, we have to sit listening to consultants who recite their creed under the glare of a thousand power point slides.'

That, it seems, if these teachers were a representative group, is how it is these days. What matters now isn't the contribution English and history can make to a pupil's intellectual and emotional development. The idea that English teachers might want to instil a love of literature in their pupils doesn't cut much ice in official circles.

We live, apparently, in an 'increasingly competitive global economy'. We need schools to churn out employees with the right skills and attitudes. Targets are set, strategies devised. The teacher's job is to comply and deliver.

You love your subject? You want to share that love with others? Forget teaching. That is the bleak message I heard in the working groups and bars of our Buxton hotel. If things don't change, the advice these teachers were giving to graduates contemplating a career in teaching was loud and clear: don't.

The tragedy is that their despair was clearly borne out of their passion and commitment. If they had not been so idealistic, they would not have cared so much.

'Some of you,' the Prince said in his opening address, 'may be wondering why I set up these summer schools.' He paused, and looked up with a wry smile. 'Given the way the media report my initiatives, I sometimes wonder myself.'

The answer is that teachers are rarely, if ever, encouraged to reflect on the nature of their subjects and their responsibilities as teachers. What is it to teach English and history? Why are these subjects so important? The summer schools offer an opportunity to discuss these fundamental questions and to listen to eminent historians and literary figures.

Where else could you find historians Anthony Beevor, Simon Schama, David Starkey and Niall Ferguson, Christopher Ricks, the next Oxford University Professor of Poetry, crime novelist PD James and playwright Tom Stoppard? The Prince's own speech was well received. 'I didn't expect him to be so well-informed or so outspoken', said one delegate. It was clear that he understood the day-to-day pressures under which teachers have to work: the ceaseless flow of initiatives that, more often than not, peddle wacky theories that solve nothing, the collapse of authority in society; above all, perhaps, the bleak utilitarianism of so much of our contemporary debate.

His vision of a state education dedicated to the transmission of worthwhile knowledge in which children engage with 'the best that has been thought and written' drew particular applause, as did his ridicule of the re-invention of the teacher as a 'coach' or 'learning mentor', whose job it is to facilitate the child's voyage of self-discovery.

Anthony O'Hear, Head of Education at Buckingham University, spoke about the relevance of great art, arguing that we must learn to suspend our contemporary preoccupations and attend to the actuality of the masterpiece before us.

My own contribution was, I have to confess, less sublime. I put my foot in it immediately. 'The Tomlinson report into the future of 14-19 education,' I thundered, 'is an abomination, a tissue of assertion masquerading as an argument, a compendium of the most offensive educational clichés.' Who was sitting at the back of the hall? My ex-colleague, Mike Tomlinson. Sadly, he declined the invitation to defend himself, preferring to gaze at the floor in sorrowful incredulity.

The rain fell outside. The conference days passed. David Hopkins – the senior adviser to Charles Clarke, the Education Secretary – turned up and wished that he had not. The questions were too pointed, the mood of the conference too obvious. It was a pity his ministerial masters could not fit this year's summer school into their 'busy schedules'. If they had been there, they might have learnt something.

Should the Prince be hosting such an occasion? Of course he should. And I say that as a relative outsider attending my first summer school, not as the Svengali-like adviser some sections of the press imagine me to be.

Education matters. The future of our nation depends on the experiences that our teachers offer pupils. If they are compelled to attend conferences, as they are, as part of the 'key stage three strategy', designed to convince them that lessons should have 'a beginning, middle and an end', it is unlikely that those pupils will be particularly enriched.

Who else, other than the Prince could persuade so many of the great and the good to come and talk at a conference for teachers? Does anyone really think that teachers should be denied this unique opportunity? My own view, for what it is worth, is that the only question that is worth asking is: 'How can the experience be extended?' How can more teachers be offered this immensely rewarding experience? How can those who have attended be supported when they go back into their schools? The daily grind creeps up with horrible rapidity.

Stephen Miles told us about a conversation he had had with some of his pupils. They had asked him why they could not spend more time reading the literature that mattered to them. Miles explained to them that he had government consultants telling him what he should teach and how he should teach it. There was, he said, a long pause, a long embarrassing pause.

'Don't you find that degrading?' asked one. Miles smiled. 'I didn't,' he confessed, 'know what to say.'

***

These comments on teaching, prompted by issues of the day and questions from his readers, appeared in his weekly blogs for *The Sunday Times.*

Teaching includes marking – how else do we learn from our mistakes?

September 2011

We have spent the last hour or two searching for one of my old school exercise books. Light green cover, Wallington County Grammar School for Boys, printed near the top, 'C. A. Woodhead' and 'English', somewhere in the middle. Oh, and my class '4 Special 1'. In fact, I was in the 3rd form rather than the 4th form. The school did not have a 1st form because it wanted to have two 5th forms: an upper and a lower fifth. Such were the pretensions of grammar schools in the 1950s as they tried to emulate their public school rivals.

I was looking for this exercise book because of a letter a *Sunday Times* reader sent me last week. The reader wanted to know why it was that the written work, such as it was, at the primary school where she was a governor never seemed to be marked. Surely, she asked, every teacher set their pupils written work and then commented on the success of the ideas expressed and the accuracy of the spelling, punctuation and grammar?

That was certainly the case back at Wallington in 1960. We had to do an English essay each week and our teachers would comment on both content and linguistic accuracy. These comments mattered to me as a pupil. The particular book I have been trying to find contained an essay on going to the dentist. I had written in it about the relief of leaving the surgery, albeit with an 'unfamiliar' mouth. My teacher, Mr Evans, had underlined 'unfamiliar' and congratulated me in the margin on my excellent choice of adjective. Looking back, I don't think it is over-egging it to say that the moment I read his praise was one of the key experiences in making me think, as I have thought every day of my adult life, about the importance of the words we use.

Now, though, as this primary school governor has discovered, systematic, regular, engaged marking is no longer the norm in many schools, primary and secondary. Some teachers argue that to identify and correct mistakes undermines the self-confidence of the pupil. Others, like, apparently, the teachers in my reader's school, worship at the shrine of an American educator called Bob Slavin, who believes that it is far better for children to learn from each other than it is for them to learn from a teacher.

The question I ask myself is: 'how is it that anyone can come to believe what at best is a desperately partial truth?' When Labour was in power a unit called 'the Standards and Effectiveness Unit' used to exist at the Department for Education. Its mission, as its name suggests, was to promote better standards of teaching across the nation's schools. It was headed by a man called David Hopkins, whose guru was, yes, you have guessed it, Bob Slavin.

Professor Hopkins and his Standards and Effectiveness Unit have disappeared from the scene. The DfE and the ideas its inhabitants promoted under Labour remain. Teachers in too many schools think, for example, that they should not, as an article of educational faith, mark their children's work in the way I was fortunate enough to have my work marked when I was a child.

We have, moreover, a government which does not appear to have learnt the lesson of thirteen years of Labour educational misrule. Last week, Nick Gibb stood up at the Liberal Democrats conference and boasted about the fact that £50 million had been found to run summer schools for disadvantaged children who might otherwise be out in the streets pinching the latest trainers from the shops they have set on fire. These kids, he told his ecstatic audience, are the ones who 'have fallen through the cracks'. Indeed, they have, and no amount of summer school cash is going to pull them back out. The solution, as always in education, is to challenge the educational ideas that have caused the problem in the first place. Michael Gove has made a start, but very little has been achieved. In the Department for Education and its quangos, in university departments of education, and in local authorities, 'experts' like Professor Hopkins continue to promulgate 'ideas', like that of children learning from each other, which undermine the ability of teachers to teach and the possibility that children will ever learn.

***

Teachers should not bow to the great god, Relevance

February 2012

Rod Bristow, President of Pearson UK, the company which owns the exam board, Edexcel, thinks that maths has become 'a meaningless subject' for most young people, 'a series of disconnected techniques and formulae'.

'twas ever thus, I am afraid, Rod. The day I learnt that I had scraped an O level pass in maths remains in my mind as one of the happiest in my life. I had no idea how different mathematical concepts hung together or what the point of the subject might conceivably be.

Mr Bristow thinks that: 'We must show how maths is applied in careers, from construction to web design. We need to embed the sort of mathematical literacy that enables young people to see the connection between an abstract formula and the interest rate on their credit card'. Anne Watson, who is apparently Professor of Maths Education at Oxford University, agrees with him. She wants maths lessons to focus on things like spreadsheet design, problem solving skills and the need to 'adapt to new technologies'.

In other words, if we all bowed down before the great god 'Relevance', all would be well in the world of education. Suddenly, miraculously, the mathematically disaffected would be swept by a golden light of intelligence and understanding. 'Ah, a simultaneous equation! Excellent! Just what I will need when I am problem solving my way through adult life'. And, if everything can be rendered 'technological', so much the better, because we all know that the new technologies are going to transform education into a bright new world of instantaneous gratification.

My problem with maths had nothing to do with the fact that nothing we did in mathematics lessons connected with anything in the rest of my life. Nothing I did in any other lessons connected with anything. This did not worry me in the slightest. School was a major part of my life and what happened at school was as real and important as anything else. I might not have enjoyed it all, and I certainly didn't enjoy maths lessons very much, but I never for one moment thought that the problem was a disconnect between abstract formulae and the interest on my credit card (not that the latter, of course, existed in those distant days).

No, my problem was that I spent my second year at grammar school enjoying myself, playing the fool, in maths lessons. My maths teacher did not have any idea how to control the class and the temptation was just too great. In a sequential subject like maths, you cannot afford to skip a year's instruction. I never caught up. In a sense it was my fault; in a more fundamental sense it was the teacher's, who should have been competent in his job.

If we want more children to enjoy maths, we need better maths teachers. The challenge is that simple and that difficult. To waffle on about how maths must be made more relevant is to bang yet another nail into the concept of education which should be driving our struggle to reform the mediocrity of current practice. What happens in the classroom should be alien and remote and, therefore, challenging and exciting. The exact opposite, in fact, of what Rod Bristow and Professor Watson would have us believe.

***

What, actually, is 'mathematical reasoning'?

July 2012

Fifty years ago I suffered serious and repeated acts of educational abuse. My human rights as a 'learner' to determine what and how I learnt and, indeed, what counted as right answers in mathematics or grammatical accuracy in English and foreign languages, were denied. I was subjected to inhuman and degrading incidents of rote learning.

In the classroom next to the staffroom at Wallington County Grammar School for Boys, I was forced, for example, in Latin lessons, to 'look out at the roses and repeat after me: subject, object, odds and ends, verb'. The structure of a Latin sentence. Hammered, relentlessly, remorselessly, mindlessly, lesson after lesson, into my poor brain. The fact that, all these years on, I still remember the mantra I was forced to mutter shows the extent of the trauma I experienced.

Along with all other right-minded and progressive educationalists, I hoped that the practice of rote learning had been banished from every school in the land. But no. Education Minister, Nick Gibb, has been encouraging teachers to return to this inhuman past. Children, he has been saying, might learn their tables quicker and more effectively if they spent time chanting them as I did back in the 1950s.

Thank God for research emanating from the Oxford University Department of Educational Studies, which was published last week. What matters, the researchers tell us, is not the mastery of multiplication tables; it is the development of 'mathematical reasoning'. As one newspaper report put it: 'Children taught maths by rote learning times tables do worse at exams because they risk failing to understand the subject'.

Quite right, I thought, and applauded loudly when I read this. None of the newspaper reports I saw, however, told me what 'mathematical reasoning' actually was. So, fascinated by this new illumination from the research community, I did a little research on the Internet.

None of the sites I found offered any definition. I found, though, much intriguing material. The following extracts are typical. 'Students must develop a sense making orientation'. They 'must construct meaningful ways of thinking about mathematics'. The class should 'determine' whether 'solutions' made up by students 'make sense'. 'Teachers must be non-judgemental' and 'should not explain'. Their responsibility is to 'promote intellectual autonomy'. The aim is for the teacher to move from being a 'dispenser of knowledge' to a 'facilitator' so that they 'put students in charge of their learning'.

I should add that all of the above has been endorsed by Randy Harter, the past President of the North Carolina Council of Teachers of Mathematics. Wouldn't it be wonderful if *Sunday Times* readers were to club together to fund a Ministerial trip to North Carolina so that Nick Gibb could be helped to see the progressive light?

***

Continuing Professional Development is a multimillion pound industry

January 2013

What with the weather and living up an impassable track, half way up a mountain in Wales, and the ravages of Motor Neurone Disease, I don't get out much these days. Sometimes people do come to see us, though. Christine ferries them up the track in our Toyota pick-up and we sit round the fire chewing the cud.

Last Saturday was such an occasion. The conversation turned, as, depressingly, it so often does when I am around, to education. 'Why is it', someone asked, 'that my children's teachers are away from school so often on what, I am told, is known as "continuing professional development"?'

Good question, I thought. I would be fascinated to know just how many millions of pounds of taxpayers' money are spent every year on

CPD (as it is known in the trade) and how many hundreds of thousands of pupils sit bored in front of a supply teacher, filling in a tedious worksheet, instead of being taught by their proper teacher.

The educational establishment, of course, is all for CPD. They would be, wouldn't they? It is a multimillion pound industry that gives the academics, the advisers and the consultants a very comfortable living. Last week, I noticed in a national newspaper that Sir Tim Brighouse, who was once the London Commissioner of Schools, and Bob Moon, the Emeritus Professor of Education at the Open University, have criticised the current provision of CPD for teachers as 'haphazard, poorly planned and lacking strategic direction'. They want, apparently, a body such as a 'National Teaching Institute' to be established in order to provide a sense of direction and the structures needed in order to ensure that England's teachers have world class CPD.

Whenever I read the word 'strategic', I flinch. We do not need a great national debate about a new strategy for training teachers in service. We need a recognition that teachers spend far too much time out of school attending courses which contribute, I agree, little or nothing to their effectiveness in the classroom. We need, further, to recognise that teaching is not a profession where people have to attend courses all the time in order to keep up with the latest developments. Good teaching in the 21st century is not very different from teaching in the 20th or, for that matter, the 19th century. We need teachers with a knowledge and passion for their subject, high expectations of their pupils and a mastery of the craft of the classroom.

The best way to develop the latter is to create a school culture where teachers are encouraged to open their classroom doors to their colleagues and engage, every day of the working year, in a professional debate about the strengths and weaknesses of their practice. My good friend, Peter Ireland, developed such a culture when he was Head of The Nelson Thomlinson School in Wigton. He even found the money to build a special classroom which had a one way mirror down one side. His teachers would volunteer to teach sample lessons, which were observed by their colleagues behind the mirror. When I visited I was amazed by the intensity and excitement of the discussion as colleagues talked about how they could work together to help their students to achieve more.

Parents who are sick of teacher absence on CPD should band together and ask their school's headteacher why these unacceptable levels of teacher absence are necessary when the best schools are so effective in training their teachers on site.

The track leading to our house in north Wales.

***

Most teachers these days see themselves as facilitators

April 2013

'I do not want to create a society of robots who just know stuff'. In that it takes a kind of genius to sum up the whole educational zeitgeist in one short sentence, this delegate to the National Union of Teachers' Easter conference deserves our congratulations.

He or she no doubt received rapturous applause from the couple of thousand teachers packed into the conference hall. Who, after all, needs to know 'stuff' when everything that has ever been known is instantaneously available on the Internet? Who, in their right mind, would want students, in all their impressionable ignorance, to be initiated into forms of worthwhile knowledge by teachers who are older and wiser? Our children should, shouldn't they, be encouraged to discover things for themselves and come to their own unassisted conclusions? We do not want unthinking little 'robots', do we?

I was fortunate enough to attend a grammar school in south London fifty-odd years ago. My teachers might, I suppose, have dragged anxiously on their cigarettes in their smoke-filled staffroom, pondering the nature of the educational enterprise. Somehow, I doubt it. We went to school to be taught things that mattered by men who were passionate about the subjects they taught. Some, inevitably, were not very good teachers. But the ideal was clear. This was a community in which the importance of knowledge and the fact that education depended upon the young submitting to the authority of experts and enthusiasts was taken for granted.

A lot has changed over the last fifty years in education. There are still schools which hold on to the idea that knowledge matters and the authority of the teacher must be absolute. But they are few and far between. The teacher who spoke at the NUT conference has become the norm. The Secretary of State for Education's proposals for a new National Curriculum rooted in worthwhile knowledge have provoked venomous opposition. A hundred academics working in university departments of education recently signed a letter to national newspapers dismissing Mr Gove and his wretched curriculum as a throwback to the educational dark ages when teachers, they allege, did nothing but cram facts into their pupils' heads to be regurgitated in examinations and, in later life, in pub quizzes.

One of the greatest ironies of the current educational debate is that those who espouse most passionately the central importance of teaching the young how to think for themselves demonstrate such a lamentable inability to reflect on the absurdity of their own arguments. The ability to think demands a basic knowledge of the thing one is thinking about. I have opinions on, for example, the topic of global warming, but I do not have the scientific knowledge to think, in any meaningful sense of the word, about the strengths and weaknesses of opposing arguments.

Knowledge matters. The purpose of education is, as Richard Peters and Paul Hirst argued many years ago, to initiate the young into the different ways in which over the centuries men have organised their experience and understanding of the world. This initiation depends upon the ability of teachers to explain and inspire and the willingness of the young to engage in this enterprise with a proper humility.

Most people who think at all about education, but who are not teachers or academics working within university departments of education, would probably raise an eyebrow at the idea that anybody could believe anything different. But most teachers in this second decade of the 21st century have been brainwashed into a Pavlovian rejection of what they believe to be an outdated and authoritarian view. They see their job as facilitators rather than teachers who have an authority in their subject and over their students. They aspire to a democratic relationship in which everyone in the classroom is a 'learner' engaged in the discovery of new knowledge and personal insights.

Standards in our schools will not rise until these beliefs are defeated. This is why Michael Gove's examination reforms are so important. The changes he is making to the National Curriculum are fundamental, but the lesson of the last twenty years is that a National Curriculum does not have a significant impact on the ideas that underpin the teacher's practice. High stake public examinations have to be taken seriously. They are the single most important weapon in the war of ideas about education that has to be won if our children are to fulfil their potential.

***

We need a less romantic view ….

October 2013

Last week, figures released by the OECD revealed that the 55–65 age group in England had stronger literacy and numeracy skills than 16 to 24 year olds, even though the younger group had much better qualifications.

These days, I find it hard not to yawn and turn the page. There is so much evidence now to show that the last thirty years of education reforms have not had the necessary impact, that billions of pounds of taxpayers' money have been squandered, that the ever improving GCSE statistics mean nothing. But why is it so hard to improve things in education?

A day or so after the OECD statistics were published, I received an email from a *Sunday Times* reader who is something of an expert in this area. He wrote that standards in maths are

'dire...because the teaching is vague and unfocused in primaries. It is a kind of discovery learning, what the children are supposed to discover being for them to find out'.

He went on to say that he had

'...visited some German and Dutch schools recently, both in poor areas. The approach of the schools was impressive, focused and direct. The over-professionalisation which we suffer from was absent. The teachers didn't go about kidding on they were something terrifically special. This went up to education officer level. They said, pupils need to add so we teach them to add, that's it, and then they looked at me as if I were thinking there might be more to it. But I was just thinking, jings, that's fabulous. I asked a number of pupils in the German school what they thought of their big sums – 'grossartig!' they enthused (German likes lots of exclamation marks). None seemed tortured or depressed or craving to learn unit number bonds by means of painting a picture of social cohesion or global warming. Maybe they were just happy that they could actually do things'.

One of the most important things Michael Gove's special adviser, Dominic Cummings, wrote in the fascinating essay he published a few days ago was that we are mad to pretend that every teacher can be brilliant and inspirational. The world of teacher training loves to pretend that the key to better student learning is the development of 'reflective practitioners' – men and women who spend hours every night pondering the magic of their craft. Cummings argues that it would make a great deal more sense if we adopted a less romantic view of the teaching profession and required schools to use programmes of instruction which are known to work. Teachers complain about the pressure they are under but seem prepared to die in the ditch in a battle to protect their sacrosanct autonomy. We should rescue them from the absurdity of their collective self-delusion.

The key, as the reader who emailed me suggests, is to deflate the professional self-aggrandisement and return to a basic, common-sense approach that cuts through, for example, the widespread assumption that the teaching of basic mathematics should be embedded in a trans-disciplinary effort to ensure that our children are indoctrinated into a proper stance towards the key issues of the day, such as social cohesion and global warming.

***

Our ability to grapple with what was difficult was what counted

December 2013

I would rather be meandering through country lanes than flogging up a motorway. I prefer to turn the pages of a book than to push the buttons of a Kindle. I never did understand why John Major's pastoral idyll of cricket on the village green and warm beer attracted so much scorn and ridicule.

Romantic and nostalgic, I am more than ready to confess that I am out of synch with our tower block and technological times. I do not think, though, that there has ever been a golden age when it comes to education.

A couple of days ago, a friend asked me a question. 'How is it', he said, 'that we have once again done badly in the PISA league tables when ministers tell us that we have the best generation of teachers we have ever had?'

Good question, I thought. The quality of the teaching a child receives is the key determinant of the educational progress that child makes. Not every child will make the same progress, but whatever their innate ability, they are going to do better if they have a good teacher. So, if it is true that we have the best teachers we have ever had, then our poor PISA performance is indeed puzzling.

But the assertion that today's teachers are better than any teachers at any time in the past is nonsense. There is no evidence whatsoever to support it. Tests and examinations have changed so dramatically over the years that examination data offers no reliable indication of how students have done and their teachers have taught. There was no systematic Ofsted inspection of teachers prior to the early 1990s and, while the current system sees schools inspected more regularly, it delivers very little reliable data on the quality of teaching. Ofsted inspection of teacher training focuses more on compliance and policies than it does on the competence of the trainee teacher.

The fact that this statement has gone unchallenged tells us more about the need to convince ourselves that things are getting better in the world of education than it does about what is actually happening.

This is not to say that, when I look back at my own school days at a grammar school in south London in the 1950s and 60s, I think standards of teaching were necessarily higher. I had several teachers who were unable to control the admittedly rather difficult class I was in. Others wrote notes on the board or dictated from a dog-eared collection of lesson plans. We were expected to sit and copy. One or two took a delight in humiliating children and should not have been in the profession.

Conversely, there were men (and all our teachers were men) who were quite simply inspirational. Their knowledge and enthusiasm were palpable and their interest in us as pupils was hugely supportive. I guess my school was, in fact, much like any other school, then and now. There was a very wide spread of teaching quality from the very best to the unacceptable.

What was different was the sense that it was all worthwhile. I didn't always think this as a 13 or 14 year old, but the ethos of the school was strong. The subjects we studied mattered, not because they might lead us towards a future job, but because they had intrinsic worth. It was the subject, too, that mattered most, not the views we had as pupils about the knowledge we were taught. We were encouraged to think, but it was our ability to grapple with what was difficult rather than our personal views about anything that counted.

This is a real difference between then and now. We live in a materialistic and utilitarian age and it is the relevance of the classroom to the world of work that dominates our view of education. It surprises me that given this culture so many intellectually able young men and women continue to choose to enter the teaching profession. If we really want the best generation of teachers ever, we need to change our concept of education and our sense of what a teacher should do.

***

The wider the range of ability in the class the harder it is to teach

September 2014

Sometimes I wonder whether the educational researchers who pronounce upon how schools should be run and children taught have any idea at all about what it is to teach real children in a real classroom.

Take mixed ability teaching, which was in the news last week because of a rather mysterious leak which the Education Minister, Nicky Morgan, was forced to deny in the Commons. The story was that Number 10 was keen to include in the Conservative manifesto for the next election the proposal that all secondary schools should be forced to group their pupils in ability sets. For the record, Morgan denied that she had any intention of doing any such thing.

Mixed ability teaching is one of those perennial education issues that polarises opinion. It was utterly predictable, though, that Professor Chris Husbands, from the Institute of Education in London, remarked that, while the evidence was inconclusive, it seemed that setting was of some benefit to academic pupils but damaging to the less able. Professor Dylan Williams made the point that setting was another way in which middle class parents managed to exert their influence to ensure that their children had the best teachers. So, for these two leading academics, setting is a bad thing because it is one more nail in the coffin of the disadvantaged and the less able.

It is a good many years now since I actually taught, but I have clear memories of trying to teach English to a class of 15 year olds which included a boy who could barely read and a girl who told me that I really must read John Fowles' latest novel, *The Magus*. Trying to plan lessons which engaged the most able and the least able in this class was a daunting and unsatisfactory challenge.

Whatever the research might say, the common sense truth is obvious. No class is ever going to have children of exactly the same ability, but the wider the range of ability in the class the harder it is for the teacher to teach. It is pretty obvious, too, that whilst children can end up feeling unloved and rejected in a low ability set, they can also find the going pretty tough if they are forced, lesson after lesson, to compete with their more able peers.

Does this mean that, whatever Ms Morgan's denials, Number 10 has lit upon a good election wheeze? It does not. The whole thrust of recent education reforms has been to free headteachers from the Whitehall diktat that burdened them when Labour was in power. I find it inconceivable that a Conservative government would want to reverse this trend and tell schools how they should organise their pupils.

The key to higher standards is to let good ideas flourish in a market where parents have a genuine opportunity to choose between schools. The schools that use the best methods to organise and teach their students will be the most popular with parents. Those that stick to cherished ideological beliefs that do not deliver will lose students to their more popular rivals.

This, again, is a statement of the obvious, but no doubt dozens of educational researchers are seeking evidence to prove me wrong, even as I write.

***

We need to find ways to minimise the influence of the Blob

November 2014

In the mid 1950s, the American sociologist, Leon Festinger, infiltrated an apocalyptic sect called 'the Seekers'. It was led by a suburban housewife, Dorothy Martin, who claimed to have received messages from 'the Guardians', a group of superior beings from another planet, telling her the precise date when the world would end.

He wrote a book about the sect, called *When Prophecy Fails*. It is a fascinating study of how human beings react when cherished beliefs do not deliver the expected results.

One might have expected the sect members to have decided that Mrs Martin's messages from the Guardians were discredited. Far from it. She explained to them that the end of the world had been averted by 'the force of good and light', and that they themselves had played an important part in this wonderful event. They continued to proselytise their message with renewed vigour, undaunted by what most of us would see as compelling evidence to the contrary.

This study led Festinger to develop his theory of 'cognitive dissonance'. Put briefly, this theory seeks to explain why human beings who have deeply held convictions which are crucial to their everyday actions and behaviour find it so hard to react rationally to evidence which challenges their beliefs.

In a way, it is obvious. The existence of 'dissonance' is psychologically uncomfortable and it may, therefore, be easier for the believer to seek reinforcement for their beliefs than to accept that they were wrong. They will, furthermore, and again naturally enough, seek to avoid evidence and argument that increases the dissonance, whilst simultaneously trying to bolster belief through contact with fellow believers.

What brought Festinger and his book, *When Prophecy Fails*, to my mind was a report published by the Sutton Trust last week which reviewed a good deal of evidence about educational theories that have dominated thinking about teaching and learning over the last two or three decades. The report tells us that effective teaching depends on the subject knowledge of the teacher and their mastery of the craft of the classroom. Yes, I thought, I was saying this twenty years ago, and precious little good it did me. To most of us, it is a statement of the obvious, but not, I am afraid, to the theorists and pundits who have driven education policy in recent times.

They prefer to believe, to quote some of the theories discredited by research that the Sutton Trust report lists, that: lavish and indiscriminate praise turns unmotivated students into committed and enthusiastic seekers after knowledge; it is better to allow children to discover things for themselves than ever to cut through the fog of time-wasting ignorance and actually tell them anything; the teacher must cater for every individual 'learning style' in a class of thirty or more students; and that 'active' learning, in which, for example, a group of bedraggled teenagers spends their morning counting the number of delivery vans parked in a suburban high street, is preferable to time spent 'passively' listening to a teacher explain and inspire.

Cognitive dissonance, I am afraid, once more raises its ugly head, and there is no magic bullet. The equivalent in our education system to the suburban housewife who believed she had extraterrestrial authority to promulgate her delusional beliefs is what has become known as the Blob[*], leading figures in the world of education who have had, and continue to have, huge influence on how children are taught.

We need to find ways to minimise this influence and to maximise the influence of the pragmatic headteachers who lead our most effective schools. This is what Michael Gove was trying to do in shifting teacher training into schools, encouraging the development of free schools and academies, and introducing more rigorous, knowledge-based examinations. He made a hugely important start, but it was only a start.

The question now, as the next election approaches, is which of the political parties understands the extent to which the prophecies have failed and is determined enough to continue the drive to short-circuit the influence of the prophets.

***

---

[*] The term 'the Blob' was coined by an American commentator on education, who observed that the educational establishment, aggressive in its self-righteousness and fierce in its determination to protect its own vested interest, was harder than 'a greased steer' to wrestle to the ground. I pinched the term when I wrote *Class War*, the book I published after I resigned as Chief Inspector, and in recent years it has gained some currency.

A charismatic teacher

March 2013

I never met Theodore Zinn, but, reading his obituary a week or two ago, I very much wish that I had.

From 1950 to 1983 Zinn taught Classics at Westminster. The photographs accompanying the obituary show a man sitting at a desk in a book-lined room, addressing a horseshoe of students. He was clearly loved by generations of those he taught and was, it seems, not only a scholar with a formidable intellect, but a kind and generous man with a sense of humour. He must have had remarkable charisma to persuade teachers and parents to sit watching plays performed in Latin when they did not understand a word of the language.

I do not think that there was ever a golden age in education, but reading this obituary I was left with a sense of what has now been more or less lost. There are, of course, dedicated and highly effective teachers in our schools. There may well be some who have the individuality and commitment of Theodore Zinn. Ours, however, is the age of relevance and accessibility and lessons which depend more on the technology than the teacher.

Zinn would not, I suspect, be a great fan of Firefly or iSAMS. I am certain that the impact of his lessons stemmed from the force of his personality and the love which he had for the language and the literature he taught. All great lessons depend upon these things. The rest is flim flam.

But it is not just a matter of lowered expectations and the worship of the great god of technology. That book-lined classroom, with the teacher at the front behind a desk, evokes a sense of something I can only call deference. We don't do deference these days, do we? What matters more than the substance of the ideas studied is the student's personal opinion. If you want to know why things have gone wrong in education, here is the place to start.

You cannot have a true education without a proper sense of deference. Real education requires the student to submit himself to the mastery of new ideas and to respect the teacher as an authority in his or her subject. That respect has, of course, to be earned, but those who see the relationship between the teacher and the student as something which has to be outgrown as soon as possible are profoundly misguided. Many in the world of education believe that the purpose of education is to teach children how to learn on their own, to equip them with so called learning skills, and to offer them the joy of a curriculum which they 'personalise' in terms of their individual interests.

It is all nonsense. I imagine that Theodore Zinn must have contemplated this new world which emerged towards the end of his teaching career with some bemusement. The question is whether the scholarship he embodied has gone forever. Is there any way in which it can be rediscovered and brought back into our schools?

***

And headteachers – the nearest thing to a magic wand

December 2012 *[Abridged]*

I was sitting in my office soon after I had been appointed to my first senior post in a local authority wondering what the day would bring, when the phone rang. It was the headteacher of a small primary school in the south of the county. He sounded flustered. The school bus had turned up at his school gate, but there were no children on board. He had, it seemed, no pupils. 'Do you know', he asked rather plaintively, 'what is going on?'

I didn't, but I had hardly put the phone down when it rang again. This time it was the headteacher of the village school next to the pupil-less school. 'I seem', this Head said, 'to have an extra thirty-two children. Do you know what is going on?'

It rapidly became clear what was going on. The parents of the first headteacher's school had been complaining about educational standards for some time. They had become frustrated at our lack of action and had decided to take matters into their own hands. Their children were no longer going to attend what in their view was a substandard school and that was that as far as they were concerned.

Chris as a local authority senior adviser in the 1980s.

A week or two later I attended a conference in Birmingham where Sir (as he was then) Keith Joseph was the lead speaker. He talked about the fundamental importance of the headteacher. 'The nearest thing to a magic wand', he said, 'we have in education is a good Head'. Driving back, I thought about what he had said in the light of our little local difficulty. The headteacher is the key figure in any school. If he is offering strong leadership and relating positively to the parent community all is well; if he is not, then no amount of external support or financial investment in new facilities and extra resources is going to make the slightest difference.

My experience as Chief Inspector confirmed time and time again this obvious truth. Schools that failed our inspections almost invariably failed because the leadership was weak. I was, therefore, enthusiastic when the last Government proposed to create a National College of School Leadership. I liked the idea of an institution where heads and aspirant heads could meet to think about what leadership in a school means. I wanted to find ways to move discussion beyond the platitudes that so often constrain thinking about leadership, to encourage people to be honest about themselves and their schools, to reflect on the challenges they faced in working with staff to improve teaching, and, crucially, to explore their individual thinking about the nature of the educational enterprise.

In the event, the College has been a disaster. It is now very much at the heart of the educational problem Michael Gove has inherited. Why? Because it has sought to support every new government initiative that has been proposed over the last decade. It could not have focused more enthusiastically on the political message. To give just one example, a recent NCSL corporate plan stated that the College 'will work…to identify and support those leaders who have yet to engage in the Every Child Matters and extended schools agenda'. The latter were key elements in the last Government's education reforms. You may not want our support, but we know where you are and you are going to get it. Am I alone in finding this Big Brother attitude rather sinister?

Aspirant heads have to achieve a College qualification before they can be appointed to a state school. This requires them to attend a 48 hour residential conference which ignores the here and now, the challenges and opportunities headteachers face today, in favour of a vision of 'the school of the future', though delegates are warned to be wary of the concept of a 'school' for 'the very use of the word can limit our thinking to what we understand goes with a school' and 'in the future, such a concept may become rapidly outdated'. Their noses are rubbed in the 'personalised learning agenda', the ever increasing potential of technology, the exciting prospect of community schools, which address 'the needs of individuals, families and groups in a holistic way' and the importance of what is known in the jargon as 'distributive leadership'.

Michael Gove wants to free state education from the ideological and bureaucratic shackles of state control. He should have announced the closure of the NCSL on his first day in office. Headteachers matter. They are, as his predecessor, Lord Joseph, said, the nearest thing to a magic wand we've got. When is the penny going to drop?

***

You have to be a warrior and a battler

July 2012

Sir Michael Wilshaw, the Chief Inspector of Schools, is right: the best headteachers are 'often quite odd people'.

Mind you, there are different sorts of oddness. I spent two terms working in a secondary modern school before I went to university. I have a vivid memory of the Head, leaping, one morning, from the stage during assembly, brandishing his cane above his head, shouting: 'Sing, damn you, sing!' Would Sir Michael approve? I don't know, but I can tell you that the enthusiasm with which the hymn was rendered by staff and pupils alike increased tenfold.

Today, it is 'consultative leadership' which is all the vogue. When I interviewed the first Chief Executive of the National College of School Leadership, I remember quizzing her on her overriding enthusiasm for 'empathy' as the key quality which headteachers had to possess. Sure, I remember saying, it is important for those in positions of power to understand what their colleagues are feeling, but, isn't it also important for them to be able to motivate and inspire and, from time to time, take situations and people by the scruff of the neck? She looked at me as if I were mad.

The best headteacher I ever met when I was Chief Inspector of Schools was Peter Ireland, the Head of The Nelson Thomlinson School in Wigton in Cumbria. I visited his school because I was intrigued by the intemperate tone of a letter of complaint he had written me about the patronising arrogance of two of my inspectors who had dared cross the threshold of his school. Five minutes into our initial chat over a cup of coffee, and I was bent double with laughter as he pranced around his office demonstrating how he had wanted to signify his displeasure to the puffed-up bureaucrats who had failed to understand anything of what he was trying to do.

Walking round the school, I was immediately struck by the buzz of excitement in every classroom we entered. Here was a school where the teachers knew that the quality of their teaching was the only thing that mattered. Peter had the best system of performance management I have seen in a school, and it worked because he, himself, exemplified, in everything he did, the values that mattered most to him and the school he led.

Of course, great headteachers are, as Sir Michael puts it, 'slightly maverick'. The run-of-the-mill lurk in their offices, shifting bits of paper, hiding from the real challenges which leadership involves. Leadership takes courage. It cannot be taught in national colleges. You have got it, or you haven't. Peter Ireland had it. Sir Michael, himself, from what I have heard, had exceptional courage and determination when he was Head of Mossbourne Academy. He is demonstrating similar courage now, as an outspoken Chief Inspector.

Of course, leadership should be consultative. The danger, and the reality in so many schools, is that decisions get bogged down in the consultation. Meeting after meeting is held to avoid ever reaching a conclusion. In the end, headteachers are paid to point the way forward, to inspire those who want to make the journey, and to remove those who do not. It's a cliché to say the job is lonely, but leadership always is. The buck stops with you. You have to be happy with the responsibility and confident enough in yourself not to care too much about the back-biting and the criticism.

You have to be, to quote Sir Michael once more, 'a warrior and a battler'.

***

Spare me the moral mission

April 2015

Why is it that phrases like 'a moral responsibility' and 'the moral core of headship' make me cringe?

I recently spent a couple of hours ploughing through some applications for a vacant headship post. Every letter I read made some reference to a 'moral mission'. It was as if each of the candidates had been programmed to emphasise the profundity of their vocational commitment.

This is not actually surprising, because the National College of School Leadership has been peddling this rhetoric for years now. We have a conveyer belt of aspirant headteachers who all say exactly the same things about personalised learning, wellbeing, happiness lessons, moral mission, and the rest. The days of the maverick individual who knew what they wanted to do and who had the courage of their personal convictions has long gone.

The cringe factor for me stems from my natural scepticism. There are saints in this world, and I am lucky enough to be married to one. But there are not many such people, and those who feel the need to profess their saintliness always make me suspicious. Why is it, I ask myself, that they need to make such a fuss? What have they got to hide? Why can't they let the strength of their personal motivation to run a school emerge from the details of how they would approach the job if appointed?

When I appoint a headteacher, I am looking for the sharpness of their intelligence, their ability to carry their school community with them, and their strength and resilience under fire. I will ask them why they want the job and I will push and probe to establish whether their answers are underpinned by real reflection and conviction. It is actually rather a depressing business these days, a bit like asking robots whether they believe in God.

Curriculum reform: the battle for the soul of education

Staunch defender of the subject-based curriculum, Chris Woodhead blamed the pursuit of what he called the 'holy grail of our core skills' and cross-curricular themes, and our obsession with making the curriculum 'relevant' and 'accessible' to young people for much of the decline in educational standards. In the first piece here he deplores the way the National Curriculum had already, by 2005, moved a long way from the original intention of a broad statement of the subjects that should be taught.

First published in *The Sunday Times,* April 2005

You have a 12 or 13-year old? Ask them what they know about 'the world as a global community, and the political, economic, environmental and social implications of this'. Ask them about 'the diversity of national, regional, religious and ethnic identities in the United Kingdom'. Share with them their 'reflections on the process of participating'. Then ask yourself what this toxic mix of political correctness and new age mysticism has to do with education.

The quotations are from David Blunkett's great legacy as Education Secretary: a new National Curriculum subject, citizenship. Something, he felt, had to be done to counter the yob culture and develop a sense of responsibility and national identity. As the then Chief Inspector of Schools in England, I agreed. Of course, who wouldn't? But who in their right mind would waste time on this sort of twaddle?

Some 90% of 15 to 24-year olds do not know that King John signed the Magna Carta. Under a quarter can name either the most recent monarch to abdicate (Edward VIII) or the opposing sides in the wars of the roses (York and Lancaster). Citizenship in primary schools is meant to teach children to 'feel positive about themselves' by, for example, 'producing personal diaries, profiles and portfolios of achievements'. Not, you note, through mastering new knowledge and pushing back the frontiers of what they believe they can achieve.

The National Curriculum should be a straightforward statement of what children need to be taught in the traditional subjects of the school timetable – English, maths, science, history, art, and so on. That was what the original National Curriculum more or less was.

But even when it was formulated, back in the late 1980s, it was a battle. Some educationists resented the very idea that subjects could be taught separately and what mattered was the 'seamless web of knowledge'. Others attacked the focus on subject knowledge, saying children needed to be taught 'cross-curricular' skills such as 'problem solving' which were far more important than boring facts.

The battle was, ultimately, for the soul of state education and since 1997 those of us who think that a National Curriculum should encapsulate worthwhile knowledge have suffered some pretty comprehensive defeats. That is why Michael Howard is right to call for a review of the National Curriculum, and why I have agreed to undertake that rethink if the Conservatives win the election.

Most of us would probably agree that some time in the school week should be spent on sex and careers education. What, though, of cramming in 'education for sustainable development', the teaching of 'financial capability', 'enterprise and entrepreneurial skills', the provision of 'work-related learning', the promotion of 'spiritual, moral, social and cultural development'? Oh yes, and the odd period for the banal pieties of Blunkett's citizenship curriculum.

It can't be done. These are the unworkable aspirations of politicians who will never have to deliver in the classroom. Five-year-olds are expected to develop 'entrepreneurial characteristics of tenacity, independence, innovation, imagination, risk-taking, creativity, intuition and leadership'.

I don't know about you, but 53 years on I am feeling more than a little inadequate. I would like teachers to teach children to read, and I rather suspect that they might have more success if the National Curriculum had some clear focus on phonics, shown in study after study to be the key to reading.

Under the current system children are expected to 'select and apply skills, tactics and compositional ideas' in physical education. In history what matters is not the story of the past, but the skills of the historian.

They must be taught 'to recognise that the past is represented and interpreted in different ways, and to give reasons for this'. At seven, 11 or 14, even, when most children do not have the shakiest grasp on the facts of what happened when?

And so it goes on. The rationale for the geography order makes passing reference to 'developing knowledge of places' and teaching about maps, but suggests that the subject is important because it is 'a focus within the curriculum for understanding and resolving issues about the environment and sustainable development'. David Bell, the current Chief Inspector of Schools, agrees. 'Geography,' he said recently, 'enables us to understand change, conflict, and the key issues which impact on our lives today and will affect our futures tomorrow.' His inspectors are delighted by a new GCSE course that is not 'overloaded with content'. Students are encouraged to submit poems and posters that register their feelings about these pressing contemporary concerns.

I want children to leave school knowing something. It is the depth and breadth of their understanding, not the precocity of their feeling that matters. The emphasis today is increasingly on the latter. We tell our children less and less and expect them to tell us at an earlier and earlier age what they think about massively complex issues.

The reality, of course, is that they reflect back to us what we have taught them to think and feel. The National Curriculum has become a vehicle for indoctrination and in its present form it should be abolished. The only alternative is a review that returns to what matters: the teaching of worthwhile knowledge.

***

Micky Mouse courses

I did not always appreciate it at the time, but I was lucky to have taken my O levels in the 1960s. The teachers at my grammar school spent every minute of the school day on traditional academic subjects which provided a rigorous preparation for A level and university, introduced us to a wide body of worthwhile knowledge, and had the potential to inspire us for the rest of our lives.

Micky Mouse courses and qualifications, such as Citizenship and Media Studies, Communication and Culture, or Preparation for Working Life, did not exist in those halcyon days. Now they are part of the GCSE curriculum in many, if not most secondary schools.

There are three reasons for this calamitous development.

The first is that too many schools, state and independent, are now more interested in bolstering their league table position than they are in offering their students a proper education. Courses such as the ones described above are pretty well impossible to fail and gullible parents who do not ask the right questions will assume that the school is academically successful.

Second, where my grammar school teachers wanted me to be inspired and intrigued by the fascination of what was difficult, today's teachers are prone to think that everything must be 'relevant' to the student's experience and instantaneously 'accessible'. This pernicious belief rules out ninety nine per cent of what is worth teaching.

Then, third, there is the widespread conviction that, in the age of the Internet, nobody actually has to be taught anything about anything. All schools need to do is develop in their students the 'learning skills' that, in theory at least, will open the world of scholarship to them whenever they want. So, we have GCSEs which spend more time teaching 'problem solving' skills than they do specific subject knowledge, and, as a consequence, we have thousands of 16 year olds gazing, bleary-eyed and desperate, at their computer screens as they struggle to find something to cut and paste in order to complete their latest coursework project.

A proper education focuses above all on subject knowledge. Academic GCSEs may not have the rigour of the old O level, but they do open the student's eyes to the world which exists beyond the confines of their personal experience. The more one knows about British history, the richer one's understanding of the country in which we live. The more one knows about geography, the richer one's understanding of the landscape which surrounds us. If we want our children to live full and meaningful lives, we have to teach them about the wonder of the world. We have to teach mathematics and science and literature and art.

Any parent selecting a school for their child needs to probe beyond the GCSE statistics. You need to ask the headteacher about his vision of education. You need to find out whether that vision focuses on the development of worthwhile knowledge or whether it has been corrupted by the pursuit of relevance and accessibility. You need, above all, to visit classrooms so that you can judge for yourself whether there is teaching which challenges students to master new and difficult knowledge.

If you are not persuaded that serious educational values underpin the GCSE statistics and the league table position, you should walk away. If, having read this article, you wonder whether the school your child attends has reduced the curriculum to quasi academic nonsense, you are likely to have a battle on your hands.

Gather as much evidence as you can. Talk to like-minded parents. Take your concerns to the governing body if the headteacher and teachers are not prepared to listen. The fight matters. Good luck!

***

From his weekly blogs for *The Sunday Times*

A new curriculum and the same old battles

June 2012

A reader contacted me last week to ask whether I was pleased with Michael Gove's proposals for a new primary National Curriculum. She ended by saying that I ought to be, in that this latest version of the National Curriculum reflects much of what I have been saying for the last quarter of a century.

It does, and, in principle, I am. Michael Gove's educational heart is in the right place and we should all applaud his conviction that the educational enterprise must ensure that children have the opportunity to engage with the best that has been thought and said in the past.

What impact, though, can curriculum reform have in practice? If the lessons of history are any guide to the future, the answer is little if any.

The curriculum which was published last week resembles very closely the curriculum which we tried to implement in the early 1990s. Our experience then was that the process of consultation resulted in a never-ending series of fudges and compromises. Once the curriculum was law, the teaching profession started to complain about many aspects of what the Government wanted and ministers, panicking, set up a new consultation in order to appease the wrath of the unions and the educational establishment.

We soon discovered, moreover, what ought to have been obvious from the start. The Secretary of State does not have the power to impose his will on 24,000 schools scattered round the country. He has no real levers to pull. He can huff and he can puff, but he is never going to blow the professional house down.

The old debates have already surfaced. Stephen Twigg, for example, the Labour spokesman on education, acknowledged that it was important to teach children traditional subjects, but added that time must also be found to develop 'transferrable' skills. Reading his press release brought back memories of hours spent in committees pondering the balance between what were then called 'cross-curricular' skills and basic subject knowledge. Nothing ever changes in the world of education.

We even, it seems, have a repeat of the farce which accompanied the publication of what became known as the 'Three Wise Men' report into primary education in 1991. On the day we were to meet the press, one of the wise men went awol until the last possible moment. I can remember sitting wondering whether he would tell the world that he was unhappy with what the report contained or whether he would toe the party line. Now in 2012, it is Andrew Pollard, apparently, who, having been asked by Gove to contribute to the curriculum review, is now blogging that the Secretary of State has got it all wrong.

The truth is that no government is ever going to raise educational standards through Whitehall diktat. Why do independent schools provide high standards of education? Because they have to meet the aspirations of parents who pay their fees. Politicians and their bureaucrats should remove themselves from the educational arena and allow market forces and parental choice to flourish in the state sector as they do in the world of private education.

To argue that middle class parents who can afford to pay the fees private schools charge know what they want, but that the less affluent do not know and do not care is patronising and, in my experience, factually incorrect. Of course there are feckless parents who have no interest in the future of their feral children. Most parents, however desperate their financial or personal situation, do care.

The free school initiative is an exciting idea to strengthen parental choice. It needs to be pursued with more political courage, but it is an excellent beginning. The way forward is to acknowledge the limitations of state control and to allow new schools and new providers to enter the education market, so that the state monopoly on education can be broken. Supply side reforms will deliver far more than any reconstruction of the National Curriculum, however worthy the educational vision which underpins this new curriculum might be.

***

An A level in Creative Writing is the last thing we need

February 2013

A few months ago I joked in this blog that there would soon be a GCSE examination in 'Happiness Studies'. The Headmaster of Wellington College, Anthony Seldon, had been talking and writing extensively about the need to timetable specific lessons in happiness and many schools across the country were planning to do just this. It seemed to me merely a matter of time before some bright spark decided that a curriculum innovation of this cosmic significance must be dignified by a qualification which allowed young people to demonstrate the profundity of their cognitive insight and the depth of their emotional intelligence.

Thus far, it hasn't happened. Last week, however, the Chief Executive of the exam board, AQA, announced that there was to be an A level in 'Creative Writing'. This new course, he told us, would encourage 'bold, confident writers across a range of styles'. It would cultivate 'strong writing and communication skills', which, while equipping students with the tools they might need as aspirant poets, novelists and playwrights, would also meet the demands of employers, who are constantly 'calling for sharper writing skills'.

An examination in Creative Writing is slightly less vomit inducing than a course in Happiness, but there is not much in it. In terms of pedagogic absurdity and moral and psychological vacuity they are pretty much on a par. Happiness is a God given grace. So is creativity. A level English, properly taught, will immerse students in the mysteries of poetic and narrative form. Those who have anything to say will have ample opportunity to learn how to say it. Those who are sufficiently in love with the intensity of their own ectoplasmic outpourings to sign up for a creative writing course are unlikely to have the humility and understanding to subject themselves to the study of how the inanities of self-expression can be shaped into the wonder of real literature.

The Chief Executive of AQA will, I suppose, argue that his new A level is as focused on utilitarian as it is on creative aims. Quite how he thinks the course is going to reconcile the teaching of, say, characterisation in a short story with instruction in the writing of a report for, say, a marketing manager, I am not sure. I wonder, too, why he thinks that 17 and 18 year olds who are sufficiently interested in the business of writing to study this A level have failed during the previous eleven years in primary and secondary education to master the basics of writing employers in fact require. Everything in education has these days to be justified in terms of its contribution to the GDP, but this hotch potch of a proposal simply doesn't add up.

The timing is delicious, isn't it? We have Michael Gove doing all he can to restore some intellectual rigour to the A level examination. Simultaneously, this examination board, aided and abetted by Ofqual, the body which is meant to regulate the credibility of public examinations, developing a new A level which runs counter to everything he is trying to do. One step forward, two back. He needs to get a tighter grip on every aspect of the public examination system and he should start with the organisation which sits at the heart of the whole mess: Ofqual.

***

Knowledge matters and knowledge is exciting

March 2013 *[Abridged]*

Like many people, I have recurrent nightmares where I am falling through never-ending space or, chased through the woods by some nameless horror, find my knees crumpling as its fetid breath warms my neck. Worse still is the dream in which I am in a room with a crowd of senior education academics. We are frozen in time. Their mouths open and shut saying exactly the same things as the decades pass. 'L'enfer, c'est les professeurs', as Sartre might have put it.

In the early 1990s I was working for the National Curriculum Council, the body which was then in charge of establishing and developing the National Curriculum. We had the temerity to suggest that the English curriculum should require teachers to introduce their children to some of the classics of English literature and we specified texts that we thought appropriate for children of different ages.

This proposal prompted an enraged letter from five hundred academics to the *Times Higher Educational Supplement*. Did we not understand, they asked, that there was no longer such a thing as a literary canon? Did we not know that all literary texts were of equal value? And who were we to exercise our amateur judgement? There were a good many more such questions, all equally indignant, but, mercifully, I have forgotten the detail. What I can remember is saying to myself that if this is the reaction from the great and the good of the academic world then we must be doing something right. We stuck to our belief that every child should have the opportunity to read some at least of the masterpieces of our national literature.

I hope that Michael Gove's reaction to the letter written last week by a hundred educationalists is similarly robust. This group of experts proclaimed that Gove's new curriculum 'could severely erode educational standards'. Somewhat hysterically, they asserted that it contains 'endless lists of spellings, facts and rules'. There will be no time, they sighed, to 'develop children's ability to think, including problem solving, critical understanding and creativity'. It will, horror of horrors, they complained, encourage rote learning. Teaching and learning will, in short, be 'dumbed down', and a new dark age will descend upon the classrooms of English schools.

What is wrong with 'rote learning'? Some of the basic building blocks of knowledge, like the times tables, are best learnt through a ritual of memorisation. 'Look out at the roses and chant after me', my Latin teacher used to say, and we would all rehearse 'amo, amas, amat, amamus, amatis, amant'. Fifty years on, I can still conjugate a fair number of Latin verbs.

I am not, for one moment, proposing that children should have 'endless' lists of facts pushed down their throats. Good teachers do not do this. They make their lessons interesting and enjoyable and the more knowledgeable and enthusiastic they are about the things they are teaching, the more their pupils will be intrigued and inspired. Knowledge matters, and knowledge is exciting. What do these academics want? To leave children to stew endlessly in their own ignorance, trying, hopelessly and helplessly, to discover everything for themselves? This is a self-evident nonsense, and I sometimes wonder how it is that people who parade this kind of pseudo argument have managed to climb to positions of academic eminence.

Sitting in a Chinese restaurant last night, I found myself gazing at some tropical fish, suspended motionless in the water and, seemingly, in time, thinking, I imagine, their not-very-exciting fishy thoughts. An image of the academics who signed last week's letter imprinted itself on my mind. Sadly, it rather put me off my dim sum.

***

How much does any of us understand?

May 2013

Towards the end of his life, my father and I developed an exchange that became something of a running gag between us. He would look across to me when I was working on the laptop and ask 'How does the Internet work, then?' I would smile sheepishly, shrug, and reply that I didn't have the faintest idea. Or, on a visit to Rye, I would ask him whether Mermaid

Street was named after the famous pub halfway up the hill on the left. He, of course, wouldn't know the answer. History, politics, anything mechanical; anything at all, really, neither of us, it seemed, could explain the mysteries of the world which bore in upon us from all sides.

Mr Gove thinks that knowing things matters. So do I, and so did my father. The more one knows, the richer one's experience of the world. Critics of Mr Gove's new National Curriculum think otherwise. They appear to believe that knowing things helps one to survive in a pub quiz, but has no other useful function. They draw a sharp distinction between knowledge and understanding, as if, almost, the former militated against the latter.

So, I read recently, the proposed reforms to the National Curriculum Order for Mathematics will force children to assimilate knowledge without any true understanding. But does this distinction between knowledge and understanding stand scrutiny? I learnt my tables by rote in primary school and had, I suppose, some vague inkling of what seven times eight, say, meant in the real world. I knew and I understood that the letters c-a-t represented the animal we had at home, which, when it was feeling amiable, would sit on my lap. How much, though, do children really understand? How much does any of us understand? How much do we need to understand?

The things that matter most are, by definition almost, beyond human understanding. I have been reading and re-reading *King Lear* for more than fifty years. I have been listening to Beethoven's late quartets for almost as long. Do I understand either work of art better now I am in my late sixties than I did when I first encountered them as a teenager? I cannot say that I do, and I do not think that it matters in the slightest.

If you view the world as a crossword puzzle to be solved, then, yes, nailing things down, coming to some definite interpretation or understanding matters. The progress of science certainly depends upon hypotheses that the scientists would like to believe encapsulate a definitive understanding. Literature, art, music, religion, the murkiness of one's own existence; these things are different. Their meaning and significance eludes us and that is the fascination of our existence. I want to know as much as I can, but it doesn't bother me at all that age has failed to deliver any real insight into my experience.

The last time I saw my father alive, he woke up once. 'What are you doing here?' he asked. I told him that I had come down to see him, not wanting actually to admit that I had come to say goodbye. What did that act of saying goodbye mean? I didn't know then, on that grey January afternoon. I do not know now, nine years on. Does it matter? No, not in the least. It is one more mystery to reflect upon.

***

We get the schools we deserve

August 2013

I have never been quite sure what I think about the old adage that we get the politicians we deserve. Given that we live in a democracy, we have an obvious responsibility, collective if not individual, for the government we have chosen. How real, though, is that choice when the political parties fight for the middle ground and so few politicians have the courage of their own convictions? When there are no real alternatives, choice becomes meaningless and the notion of any responsibility is correspondingly diminished.

What is all too clear is that we get the schools we deserve. We like to pretend that schools can solve our social and economic ills. They cannot. Education is more a mirror in which are reflected the values and aspirations that drive our society than it is a force for transformational change.

When Labour was in power, ministers expected us to applaud the idea that lessons in social and emotional learning would ensure that all children left school happy and contented. Citizenship was introduced as a subject into the National Curriculum in order to resuscitate the ideals of democracy. Children were to be taught 'how to learn' so as to become 'lifelong learners', active in their pursuit of intellectual satisfaction until their dying days.

It is easy to ridicule this kind of utopian delusion, though, significantly, few did through the Labour years or, for that matter, do now and Michael Gove himself, marching perhaps to the Liberal Democrat drum, has been known to articulate similar enthusiasms.

But the rot is far more fundamental. Education is a transaction between the generations in which the young are initiated into aspects of our culture upon which our humanity depends. It demands teachers who are authorities in their subject and who have a real authority over their pupils. Pupils, for their part, must have the patience and humility to master knowledge which is demanding and, at first sight at least, often irrelevant to their immediate preoccupations.

We are not comfortable as a society with any of the above. We sneer at the notion of authority. The idea that all children should be exposed to great literature is dismissed by academics as elitist. We dismiss, in this technological age, the whole concept of knowledge. Everything we ever need to know, so the argument goes, is available on the Internet, so why should we ask children to try and remember anything? We want instant gratification. We spend our weekends in shopping malls lusting after the material trinkets that we believe will bring us the satisfaction we crave. We nonetheless think that our schools can pursue ideals that run counter to everything we say and do in our adult lives.

The novelist and philosopher, Iris Murdoch, once asked whether a belief in a serious education could survive in a democracy. She wrote that: 'Education is no longer seen as the road to freedom; it is seen as the road to a higher salary'. She was, I am afraid, right. We cannot expect schools to deliver high educational ideals until we are prepared to be honest about what we really value.

***

Self-esteem comes from knowing something

September 2013

You probably will not remember the late Baroness Blatch, a Conservative politician in the 1990s. Why should you? She was, after all, only a minister at the Department for Education, and secretaries of state move on with such mystifying rapidity and minimal impact that they themselves, the man or woman in charge, disappear into the mist once they depart office.

I came to know Emily Blatch well when I was running the National Curriculum Council and, subsequently, the School Curriculum and

Assessment Authority. She was the minister in charge of the National Curriculum and she had strong views on what needed to be done. Indeed, she was a politician with genuine convictions, a keen understanding of what was going on in the real world of schools, and an exceptional eye for detail. She died some years ago of a brain tumour, and I miss her a great deal.

I thought of Emily last week when I read that the National Institute for Clinical Excellence (NICE) had issued guidance to schools about the need to monitor children's 'well-being' in a 'systematic' fashion. Emily Blatch was infuriated by the reams of guidance and advice that the organisations I was responsible for insisted on sending to schools. Nobody reads it, she would fume, adding that on balance this was probably a good thing because if teachers did plough through our mountains of paperwork their minds would be filled with exactly the kind of nonsense we were trying to eliminate.

She would certainly have fumed if she had been around to hear what NICE has been up to. The whole notion of 'well-being' would have prompted a snort of derision. Like any good teacher, she took the view that the best thing you could do in school to foster a child's self-esteem and happiness was to teach them something. Teachers were paid to teach, and the last thing we should be doing is encouraging them to see themselves as facilitators, counsellors and social workers.

How is it that these government quangos and agencies all take it upon themselves to deluge their constituencies with words of supposed wisdom? NICE was set up to determine the drugs the NHS should fund, not to pontificate on well-being in schools. The moral is clear, and Michael Gove, who is also a brave politician with real conviction, should remember the work Baroness Blatch began and continue the battle (and it is a battle) to silence the voice of bureaucracies that think they know better than the professionals they purport to advise.

***

How can 12 year olds 'create new knowledge'?

January 2014

You have probably never heard of Michael Fullan. He is a professor at the University of Toronto who travels the world giving lectures about what schools should be like in the 21ˢᵗ century. Many teachers, educational administrators and politicians think that he has access to divine wisdom on all things educational.

His latest publication is a report summarising interviews he has conducted with teachers in twelve countries around the globe. 'Many of the teachers we interviewed', he writes, 'had students who were no longer willing to accept the role of being passive receivers of learning defined by someone else'. He argues that traditional didactic methods of teaching no longer work in a world where 'young people are digitally connected to overwhelming amounts of information and ideas'. They are, he believes, 'unimpressed by pre-packaged, de-personalised learning experiences'. What we need are the new methods which are emerging in the classrooms of progressive teachers who encourage their students to tutor each other while helping them to 'master the process of learning' and to 'create new knowledge'.

Let me re-phrase some of this. Fullan does not think that the young should be initiated into the subjects which make up the conventional school curriculum. The laws, for example, of science have been discovered and defined by someone else and are unacceptable, therefore, to a generation which wants to define its own knowledge. Their experiences in the classroom must be driven by their personal whim if they are to have any meaning or interest. The teacher's job is to help their students, in, of course, a spirit of partnership, to develop the skills they need to drive their own learning.

People have been saying this sort of thing for a long time now. Not many teachers will stand up in public and defend the classroom in which somebody who knows and loves their subject inspires their students with a sense of how exciting history or physics or whatever can be. The irony, for me, is that those, like Fullan, who promote the importance of learning skills such as the ability to think, never, it seems, think for themselves. Do they really think that the accumulated wisdom of the last twenty centuries can be discovered anew by each generation? Do they think that 12 year olds can really 'create new knowledge'?

Fullan's report was commissioned by the education company, Pearsons. You may have heard of Sir Michael Barber, who is the chief educational adviser at Pearsons and who, for many years, was Tony Blair's education guru. Sir Michael has commented enthusiastically on Fullan's ideas as an important contribution to the reform of education. All I can say is that we are lucky to have a Secretary of State for Education who has condemned attacks on didactic teaching as 'shameful'.

***

The backlash against curriculum reform

April 2014 *[Abridged]*

Back and forth the pendulum moves, slowly and erratically, but inexorable in its progress.

When I went to school in the 50s and 60s, the sage stood on the stage and the class listened. The timetable consisted of separate subjects and nobody talked about cross-curricular themes or the 'seamless web of knowledge'.

All this, of course, was a very long time ago and the past is, without doubt, another country.

In the 60s and 70s, and through into the 80s, the climate changed. The pendulum swung away from what many saw, and continue to see, as this didactic and knowledge obsessed vision of education to an approach which placed the child, as learner, at the heart of things.

I remember going for an interview for a teaching job in the 1970s where I was asked whether 'the product' (the knowledge that the child mastered) was more important than 'the process' (the skills learnt and the attitudes developed). The expected answer was clear, and I wanted the job. Of course, I said, it is the process.

At the time I believed it, too. As a young teacher and lecturer in education, I wanted to help children express themselves and I was more interested in their opinions and feelings than I was their punctuation and grammar.

Then, in the 1990s, doubts set in amongst politicians and businessmen and the reforms of the National Curriculum and school inspection began. They are being continued energetically by the current Secretary of State for Education, Michael Gove.

But, simultaneously, there is a backlash against this alleged return to what David Blunkett called, last week, the prep school education of the 1950s. According to the current Chief Inspector of Schools, Sir Michael Wilshaw, middle class parents obsess anxiously about the dangers of a pre school education which involves anything other than learning through play. Our children are said to have been tested to within an inch of their lives. We must place more emphasis on happiness and well-being and emotional intelligence than upon the knowledge encapsulated into the different subject disciplines.

I sometimes wonder whether the nature of our educational vision makes any significant contribution to our sense of ourselves as a nation. I used to think that it did, and in optimistic moments still do. But the reality, I fear, is that our sense of what we want for our children reflects the underlying values of the society in which we live. That society is flabby, self-indulgent and materialistic. The pendulum has swung a long way from the austerity of my post-war childhood, and Michael Gove has an uphill task in seeking to recreate an education and a nation which is remote from our celebrity-obsessed culture.

***

Craft subjects have been over intellectualised

November 2014

Here is a confession.

Back in the late 1980s, when the first National Curriculum began to be developed, I was in favour. I thought that a National Curriculum could help iron out an unacceptable eccentricity of local provision in which the subjects children were taught depended too often on the availability and whim of the teachers employed in the school they attended, and that, if expectations were set high enough, it could help to raise standards.

Ironically, the argument made by the late Professor Ted Wragg and many other educationalists, that a National Curriculum amounted to an unacceptable intrusion into the professional world of education, did not worry me in the slightest.

It should have done. The history of the National Curriculum is a story of how the various bodies charged with overseeing the curriculum and the various politicians responsible for overseeing those bodies have been duped by the professionals.

Take craft subjects. Prior to the National Curriculum, children went into workshops and learned woodworking, metalwork, cookery, and so on. This was not good enough for the experts who thought that the whole notion of craft education had to be revolutionised.

The introduction of the National Curriculum gave them an opportunity to attack the traditional focus on craft skills. What emerged in its place was a curriculum based on 'design and make' assignments.

One such assignment was to design your own airport. It is hard to imagine anything more farcical. What student really has any idea of the complexities of an airport or of how to translate their vague fantasies into a meaningful design, let along any tangible product?

But then, as now, many believe that the actual skills upon which real craftwork depends are much less important than the development of 'pro-learning capabilities', 'learning to learn strategies', or a 'growth mindset', whatever any of these terms might mean. What matters, according to one list I have just read, is the cultivation of attributes such as 'honesty, trustworthiness, kindness, tolerance, empathy', 'patience, self-discipline' and 'determination, curiosity, creativity and collaboration'. In short, the creation of a perfect human being.

Perhaps, however, things are about to change for the better. In a letter to *The Times* published last week, about 100 academics and figures from the art world set out a manifesto to protect Britain's 'world-leading craft status'. The signatories – who include the television presenter Kirstie Allsopp – say that craft education is at risk. Personally, I would add the words 'of extinction' to this statement, but I applaud the sentiment.

The number sitting craft-related GCSEs has fallen by 25 per cent in six years, and university craft courses by 46 per cent. It is hardly surprising that Rosy Greenlees, the executive director of the Crafts Council, is saying that the stream of young talented craftsmen and women is in danger of drying up and that we need to get craft back into our schools.

This means rescuing crafts from the last twenty-five years of educational thinking. Let's teach the practical skills upon which every craft depends and let's stop over intellectualising these activities and pretending that their main role is to develop character attributes that most of us will never possess and which are, in any case, probably unteachable.

***

The tyranny of the majority

January 2015

For better or for worse, I have a highly developed sense of the ridiculous. I am fond of cartoons which strip the subject bare, revealing what lies beneath the pomp and circumstance. But the cartoons I like best are almost always the ones that play to my prejudice. I cannot actually recall a cartoon which has caused me to re-think my attitude towards an issue or a person.

I am happy to man the barricades to defend freedom of expression. We need, though, to remember that with freedom comes responsibility. The greater the freedom, the more important it is that we think about the consequences of what we say or draw, and exercise, where necessary, some self-restraint.

It is also worth remembering, as Orwell told us, that one of the defining characteristics of our Englishness is hypocrisy. The attack on the French satirical magazine prompted, rightly, near universal disgust, but many of the disgusted seemed to have forgotten that our determination to protect the freedom of the individual to say whatever they want to say does not extend in England very far into many issues concerning sexuality and race. Breach the conventions of political correctness and you will suffer the consequences. You will not be shot, but you can expect a degree of social and professional isolation.

We who live in liberal Western democracies experience our own tyranny. It is called the tyranny of the majority. It does not compare, of course, to the tyranny of Islamic fundamentalism, but it is real and it is powerful.

As a teacher, I have always worried about the discussion of controversial issues in the classroom. There is the danger that the teacher responsible for chairing the discussion slips from what should be a position of neutrality into a stance which is partisan and possibly indoctrinatory. But the greater danger is that of the majority student view. It takes a brave fifteen year old to stand out against the crowd.

There is also the fact that the young are programmed to sneer. I think it was Orwell, again, though I can't remember where, who wrote about how easy it is to encourage people to ridicule patriotism. The young like to ridicule. They like cartoons which compress complex issues into a comical caricature. As I have confessed, I do too. But sometimes the complexity is such that the individual opinion, which may well be grounded in little or no evidence or understanding, is less important than the inculcation of something which I can only call a patience or a humility or, in some cases, a reverence. These are not words which you find in many educational treatises.

Yes, the young should be helped to think for themselves. They should be applauded when they point the finger of fun at adult pretension. But in a democratic age where everybody's opinion is judged to be as worthy as everybody else's and where freedom of expression is lauded as the ultimate liberal virtue we must defend, teachers need also to recognise that there are dangers here which might be as threatening as fundamentalist aggression.

***

Inspectors' focus on the promotion of British values is dubious

January 2015

Two headlines struck me last week. The first told me that 'NHS advisers ask callers: are you conscious?' The second said that 'Ofsted Trojan Horse inspectors asked 10-year olds: 'What do lesbians do?'. Which, I asked myself, was the more stupid?

I do not recall being asked whether I was unconscious when I phoned the 111 helpline last November. I can tell you that by the end of the questions I had been asked, I had been reduced to a cataleptic trance. I had more or less lost the will to live. Maybe this is the devious game plan. Finish the patients off before they have a chance to clog up the A&E corridors.

There are two things to say about Ofsted questioning 10-year olds on their knowledge of lesbian sex. The first is that, speaking personally, I had no knowledge of or interest in lesbian sex when I was 10 years old, and at 68 the situation has not changed. Decisions about sex education should be left to, in the first place, parents and, in the second, to the schools parents choose for their children.

The article under this headline described the anger of a church school at the intrusive nature of the Ofsted approach. Its sixth formers described how the inspectors seemed to be manipulating every conversation towards the question of whether the school was promoting 'British values', and, in particular, whether they had been educated into a tolerant attitude towards everything to do with sexual diversity.

Does this Government really want its inspectors to be asking such inappropriate and fatuous questions? More fundamentally, should Ofsted be used to enforce political diktat? The Government has decided that the promotion of 'British values' should be central to the work of schools. Ofsted has been instructed to make sure, through the threat of its inspections, that this happens.

It's a tricky one, this. An elected Parliament has a perfect right, in my view, to challenge the assumptions of the educational establishment and to define the broad sweep of a National Curriculum. It follows then that

Ofsted as the educational watchdog should inspect and comment upon how schools are responding to this political decision. But the subjects of the National Curriculum encapsulate, in outline at least, a national consensus, public and professional, about what teachers should be teaching. The 'British values' debate is far more controversial and far less central to what traditionally constitutes the school curriculum. Sex education has always been the most controversial aspect of the National Curriculum. For politicians to assume that they can dictate what students should be taught about lesbian sex and when they should be taught it is a step too far.

A big step. What is worse is that schools can be failed if they are not deemed to be dancing sufficiently vigorously to the Government tune. Ofsted should be focusing on the quality of leadership and teaching and the progress children are making as they learn their maths and their history, not on controversial aspects of personal, social and health education. Its inspectors ought to be paying a great deal more respect to the ethos of the schools they inspect rather than being castigated for their failure to bend their values and beliefs to the Government agenda.

My answer to the question I posed in my first paragraph is that the two stories are equally stupid, but the inspection issue is the more insidious and pernicious.

A Changing Culture

Many of Chris Woodhead's topics were aspects of the culture in schools. He often looked back on the character building engendered by the fostering of competitiveness, ambition and risk-taking at his own school, and worried about the effects of current attitudes to homework, detention and behaviour and the over-protection of children from failure. The editors published this piece for The Sunday Times *under the headline: 'Well done class, you learnt zilch'.*

First published in *The Sunday Times,* April 2007 *[Abridged]*

Well, all I can say is that I hope you are counting. How many times have you praised your out-of-control little monster today? If government advice on school discipline published last week applies, as logically it should, in the home, then parents across the country will need to keep a constant check on their response to the undesirable behaviour of their offspring.

Five to one is the ratio of praise to punishment, ladies and gentlemen. Criticise rarely; keep punishment to the barest possible minimum; praise and reward however monstrous the offence. Follow the latest ministerial guidance and your children will understand the difference between right and wrong and learn to act with adult responsibility in every circumstance. Just pat them on the head and tell them how wonderful they are.

I have no idea how long it took to produce last week's bulky guidance, but I can guess: months. Experts from across the country will have travelled first class to meeting after meeting. They will have been wined and dined, and, their deliberations finally brought to a carefully minuted close, they will have laid their weary heads onto the pillow of some five star hotel. Who knows what it all cost? Nobody will ever ask, and, in any case, Alan Johnson, the education secretary, will have generated a headline or two, so who cares?

Do teachers need to be told that praise can motivate? Do politicians and their advisers really think they have access to a fund of practical wisdom and advice that has somehow eluded those who actually do the job?

Of course it is important to praise children, and, looking back as a parent and a teacher, I would be the first to admit that I probably did not praise enough. Few of us do. Time and again, as an inspector, I can remember watching a flicker of disappointment cross a child's face when the teacher more or less ignored their answer to a question. A little recognition goes a long way, and everyone who has responsibility for children needs to remind themselves of this commonsense truth.

To that extent the government's advice is sensible. How, though, did it come up with this 5:1 statistic? Did Johnson's officials sit in classrooms checking out the ratio of praise to punishment? I very much doubt it. This is a finger-in-the-wind generalisation that is meaningless in any specific circumstance.

Meaningless, and, what is worse, insidious. Yes, children should be praised when they do something good. To suggest it is somehow wrong to punish them when they do something bad, or, more dangerous still, actually to reward unacceptable behaviour, is to send a message that is not so much stupid as dangerous.

Children need boundaries. They need to know what they are allowed to do and what they are not allowed to do. And they need to understand that if they choose to break the rules the consequences are unpleasant.

Talk to any headteacher who has turned round a failing school. The first thing they will tell you is that they had to deal with pupils who would not accept the conventions of normal schooling. Without order, nothing. It is not rocket science.

Punctuality, attendance, uniform, behaviour: the heads would make their expectations clear, and they would ensure everyone knew what would happen to those who stepped out of line. Good behaviour would be praised and bad behaviour punished. Make the rules clear and apply them fairly. Children know where they are and teachers can start teaching again.

Our Secretary of State for Education appears to believe self-esteem is more important than real ability. It is not. Recent American research suggests that parents and teachers who lavish praise, even when it is deserved, may be undermining the ability of their children to persevere when the going gets tough. Pupils who have come to feel they are 'smart' tend to back off when they are confronted by a new challenge that they cannot immediately crack. Effort matters as much as innate ability, and an exaggerated sense of one's own abilities undermines the need to try in the most damaging way possible.

One American advocate of the importance of self-esteem, Roy Baumeister, has reviewed psychological and educational studies into the supposed significance of encouraging high self-esteem and has come to the conclusion that much of this work is conceptually and empirically flawed. The result of his review, he says, was 'the biggest disappointment' of his career, but it was unavoidable: 'having high self-esteem does not improve grades or career achievement'.

Such research simply confirms what every sensible parent and teacher knows: it is unhelpful, and, in the long run, cruel to delude anyone. Children who make mistakes in maths need to have those mistakes pointed out to them, just as children who misbehave need to be punished for their misbehaviour. How else will they learn?

I doubt Alan Johnson is capable of making much progress, but a spell on what I believe is now called the 'naughty step' might encourage him to reflect on the idiocy of his latest pronouncements.

***

Risk and learning from failure

One summer afternoon in 1957, an 11-year-old boy was sitting on his bicycle at the top of Westerham Hill in Kent. The Sevenoaks Weald stretched out in front of him, an unknown land. He wondered whether he would ever have the energy to climb back up the hill if he had the courage to freewheel down into this new, unchartered territory. He concluded that there was only one way to find out. The descent was exhilarating; the slog back exhausting. He made it, though, and that night, drifting off into sleep, his mind was full of what he had achieved.

That boy was me. I count myself lucky to have grown up at a time when children had much more freedom to explore the world for themselves without the fret of adult supervision. Today, we agonise over the dangers they face. Teachers are reluctant to take pupils on outdoor activities because of the threat of legal action following the most minor of accidents. Parents ferry their children to and from school. We strive to eliminate all risk and, in so doing, we deny our children the satisfaction of overcoming self-doubt and the possibility of growing into self-confident adults.

Cycling gave Chris independence and freedom to explore the countryside.

Yes, of course, there are dangers out there and we as adults have a responsibility to protect the young. But let's keep those dangers in perspective and let's think about how we can challenge our children to attempt more than they think they can achieve.

What, though, if they try and they fail? Won't their self-esteem be damaged for life? Trainee teachers are told that children should never fail. They should never be exposed to any negative comment, however pitiful their effort might be. Again, I look back on my own childhood and I am grateful for the realism and the honesty my teachers showed me. In a recent international survey of pupils' mathematical ability, children from England came near the bottom of the table on every aspect except for their own estimate of how good they were at the subject, on which they came near the top. This is the Alice in Wonderland world in which our children live. Nobody tells them the truth about the reality of their achievements, so they have no idea of whether they are really any good or what constitutes real excellence in anything.

It is a cliché, but it is true. We learn more from failure than we do from success. The experience of being beaten by somebody else for a prize we coveted is inevitably painful, but if we can summon the resilience and honesty to think through how we could have done better, then next time the triumph might be ours.

I look at my grandchildren and I want their childhood to be full of happiness. But I also want them to learn how to deal with the disappointments that are inevitably a part of life. I want them to have the opportunity to test themselves against real challenges. I want them to know that if you try, more often than not, you do in the end succeed and that, if you've really done your best, it does not matter if you do not.

Aren't these the lessons we all have to learn if we are going to have a chance of coping with the real life grown-up world? When we try to protect our children from reality we act, no doubt, from the best possible motives, but we are in fact condemning them to a life of underachievement and self-delusion.

I applaud the fact that the Government appears to have woken up to the damage our cotton wool culture is doing to our children. Education Minister, Michael Gove, is determined to free teachers from the health and safety regulation which currently makes it so difficult for them to offer their pupils the excitement that comes from real challenge. But, in the end, if we want real change, then it is down to us, as parents and grandparents. You are fed up with reports that tell you nothing about your child's real strengths and, equally important, weaknesses? You want there to be genuinely competitive sports days? You want lessons which stretch and inspire? Then, you have no option. Talk to other parents. Club together. Let the headteacher and the school's governing body know the kind of education you want for your children.

But it is not just what happens at school that matters. As a parent, the real responsibility is yours. Thirty years ago, my daughter and I climbed the hill behind the cottage we were staying at in Cornwall. Dusk was falling. We took torches and I told her that we had to jump from rock to rock to avoid the monsters that lurked in the bracken. She still talks about that evening. It cost nothing. It involved minimal imagination on my part. For her, it was, as the light faded, exciting and challenging. Every day could be exciting and challenging for our children. It is down to us. Can we transform the tedium of the everyday into an inspiration? That is the challenge we face as parents.

***

From his weekly blogs for *The Sunday Times*

Our ability to cope is grounded in our fortitude and courage

November 2010

When Anthony Seldon, the Master of Wellington College, announced that his pupils were to be taught how to be happy, he said that: 'happiness is the contemporary buzzword. Every media outlet is discussing whether it should be an objective of government policy and whether it can be taught. It can be and must be, in our opinion'.

The happiness curriculum at Wellington College requires pupils to study lives which (I quote from the school's website) 'go particularly well', in order to 'develop and apply strategies and skills that promote all round progress in a person's psychological, physical and social life'. Pupils are taught some 'positive psychology' and are encouraged to reflect, amongst other things, upon their 'relationship with their past, present, future and fantasy lives'. There is, as far as I am aware, no GCSE as yet in Happiness Studies, but one is no doubt being developed even as I write.

Now Mr Cameron has jumped upon the happiness bandwagon. Approximately £2 million of taxpayers' money is to be spent on a survey designed to establish whether as a nation we are happy, and, presumably, whether we are getting happier under the austerity measures introduced by Mr Cameron's government. Nobody seems very clear quite how the survey is to be conducted, what questions are to be asked, and so on, but, never mind. We all need to be happy and Mr Cameron needs to know whether he is making a personal contribution to our collective euphoria.

If I had had the good fortune to sit in on a few of Anthony Seldon's happiness lessons, would I be better equipped to deal with the trials and tribulations of Motor Neurone Disease? Somehow, I suspect not. Years ago, I read a remarkable book called *Solitary Confinement* by Christopher Burney. Burney was a British agent who, caught by the Germans, experienced months of solitary confinement in occupied France. His survival depended in part upon luck, but to a very great extent upon his courage, his fortitude and his ability to spend days and weeks exploring the content of his own richly stocked mind. 'Down on the bedrock', he wrote, if my memory serves me correctly, 'life becomes a love affair of the mind'.

It is. Happiness is such a pathetic, inadequate concept. Our sense of ourselves as worthwhile human beings comes from what we achieve and how we cope with the unhappiness that life throws at us. Our ability to cope is grounded in our fortitude and courage, not in our mastery of 'strategies and skills that promote all round progress in' our 'psychological and physical and social life'.

More fundamentally, why are we so preoccupied with our happiness? Driving into my first teaching job in Shrewsbury in 1969, I used to look at the cows grazing in the fields and wonder if they were happier than I was. It seemed to me then, and it seems to me now, that the greater the degree of self-awareness the less likely it is that one will be happy. The unexamined life, as someone once said, is not worth living.

As for my happiness depending on the decisions of politicians, I can only say that I never thought I would hear a Conservative Prime Minister parrot such arrogant nonsense.

***

Failure teaches you the lesson of humility

May 2011

One of the pleasures of my weekly question and answer column is the correspondence it generates with readers. A recent example was a message from Caroline Whateley-Smith, prompted by the ongoing debate about medical school admissions. Caroline wrote that: 'Sometimes people just have to accept failure and it often does people no harm to fail at something and just accept that there are a lot of other people out there with qualifications and qualities that are as good as theirs and they don't get anything by right'.

The vagaries and lack of transparency which seem to me to characterise medical school admissions worry me a great deal, but I could not agree more with what Caroline wrote to me. When my Latin and French let me down and Kings College, Cambridge wrote to me to say that they could not offer me a place, I can remember sitting in my bedroom in a state of terminal despair. Looking back, the fact that I had to pick myself up and get on with it helped me to learn what is, as Caroline says, one of the most important lessons of life.

It isn't actually true to say that success is easy. It isn't. Success in my experience, at least, can and does corrupt. The higher you climb up the greasy pole, the easier it is to kid yourself that you are really somebody special. The truth, as Eliot put it in *The Four Quartets*, is that, 'the only wisdom is the wisdom of humility'. Failure, if you are prepared to learn, teaches you the lesson of humility. That is why it is so important.

It is why, too, the contemporary educational zeitgeist is so wrong. These days we obsess about the self-esteem of our children. I have sat in classrooms watching teachers squirm with anxiety as they agonise over how to respond to an answer one of their pupils has given which is completely wrong. They are desperately concerned not to embarrass or humiliate the child. This sentiment is good, but if it leads to a response which does not make it clear that a mistake has been made then we have a very big problem. The child, and possibly the class as a whole, may continue to think that a wrong answer is the right answer and, what is even more serious, an opportunity has been lost for everyone to learn about how getting it wrong, making mistakes, is an essential part of learning and growing up.

I almost wrote 'failure'. My nerve failed me. We can't talk about failure. We pussyfoot around the issue, as we did when I was Chief Inspector, euphemistically labelling failing schools as 'schools in special measures'. Crazy, isn't it? The language we use matters. Euphemisms distance us from reality, and the one thing education should do is strip the world of fantasy and pretence.

***

Pushing the boundaries of our understanding means taking risks

November 2011

I cannot recall when somebody first asked me whether I felt 'comfortable' about some change to something or other they were proposing. I do know that I felt distinctly uncomfortable at the assumption that I should feel comfortable. So, too, with the idea of 'ownership'. Why is it that, these days, a preoccupation with our collective comfort zone has come to rule the managerial and educational roost?

Actually, with regard to 'change management' (another ghastly phrase), the very fact that we talk so much about management and so little about leadership says it all. If you want to have any significant impact on the culture of an organisation, you have to take risks in the challenge that you present to your colleagues and you have to have sufficient confidence in those colleagues to assume that they will be prepared themselves to take the risk of confronting something that, if it is worthwhile, has by definition to be uncomfortable.

So, too, with education. The consensus today is that the education we offer our children must be 'relevant' and 'accessible'. We must never, that is, expose our children to ideas which they will find difficult and demanding. The truth is that what is not difficult and demanding is not educational. To believe that everything must be immediately understood and 'owned' leads to classrooms full of children who are both self-satisfied and bored.

Years ago, teaching at Oxford, in the Department of Educational Studies at Oxford University, my colleague on the top floor of our offices in Norham Gardens was Robin Hodgkin, author of a book called *Reconnaissance on an Educational Frontier*. Robin, who by then was nearing the end of his career, was a remarkable man. A leading mountaineer before the Second World War, who had lost many of his fingers to frostbite, he went on to be the Headmaster of the Quaker boarding school, Abbotsholme, and to lecture at Oxford.

His basic idea was both simple and immensely important. As human beings and educators, we have to look to our own intellectual horizons and we have, throughout our lives, to push the boundaries of our understanding. We have to create classrooms in which children are encouraged to take the risks that are necessary to do this for themselves.

There, I've said it. I have used the word 'risk'. The word which, except in the context of risk averse, risk avoidance or risk assessment, has been banished from the educational and managerial lexicon.

We fill in our health and safety forms to cover ourselves from any risk if anything goes wrong. We weave webs of bureaucracy and submerge ourselves in pyramids of paperwork so that there is always evidence that we have thought ahead and minimised the threat of anything ever going wrong.

Things still do, of course – go wrong. Nothing much, though, is achieved. It never will be while we live in a culture where managers and teachers alike believe that everybody must be comfortable, everything must be owned, nobody should be exposed to the challenge of uncertainty and risk.

***

Training hard and learning important truths

March 2012

The men's 1500 metres gold medal at the 1960 Rome Olympics was won by the Australian runner, Herb Elliot. Herb was my hero. I read passages of his autobiography, *The Golden Mile*, so often that I could rehearse them by heart. I visualised myself running up and down the sand dunes at his training camp outside Melbourne. There was nothing my 13-year-old self wanted more than to emulate his achievements.

Day after day, I would run round Beddington Park after school, through the mud of The Spinney, back over the close-cut grass, sprinting along Croydon Road to the school gates, imagining I was drawing away from my competitors to break the tape in some national, or, better still, international race. At weekends, I would disappear into Selsdon Bird Sanctuary to loop round various circuits I had devised or to run up and down a particularly steep hill at the far end of the woods until my legs buckled and my lungs gasped for air.

To an extent, my training paid off. I won a fair number of school cross-country races and, in or around 1962, managed to win the Surrey half mile championship at Motspur Park. Looking back, I wish I had continued to run and to train after I had left school. I would never have become a Herb Elliot, but I could, I know, have achieved a fair bit more athletically than I did.

We all, I suppose, regret the things we did not do. I am simply grateful for the pleasure running gave me and, what is more important, the lessons training and competing taught me.

I can remember the exact moment during a cross-country race over Farthing Downs, near Coulsdon in Surrey, when, trying to keep up with a stronger runner, a question came into my mind which haunted me for months after. The question was: how do we determine the strength of our will, as opposed to the ability of our body? Did I win races because I was physically a better runner than my competitors, or because I was more prepared to suffer than they were? And, follow-up question, what is it that explains the willingness to suffer?

The answer to the latter question, I concluded, was that, the more you wanted something, the more you were prepared to push yourself to the limit. There was no answer, of course, to the first question. None of us can ever know how much it is mental determination rather than any specific ability that carries us through. I knew, however, as a 13 year old, that without the hunger to succeed and the concomitant willpower, nothing could ever be accomplished.

There were no lessons in citizenship at Wallington Grammar School. Nobody thought to teach us how to be happy. The idea that children needed to 'learn how to learn', thankfully, had not yet been invented. What the school did do was give me the opportunity to learn for myself what I still think is the most important truth of all. We get out of life what we put into it, and instantaneous gratification can never compare with the sense of fulfilment which follows real blood, sweat and tears.

***

The manipulation of language – from student to active learner

July 2012

Have you noticed? The word 'student' has been vaporised from all public discourse on education. Everyone from the three year old in their sandpit to the postgraduate student in the university library has now become a 'learner'.

This is a perfect example of how the educational and political establishment manipulates language in order to impose its view on what should be happening in our schools and universities.

Read any Ofsted inspection report and you are likely to find a statement that there should be less 'didactic teaching' and more 'active learning'. The underlying assumption is that what matters is learning and not teaching, and, furthermore, that teaching is no more than a tedious regurgitation of fact. So we have learners lining the pavement of our high streets with their clipboards, investigating the flow of traffic and the habits of shoppers. Active learners out on a mission to make sense of the world, liberated from the restrictive confines of a classroom where the teacher is telling them things they do not know and will never, left to their own devices, find out.

To tell is not necessarily to regurgitate fact. Skilled teachers intrigue and inspire. They use questions to involve their students. They engage with the answers they are given, using misconceptions to develop the collective understanding of the class. Their lessons do not in any way resemble the dictated notes we can all remember from weaker teachers in our own days at school.

The verb, 'to study', implies an act of submission. Much as a pilgrim seeks revelation at a holy site, the student acknowledges the mystery and value of a body of knowledge and, setting aside their own thoughts and feelings, seeks to engage with that which is worth the struggle to understand. The 'active learner', on the other hand, constructs their own world view. Learning has to be 'personalised'. What matters are the views and opinions of the learner, however ignorant and confused that learner may be.

Knowledge is deemed to be less important than skills. If, the argument goes, we teach the young to become active learners, they will have the necessary skills to discover for themselves the knowledge they need as they move through life. I have never understood what these learning skills actually are, but this is the doctrine of the day.

If Michael Gove wants to raise standards in our schools, then he should issue an edict, banishing the word 'learner' from any document published by his department and its many quangos. This act would cut through the intellectual corruption and signal a new beginning.

***

We should encourage competition and foster elites

August 2012

I have a question to ask. At the very mention of the words 'competition' and 'elite', most teachers and many parents reach for the crucifix and garlic cloves. Olympic mania, nonetheless, sweeps the nation. We watch Bradley Wiggins grind the opposition into the tarmac of south-west London roads and we celebrate his triumph as he stands on the podium to receive his gold medal. How are these double standards to be explained?

We seem to think that competition is good for adults, but is an evil from which children must be protected. I have not pondered the psychological research, but common sense and everyday living tell me that: one, children vary enormously in their abilities, physical and intellectual; two, that they have a natural instinct to compete; and, three, that the experience of failure is as important in growing up as the taste of success.

Why, then, don't we encourage competition in our schools, motivate children through the struggle for success and offer everyone the chance to learn through failure?

I am not saying that a teacher should set out each day to humiliate his pupils. Sarcasm, vindictiveness, bullying, are unacceptable in any classroom. Equally, however, I think we do our children no good when we cosset them in pedagogic cotton wool.

When our pupils come near the bottom in an international comparison of achievements in mathematics, but near the top when they are asked whether or not they feel that they are any good at mathematics, something is very seriously wrong.

Wiggins won his gold medal through his relentless effort and remorseless honesty. Last year he was beaten by the Olympic silver medallist, Tony Martin. The memory of that failure must have helped drive the pedals as he powered to his remarkable success. At a different level, it is the same for us all and for our children. If we want to triumph, we have to overcome adversity.

I want our children to have that opportunity. The most powerful legacy of these Olympics would be a re-evaluation of the importance of competition and a recognition that elites need to be fostered.

***

Children will always misbehave if they can

October 2012

What strange impulse led Michael Gove to confess his teenage sins? Was it simply that, in an act of middle-aged contrition, he wanted to bare his soul and seek absolution? Or was some investigative journalist about to out him as a cocky adolescent who spent his French lessons dreaming up ways to humiliate his teacher rather than concentrating studiously on the intricacies of the more elusive irregular verbs?

It is a mystery to me. I suppose confessing one's childhood sins is a bit better than the ludicrous post-Clinton enthusiasm that has inspired Blair, Brown and, I seem to remember, Cameron to beat their political breast, shedding tears of remorse about wickednesses committed centuries ago in our foul colonial past.

But it is still absurd. Should I apologise to my late mother for driving her demented in a railway carriage to the point where, in an attempt to give me a much deserved good hiding, she missed my four year old legs and broke her finger on the handle of the carriage door?

In fact, looking back on the teachers I did my best to humiliate at school, I have no remorse whatsoever. They deserved it. My teachers fell into three categories. There were those I liked and respected; there were the bullies and sadists who were prone to take the frustrations and failures of their personal lives out on pupils who could not answer back; and there were the incompetents. Why did we repeatedly turn the postcards our French teacher placed round the classroom to inculcate a love of France to the wall? Because it was fun. Because he couldn't stop us. Because the redder in the face and the more exasperated he became the funnier it was.

DH Lawrence was right. The teacher has to impose his stronger will upon the will of the children he teaches. If he cannot, he is finished. Anybody thinking about going into teaching should read the chapters in *The Rainbow* in which Lawrence describes the anguish of Ursula Brangwen as she struggles to recognise this basic truth about teaching.

I am not proud of much of my behaviour at Wallington Grammar School, but I know now, as an ex-teacher, that children will seize on weakness and exploit it mercilessly. It would be nice if every secondary school student could meditate upon the Secretary of State's adult apology for his bad behaviour, but they won't.

Politicians who make public apologies might feel some cathartic self-satisfaction. Their words of penitence and sorrow never have any impact on the real world.

***

Surveys of morale are not very helpful

January 2013

My grandfather fought in the First World War, my father in the Second. Neither wanted to talk much about their experiences in, respectively, the Flanders mud and the deserts of Egypt followed by the jungle of Burma. I am pretty confident, though, that neither saw the trauma they had been through as a reason for not picking up the pieces and getting on with life once they had been discharged from the army.

A post-war baby, I have never had to fight for my country. I like to think that I would have summoned up the same courage and fortitude if I had been in their position, but I simply do not know.

Chris with his father and grandparents while at Selsdon Primary School.

I have, though, had Motor Neurone Disease for the last ten years, so I have some understanding of the temptation to blame the unfairness of fate when your life is turned upside down by events beyond your control or responsibility. There are mornings when it is hard to get up to face another day in the wheelchair. There are moments when the poison of self-pity undermines resolution. But what is the point? Life is not fair, and there is no point in protesting that it should be.

Two surveys were published last week. One, by the Prince's Trust, analysed the feelings of young people struggling to find employment in these difficult economic times. The second, commissioned by the National Union of Teachers, revealed the low morale of a profession that believes, apparently, that it is undervalued and under threat.

One in four 18 to 24 year olds feels that their life has been 'permanently damaged' by the recession. One fifth think that they have no future. Not surprisingly, the latter figure rises to over two fifths amongst those who are neither in education nor employment. Only 13 per cent of the 804 teachers surveyed told YouGov that they enjoyed their time in the classroom. The vast majority blamed the Government for not trusting them to do their job as they saw fit.

I have no sympathy whatsoever with the teachers. Teaching is not, whatever the unions might say, the most stressful job in the world. Christine Blower, the NUT General Secretary, should try working in an accident and emergency unit on a Saturday night or (dare I say it?) as a hedge fund manager. No government can stand by when a fifth of 11 year olds leave primary school unable to read and there is no reason for any effective teacher to feel threatened or demoralised by any policy Michael Gove has introduced. The unemployed 19 year old, whose umpteenth job application has gone unanswered, is a different case. Like everyone else, I can appreciate, even if I cannot fully understand, the despair he or she will feel.

The fact remains that life is not fair. At some point fate is likely to kick us all in the face. It is tough now for the unemployed young, just as it was tough for demobbed soldiers in 1918 and in 1945. I have great admiration for the Prince's Trust, but the question is whether surveys such as those published last week make any contribution whatsoever to a better future for the individual or the nation. If you ask the unemployed or oppressed teachers or anyone, for that matter, who is lying flat on their back in the mud, whether they feel demoralised, you simply encourage them in their negativity and helplessness.

We reap what we sow. As a society, we have encouraged everyone to think that their fifteen minutes of celebrity fame is a basic human right. We have educationalists who say that teachers should encourage their pupils to tell them how to teach and what they should teach. We believe that the self-esteem of our children is more important than what they know and can do.

Deputy Prime Minister, Nick Clegg, might wring his hands in sorrow and pontificate about how the wickedness of bankers has 'scarred' a generation. To an extent he is right. Financial greed and collective mismanagement have wreaked appalling damage upon our economy and our society. But it is not that simple. When misfortune strikes, we either encourage people to pick themselves up and do everything in their power to move on or we tell them that it isn't their fault and that the state will magic them a better future.

Happiness lessons are the vogue now in some educational circles. Would it not be better if we forgot about happiness and tried to restore the traditional virtues of courage, fortitude and resilience?

***

Personalised learning puts the student's ego at the centre of everything

April 2013

When I was in the sixth form at school we had a period every week when we were encouraged to pontificate on the issues of the day. Needless to say, I looked forward to this opportunity. The teacher responsible once wrote in my report that I 'must learn to convince rather than cudgel an audience'. Looking back over the last fifty years, I can only congratulate him on his insight.

This was the only lesson where our personal opinions mattered. We were quite often asked what we thought about a problem or topic in a particular subject. What, for example, did we think was the most important cause of the English civil war? Was Lear 'a man more sinned against than sinning'? The aim was to elicit our thoughts and then, through Socratic questioning, to reveal why we were wrong so as to deepen our understanding of the issue. The idea that we, in our ignorance, could offer a worthwhile individual opinion never really occurred either to the teacher or to us as students.

Now, of course, the world is very different. Education has been 'personalised' so that the learner and his or her ego are at the centre of everything that happens in our classrooms. In extreme versions of this fad, teachers are told to allow their students to determine the detail of the curriculum which is to be studied, the teaching methods to be employed, and how their work is to be assessed. Whole class teaching, if it is to happen at all, must be, in the jargon, 'interactive'. The teacher, that is, must never lecture to the class. Students must be drawn into the discourse through frequent questioning so that they have their opportunity to tell the teacher and each other what they think. In English, the emphasis remains on creativity and self-expression, and, as the current controversy over the introduction of spelling and grammar tests demonstrates, there remains huge resistance to the notion that anything should be allowed to obstruct the free flow of the student's thought and feeling.

I sometimes wonder which is the chicken and which is the egg here. We live in a society where we are all encouraged to tell each other what we think. Once we bought newspapers to read about what was happening in the world. Now every article has an invitation underneath to readers to tell the editor and each other whether they agree or disagree. Radio stations fill their hours with never-ending phone-ins where listeners dredge the depths of their personal experience to bore the rest of us witless. Most of the population appear unable to survive a day without telling their family and friends what exactly they have been up to through twitters and tweets and all the rest of it.

Is this because our schools have abandoned any notion of the student as the recipient of worthwhile knowledge? The teacher as an authority in their subject whose job it is to tell those who are inevitably more ignorant things that they would not otherwise know? Or have our schools merely responded to the relativisation of knowledge and our cultish preoccupation with the importance of self-expression?

I do not know. Reading Patrick Leigh Fermor's book describing his stay in various French monasteries, *A Time for Silence*, I do know that the ceaseless chatter which fills our world has made it difficult, if not impossible, for any of us to focus on the challenge that matters more than anything else in life: the struggle to appreciate the mysteries of human experience. When we think as adults that our commentary on our lives has to be ceaseless and instantaneous and we encourage our children to think that nothing matters more than their own opinion, we need, all of us, to discover what Leigh Fermor discovered when he retreated from the noise of the world: the satisfaction that comes when we stop talking and start thinking.

***

Expectations are important but they have to be realistic

June 2013

These last few nights, I have not been sleeping very well, and I blame Michael Gove. I keep waking up asking myself the same question. 'Am I, or am I not', in the phrase Gove borrowed from Cyril Connolly, 'an enemy of promise?'

Gove was referring to the Labour politicians and educationalists who have condemned his curriculum and examination reforms as anachronistic and elitist.

Well, I am not a Labour politician and, whilst I have spent my life working in education, the educational establishment has not, to put it mildly, embraced me as a fellow traveller. I stand shoulder to shoulder, in fact, with Gove in his drive to rescue education in England from the soggy, all-must-have-prizes abyss into which it has sunk.

But, and this is the reason for my nocturnal angst, I think our expectations of children and, equally important, their teachers must be realistic.

Expectations matter in the classroom as they do in the family. If we do not believe in our children and expect them to achieve more than they themselves think they can achieve, they will never realise their full potential.

I knew this at 14, when, sitting on the top deck of the 408 bus from Wallington to Croydon, I reflected on the school day that had just passed.

I knew that there were teachers who had a low opinion of my abilities and I knew that in absolute terms they may well have been right. But I also knew that there was a law of self-fulfilling prophecy and that I was doing much better in the lessons where the teachers thought that, however irritating my adolescent waywardness might be, there was a hope of better times. We may not become the adults our parents and teachers think we will become, but the adults who preside over our childhood have a profound impact upon our lives.

To expect, on the other hand, too much of the young, to impose perhaps the identity we want for our children and pupils upon the reality of their individual abilities and aspirations, can be equally destructive. Reflect, for a moment, on this paragraph from DH Lawrence's essay, *Education of the People*, written almost a hundred years ago:

'Every teacher knows that it's worse than useless trying to educate at least fifty per cent of his scholars. Worse than useless: it is dangerous: perilously dangerous. What is the result of it? Drag a lad who has no capacity for true learning or understanding through the processes of education, and what do you produce in him, in the end? A profound contempt for education, and for all educated people. It has meant nothing to him but irritation and disgust and that which a man finds irritating and disgusting he finds odious and contemptible'.

Elsewhere in this exceptionally important essay, Lawrence observes that 'if there is a poor devil on the face of the earth it is the elementary school teacher'. It is alright, he observes, with some personal bitterness, having taught himself in what appears to have been a demanding school, for what he calls the 'high idealists' sitting in their offices in Whitehall. They don't have to translate highfalutin expectations into classroom reality. My critics may not believe it, but I never forgot the truth of what Lawrence said when I used to sit, myself, in a Whitehall office.

We have to expect more of our students and their teachers, but we also have to avoid the euphoric buzz of progressive politics and utopian myth. When Michael Gove said recently that everybody should read *Middlemarch*, I felt both elation and disappointment. It is wonderful that we have a Secretary of State who appreciates the glory of George Eliot's masterpiece, but, it is no use trying to impose what Lawrence called 'the high ideal of human existence' on a humanity that doesn't want it.

Does this conclusion make me 'an enemy of promise' or not? I was hoping that writing this blog would clarify my predicament, but I still do not know.

***

Character development cannot simply be added to the curriculum

February 2014

I spent much of last week in hospital, recovering from an operation. Lying in my bed, struggling to summon up the reserves of energy and willpower necessary to endure the next ignominious hoist into my wheelchair, I reflected on Baroness Claire Tyler's astute observation that, 'however many GCSEs you have, where you are on the character scale will have a big impact on what you achieve in life'.

I scraped eleven GCSEs, or O levels as they were then. But where am I on the character scale? Do I score top marks for fortitude and patience and courage? Or am I just another academic nerd, a product of a 1950s grammar school 'exam factory', who lacks the emotional strength to survive the vicissitudes of life.

Baroness Tyler is a member of the all-party Parliamentary group on social mobility that has just published a report, the 'Character and Resilience Manifesto', which calls for schools to focus time and energy on the development of character.

It is hard to deny that strength of character matters and that schools have a responsibility to develop more than the intellectual abilities of their students. Good schools, state and independent, have always understood this. My own grammar school, where the teachers did everything in their power to broaden the intellectual horizons of their pupils, also offered a wide range of sporting and cultural activities that added up to an extremely broad education. My lifelong interest in rock climbing was sparked, for example, by a trip to Harrisons Rocks in Kent one summer afternoon in 1960 when, desperate to disguise my trembling legs, I shook my way to the top of one of the easiest climbs on the edge, Dark Chimney.

So much for Nick Clegg's banal and predictable observation that this report will 'drive innovative thinking'. In fact, the basic assumptions upon which the report rests are highly questionable. Character traits such as fortitude and courage are not 'soft skills'. A skill is an activity, like cycling or knitting, which can be learnt. I do not think that fortitude can, in any meaningful sense of the world, be taught. It is a moral value which should underpin the aspirations a school has for its students, but it cannot be taught and should not in any explicit way be viewed as part of the formal curriculum of a school.

Harrisons Rocks in Kent, where Chris first went climbing on a school trip in 1960.

Neither does the dichotomisation of education into a preparation for exams on the one hand and the development of character on the other make any sense. The truth is that to learn anything that is worthwhile and is, therefore, challenging and difficult, one has to submit oneself to a body of knowledge which must be mastered. The student may be learning how to conjugate a Latin verb, but at the same time he is learning the most important lesson in life, which is that patience and hard work are essential if we are to engage with and understand the richness of the world in which we live.

It is all so trite. Report after report, pundit after pundit, attacks the Government's supposed preoccupation with examination success to the exclusion of everything else. Vacuous, quasi therapeutic ideals are dangled before our gullible eyes. Nobody seems to realise or remember that every good teacher engages the whole pupil. They always have and they always will.

***

The RSA is trying to make real success meaningless

March 2014 *[Abridged]*

Teachers who criticise and humiliate children should be drummed out of the profession. So should teachers who think that it is more important to bolster a child's self-esteem than it is to ensure that they really learn anything. And what about the researchers at the Royal Society of Arts (RSA) Social Brain Centre, who have just published a paper which suggests that all pupils should be given an A grade at the beginning of each year? They should be hung, drawn and quartered, intellectually and, if it can be arranged under EU legislation, physically.

The RSA argument is that people are more motivated when they are trying to avoid losing something than they are when they are struggling to improve themselves. Psychologists call this phenomenon 'loss aversion'. But why would any canny and demotivated 14 year old care about losing their A grade when they know that, however minimal their effort, they will be given a new A grade at the start of the next school year? It is obvious, moreover, that awarding everybody an A grade renders the concept of real success meaningless. A top grade should be something which is difficult to achieve and which has, therefore, real currency.

There is a school in Penzance called Mounts Bay Academy which attracted a bit of media attention last week because, like a good number of schools in the past, its teachers have been instructed to use green ink rather than red when they are marking pupil work. Red is too aggressive and threatening, and everything possible must be done to persuade children that they are doing well, even if they are not.

None of (the teachers at my grammar school) would have had any truck with the ideas the RSA is attempting to promulgate. They knew that if any of us were to learn anything our mistakes had to be pointed out to us. They would not have wished, as the RSA advocates, to replace the term 'fail' with the substitute 'not yet'. They would not have dreamed of a classroom in which teachers and pupils should sit down to discuss the 'cognitive biases' which might lead teachers to make erroneous assumptions about the ability of children from disadvantaged backgrounds. They would not wish to be seen as 'lead learners' in order to create a mindset that education is a continuous process.

The RSA bills itself as: 'an enlightenment organisation committed to finding practical solutions to today's social challenges'. There are plenty of challenges in the classrooms of our schools, but the RSA's first mistake is to see these challenges as social rather than educational. The solutions it advocates are highly unlikely to result in improved learning. Indeed, the mystery to me is how the RSA can continue to bang the enlightenment drum and theorise about education in these regressive ways.

***

What is wrong with competition?

May 2015

In his recently published book, *The Unexpected Professor,* John Carey muses on why he started to work hard when he moved to Richmond and East Sheen Grammar School for Boys. In part, he says, it was no doubt down to the excellence of the teaching, adding that a visit to the opticians and a pair of glasses which allowed him to see the blackboard might have helped too. But the real reason was probably, he thinks, the fact that he began to be competitive. He wanted to be top of the form.

Every week, his grammar school published a form by form list of how well its pupils had done in their different subjects. The grammar school I attended some ten years later than Carey did the same thing. 'I imagine', Carey writes, that, 'anything so discriminatory would be illegal nowadays, but it was certainly a stimulus to me'. It was a stimulus to me, too, though I was more anxious to avoid being at the bottom of the list than keen to be at the top. Is there a school in the country in 2015 that encourages competition through the publication of such lists? I do not know of one.

Instead, we have a society in which 35,000 children have, apparently, phoned Childline to talk about the unbearable pressures they are under from tests and examinations. A recent survey reports that 50 per cent of primary children are worried that they will not do well enough in their SATs tests. Teachers, likewise, complain that league tables and the government's insistence that underperforming schools should be held to account have made their lives intolerable.

John Carey went to grammar school as the Second World War ended. For him, and for me in the 1950s, tests were a fact of school life. Classrooms, like school playing fields, were competitive places. As a sixth-former, I was aware of competition between teachers to see who could achieve the most Oxbridge scholarships and exhibitions. I do not think that the school saw itself as competing with other schools, but I am sure that at some level there was a real desire to be thought of as the best school in the locality.

We worked hard and we played hard. Yes, there were times when I felt that I was not keeping up and that worried me. But I never thought that the system was wrong and that I was being denied the freedoms that were my right as a child. I do not think that I would have welcomed happiness and mindfulness lessons. Indeed, I suspect that I would have bunked off if I had been expected to endure any such nonsense.

What's wrong with competition? Why are we as a society so determined to talk ourselves into a panic about the fact that examinations matter, that most children need to feel a bit of pressure if they are to work as hard as they should, and that schools which compete in order to survive are likely to offer their children a better education than those which swan happily along doing their own unpressurised thing?

***

Homework and detention – I resented both at the time

June 2015

The bus drew off when I was fifteen yards or so from the stop. It was cold. It was dark. It was more than fifty years ago, too, but I can still remember standing there in the Croydon Road, cursing everyone I deemed responsible for my undeserved misery: my parents, for sending me to a school which necessitated daily journeys of an hour and a half each way; the bus conductor who had ignored my frantic gesticulations as I sprinted towards him; and, above all, the teacher who had inflicted the detention upon me which had delayed my journey home.

I had received the detention for turning in an inadequate translation of a couple of paragraphs of English into Latin. In the run-up to our O level examinations, we received somewhere between two and three hours homework a night. I did not enjoy doing this homework and I resented its imposition, but I do not recall ever questioning the principle of it being set. We had around 25 hours of teaching a week and we had 10 to 15 hours of homework, in which we were expected to consolidate what we had learned. It was a burden, all that homework, but the logic of it being set made sense, even to my resentful adolescent self.

Now we have Eve Jardine-Young, the Principal of Cheltenham Ladies' College, suggesting that homework might be one of the pressures that is creating the 'epidemic' of mental health problems which is afflicting the young. Her school is, apparently, contemplating the possibility of abolishing homework, although she has subsequently said there is no immediate prospect of that abolition.

Who knows? Maybe all those hours of sitting upstairs at my desk with Radio Luxembourg fading in and out did inflict unbearable harm upon my psychic equilibrium. Somehow, I don't think so. We worked hard and we played hard. I used to cycle sometimes at weekends past Biggin Hill airport. I wonder what the young men who had climbed, day after day, into their Spitfires, knowing that the odds of their long-term survival were minimal, would think about the 'epidemic of anxiety' that the young today are meant to be experiencing.

We cannot and we should not try to protect our children from the unavoidable pressures which life brings. I do not think that lessons in happiness can make us happy, and I simply do not understand what people mean when they talk about 'well-being'.

Our moments of happiness descend upon us, if we are lucky, from time to time, a gift from the gods. Their magic and their wonder depend upon our experience of the tedium of the everyday and the misery which is part of our human lot.

Our children need homework and detentions. That half hour I spent standing at that bus stop, in retrospect at least, was a positive experience.

Schools

Chris Woodhead believed passionately that grammar schools have contributed more to social mobility than any other institution we have known. The Conservative Party ought to recognise that and ought to have the political courage to back a revival of selective education. Here he argues that in their refusal to do so they have sacrificed grammars on the altar of compassionate Conservatism.

First published in *The Sunday Times*, May 2007

'Academic selection,' the Conservative spokesman on education David Willetts announced last week, 'entrenches advantage, it does not spread it'.

The truth is that grammar schools have contributed more to social mobility than any other institution this country has known. In the 1940s and 1950s, when there was a grammar school in every town, more young people from disadvantaged backgrounds won places at top universities than before or since. Headteachers at public schools wondered about their future. Why, they asked, would parents continue to pay huge sums of money for their child's education when a similar or better education was available at no cost in state grammar schools?

Then in 1965 Anthony Crosland vowed that if he did nothing else he would abolish every grammar school in the land. The cull began and the independent sector flourished. Now grammar schools survive, just, in Northern Ireland and in a handful of local education authorities in England.

Grammars constitute just 5% of state schools and they routinely dominate the league tables. As, of course, given their selective intake, they should. But research shows that children at grammars make better progress than their peers at comprehensive schools. In Northern Ireland pupils of all abilities routinely outperform pupils in England at GCSE and A-level.

Not so long ago Willetts, acknowledging these results, declared that he was a strong supporter of selective education. He has now changed his mind. Why? Because, he says, new evidence shows that grammar schools do not contribute to social mobility. I do not believe him.

His U-turn stems more from his party's desire to rebrand itself than it does from the pursuit of a serious policy on secondary education. Grammar schools have been jettisoned because they are thought to smack of a right-wing Conservative past. The interests of bright children from disadvantaged homes have, in one of the bitterest ironies of modern politics, been sacrificed on the altar of compassionate Conservatism.

The killer fact for Willetts is that only 2% of pupils at grammars claim free school meals. Grammar schools, he concludes, have become middle-class institutions and, therefore, a bad thing. What matters in David Cameron's desperate drive to convince the electorate that his party has discovered its social conscience is the underclass. You pay your taxes and worry about your children's future? Hard luck. It is the 2% who claim free school meals that matter to Cameron's Conservatives.

Willetts would have done well to ask himself why so few grammar school pupils claim free school meals. It is not after all a difficult question. Grammar schools are hugely oversubscribed. Children from disadvantaged backgrounds often attend underperforming primary schools. They find it difficult to compete with middle-class children who have, more often than not, benefited from a challenging intellectual environment.

The solution is equally obvious. Create more grammar schools so more children have an opportunity to benefit from the education they offer. Do more to raise levels of expectation and standards of education in our bog-standard inner-city primary schools. Encourage grammar schools to identify and support able children in poorly performing primary schools. Level the playing field.

This would have been the pragmatic solution. A common sense response would, however, have denied Cameron his clause 4. No dragon would have been slain and no headlines would have followed. Those headlines are deserved. Forget new Labour. This Conservative decision to abandon selection is old-style socialism, red in tooth and claw. If everyone cannot have it, nobody will.

Cameron and Willetts might just as well apply their argument to Oxford and Cambridge. Working-class children are underrepresented there so, whatever the contribution these institutions make to the nation's intellectual and economic life, they must be dismissed as an elitist anachronism, a blot on the face of Cameron's socially inclusive Britain. Sorry, chaps, but that is the inevitable consequence when compassionate Conservatism functions at its illogical best.

Having abandoned grammar schools, the Conservatives are now embracing Tony Blair's city academies. They have, I suppose, to offer some solution to the problems of state secondary education. That progress is woefully slow in so many academies is a little awkward. The fact that their much trumpeted independence from state control is an illusion is neither here nor there, as is the lack of convincing evidence that the involvement of a sponsor who knows little about education makes much difference. They are new, they are glitzy, they demonstrate a Conservative commitment to waste as much public money as Labour, so who cares?

The great thing for Willetts is that academies are socially inclusive and are contributing, he claims, a great deal to the holy grail of social mobility. This claim is spurious. Few have achieved half-satisfactory examination results and none has existed long enough for anyone to know what its former pupils have done with their lives.

If Willetts is suggesting that the original city technology colleges, established by the Tories, have proved to be an academic success, then he is right. But he has conveniently forgotten that these colleges were allowed to interview prospective pupils and their parents, and therefore to eliminate those deemed likely to impact negatively on results. Socially inclusive they were not.

Grammar schools succeed for two reasons. Their pupils are all academically gifted so there is peer pressure to achieve and they attract teachers with first-rate academic qualifications who want to work with such children. Some comprehensive schools can recruit similar staff and attract enough able children to replicate this kind of competition, but not many.

In particular, it is difficult for the inner-city comprehensive and city academy. It is the inner-city child who needs the grammar school the most. The middle-class child who attends a half-decent suburban comprehensive school is going to survive reasonably well. The bright boy or girl from an inner-city ghetto who has to attend his or her inner-city comprehensive or academy won't. However stunning the accommodation and cutting edge the resources, the city academy is never going to replicate the intellectual challenge of the traditional grammar school.

Lord Adonis, the architect of Blair's academy programme, must know this. Like Willetts he used to be a supporter of grammar schools, even writing a book to extol their virtues. Now, having persuaded the Conservatives that academies are the way forward, he will no doubt be hoping that Gordon Brown becomes, as rumour suggests, similarly enthusiastic.

Nowhere is there any radical thinking. No party is committed to the creation of secondary modern schools for the 21st century which offer pupils who are not academic, but who have different, practical skills, the opportunity to develop their particular talents. No party appears willing to accept that teenagers are markedly different in their abilities and aspirations and that a vocational education in a vocational school might easily come to be seen as equally desirable as an academic education in a grammar school.

No, the political debate remains locked in the old clichés about the unfairness of selection and the desperate attempt to buy our way out of educational underachievement through the establishment of ever more expensive city academies.

Cameron dismisses any discussion of grammar schools as 'pointless'. He caricatures those of us who continue to support grammar schools as being interested only in the education of 'the select few'. I can reply only that I am interested in a meritocratic society in which academically successful schools are open to every child irrespective of the parents' ability to pay.

Cameron and Willetts tell us they are going to transform every comprehensive school into just such an institution. There are just two questions we all need to ask: how are you going to do it? And how do your ideas on the reform of secondary education differ from Blair's failed initiatives? They do not, I am afraid, have an answer.

***

Here, in 2005, he reviewed a new history of comprehensive schools which showed their fundamental flaws.

First published in *The Sunday Times,* September 2005

'Someone got chucked out of the window. A girl had her hair set on fire. Someone else was shot. You know', the speaker concluded – I take ironically – 'the usual sort of school week'. This was an ex-pupil at Risinghill, reminiscing about life at the infamous London school in Radio 4's compelling history of comprehensives, Comp!, broadcast on Thursday mornings.

Not all comprehensives, even in the 1960s, pushed their progressive theories to this anarchic extreme. The problem then, as now, was more often low expectations on the part of teachers and low-level but persistent disruption from pupils.

It's the sort of aggravation that drove teacher Francis Gilbert out of his profession for four years, 'burnt out' by his time in London's comprehensives – as he graphically details in his new book, *Teacher on the Run: True Tales of Classroom Chaos.*

Some comprehensives, particularly those in middle-class suburbs, succeed. Many, perhaps most, serving inner-city communities, do not. Yet no government in the last 40 years has had the courage to reintroduce selective education.

It was not always like this. The post-war Labour education minister, Ellen Wilkinson, a veteran of the Jarrow crusade in 1936 and a firebrand of the left, was a staunch believer in grammar schools. She had gone to one herself and saw them as public schools for the poor offering a meritocratic opportunity to everyone.

They did, too. Two-thirds of grammar school pupils in the early 1950s were working class. Only four of the 21 heads of big civil service departments listed by Anthony Sampson in 1971 were ex-public school pupils. The rest had attended grammar schools.

The tragedy is that the huge success of grammar schools became, to quote the sociologist Frank Musgrove, 'apparent precisely when they were destroyed'. Social mobility in Britain, according to a report published last April by the education charity the Sutton Trust, is now lower than in any of the eight countries studied other than America.

More young people from disadvantaged homes won places at Oxford and Cambridge in 1960 than is the case today. For all the egalitarian rhetoric that accompanied the abolition of the grammar schools, the move to comprehensive education has damaged the life chances of the very children it was meant to help.

It ought to have been obvious back in 1960, but it was not.

Middle-class families whose children had failed the 11-plus grew increasingly resentful. Academics such as A H Halsey at Oxford, who claimed that the exam allocated a quarter of children to the wrong school, argued that it was impossible to decide at this early age which children would benefit from which kind of school. Administrators such as Andrew Fairbairn and Stuart Mason in Leicestershire, brooded on stories of distress caused by the selection process and were converted to the comprehensive cause.

But the real revolution began when Labour came to power in the mid-1960s. Anthony Crosland, the then Education Secretary, famously declared that he was going 'to smash every f****** grammar school in the country', and started bribing education authorities with capital grants to ensure they did his will. Some resisted, but most did not, and by the end of the 1970s 3,300 comprehensive schools had been created and 80% of pupils were being educated in them.

In retrospect it seems that the whole project was driven by political rather than educational considerations. The aim was to create a more equal society and if a few wonderful schools were destroyed in the process, so be it.

Nobody asked the question whether it might be better to keep selection and develop a more intelligent, secure mechanism to identify the children who would really benefit from an academic education. Nobody thought for a moment about the curriculum the less able would be offered in these new comprehensive schools. Nobody wondered whether it was really a good idea to create schools for 2,000 or more pupils.

If Tony Blair was serious in his education reforms, he would be asking these questions. I suspect that if he had a free hand he might, for all his public protestations to the contrary, create new grammar schools. But he hasn't. Caught between the Scylla of the 'bog-standard comprehensive', which he knows has failed, and the Charybdis of backbenchers apoplectic in their hatred of the 'elitist' 11-plus, he can only struggle manfully to square an impossible circle.

So we have 'specialist' schools that in many cases are not that different from bog-standard comprehensives and are, according to the Office for Standards in Education, failing even to teach their specialism adequately. We have city academies, which can cost the taxpayer £24m each only to deliver results little or no better than the failed school they replaced.

Ruth Kelly, the Secretary of State, apparently expects us to swoon in grateful admiration at her announcement that the Government is to shut failing schools more quickly. What will she replace them with? Presumably yet more city academies, which, since they can select only up to 10% of their pupils, share the wrongheaded notion of comprehensive schools – that children, no matter what their abilities or backgrounds, can successfully be taught together in the same classes.

The grammar school, a proven instrument of social mobility, ought to be at the heart of Blair's education strategy. It is not, and, because of ideological opposition, never will be.

Why not reform the 11-plus, re-define and properly resource the secondary modern school as a technical school for the 21st century, and introduce new grammars, particularly in inner-city areas where comprehensive schools will never attract sufficient numbers of bright pupils and academically well-qualified staff to stretch the most able? There is only one reason and that is a lack of political will. Sad, isn't it?

Forty years ago the powers that be had the courage to close Risinghill. The time is now right for similar political decisiveness.

***

From his weekly blogs for *The Sunday Times*

International comparisons are difficult to make

June 2010

Most educational research tells you more about the ideological prejudices of the researcher than it does the subject it is meant to illuminate. When the researcher attempts to make comparisons between educational standards achieved in different countries the whole business becomes even murkier. How, given differences between the make-up of populations, culture and education systems, can anybody come to a firm conclusion that one particular factor justifies the argument which is laid before us?

Last week, my colleague at the University of Buckingham, Alan Smithers, tried. His analysis of science tests taken by 15 year olds in a number of developed countries in 2006 shows, he told us, that pupils in nations (such as Austria, Germany, the Netherlands, Japan and Korea) which had some form of selective education did better than their peers in countries (such as Canada, New Zealand, Australia, France and Britain) which did not. 'There are claims', he said, 'that non-selective systems do better, but it is not true. The argument for a non-selective system over a selective system doesn't add up'.

My initial reaction was to cheer. I am a supporter of selective education and I believe Alan Smithers to be one of the more objective, and therefore credible, educational researchers. I have, however, to confess that I am not entirely persuaded by his conclusions. If Japanese students are doing better than our own, is it because Japan has a system of selective education? Or is it because the Japanese as a nation take education rather more seriously than we do in the UK? Or is the real explanation the continuing commitment to powerful whole class teaching in the classrooms of Japanese schools? I suspect it is all these things, and a thousand others.

Neither am I convinced by Smithers' policy conclusion. 'Academic selection at 11 is too sensitive, and at 16 it is too late'. Sixteen is certainly too late, but why is selection at eleven too 'sensitive'? Politically controversial, maybe. That does not make it a forbidden topic, too painful to raise in polite company. It is the politicians and educationalists, not the topic, that are too sensitive. Or, to put it more accurately, too herd-like in their unswerving commitment to the consensus of the chattering classes to look at the existing evidence and to think for themselves.

I am grateful to Alan Smithers for challenging the myth that all international comparisons demonstrate the superiority of comprehensive education, but actually we don't need new research to reveal the success of selective education. It is nearly a quarter of a century since Frank Musgrove published his analysis of the social composition of grammar schools in the mid twentieth century and the success of the working class children they educated. Grammar schools were the most powerful mechanism for social mobility this country has ever had.

The great and the good may be too coy to admit the fact, but parents need no convincing. If Michael Gove were to allow his free schools to select their pupils on grounds of academic ability, I have absolutely no doubt: we would have a grammar school in every town.

***

There is nothing magical about academies

April 2012

You have probably forgotten all about specialist schools, but they were all the rage when I was Chief Inspector in the late 1990s. Labour could not distance itself in any way from the supposed ideal of the comprehensive school. Tony Blair knew, from his own experience in his constituency in the north-east, that many comprehensive schools were failing their students abysmally. Specialist schools were the way out of this difficult political problem. They were comprehensive schools, but they were specialist schools as well and, as such, they were necessarily and immediately liberated from the failure of the comprehensive movement.

It was all nonsense, of course. The school chose its specialism, maths or music or whatever, and the very fact that it had made this choice was meant to result in a miraculous transformation in standards. Not just in the chosen specialist subject, but in every other subject in the school, too. Parents were meant to be happy to send their child, who might be passionate about art but indifferent to maths, to a school which specialised in maths. Everybody was expected to celebrate when more and more secondary schools decided to become specialist schools.

I remember talking to a secondary headteacher one evening, after some formal engagement. I asked him what he thought of the specialist school initiative. He looked at me quizzically, clearly wondering how honest he should be. Initially I got all the usual flannel: wonderful idea, will make all the difference to us, has already lifted morale, etc, etc. I smiled back at him equally quizzically and he began to realise that I would rather like him to be honest. OK, he said, the truth is, it is a nonsense. We're doing it because there's a bit of extra cash, and we can't afford to be the one secondary school in the neighbourhood which is still a bog-standard comprehensive.

This headteacher came into my mind as I read another newspaper comment piece extolling the virtues of the Government's academies initiative. Soon, the pundit opined, every secondary school in the country will be an academy and Michael Gove will have redefined the face of secondary education.

Will he? I am absolutely certain that most schools which have become academies have made the move for exactly the same reason that schools became specialist schools a decade and a half ago. They like the idea of more money and they do not want to be left behind. Oh, and a few of the more astute operators amongst our headteachers have cottoned onto the fact that if they can persuade their newly autonomous governing body to raise their salary, it could have a pretty massive impact on their pension.

There is nothing in the concept of an academy that in itself will necessarily raise standards. Successful academies, like successful schools generally, are successful because they have strong leaders and good teachers. The last Government commissioned a whole series of consultancy reports on academies at, no doubt, huge expense to the public purse. The consultants came to exactly the conclusion that I have just stated, although it took them, of course, many thousands of pages to articulate their weighty opinions.

Re-labelling a failing or mediocre product is never going to make it better. There is only one way to solve the problems in state schools, secondary and primary, and that is bottom-up. Class by class, teacher by teacher, lesson by lesson, school by school, underexpectation and ideological prejudice must be confronted.

Michael Gove has no magic wand. He should abandon any belief in the alchemical powers of rebranding and base his reforms in a properly Conservative determination to empower the parent as consumer so that the producer interest is challenged in schools across the country by parents who have real power.

***

Change in state education means wrestling with the Blob

July 2012

It was an American who first coined the term 'the Blob' to describe key figures in the educational establishment. I cannot remember his name, but I want to salute his onomatopoeic brilliance.

When I wrote *Class War*, I tried to find an alternative phrase. I failed, of course. The Blob captures the inert mindlessness and sullen, rubbery resistance of the professors and quangocrats and officials and consultants who make up the educational establishment better than any other description possibly could.

Michael Gove knew about the power of the Blob before he came to office. He has made valiant attempts to wrestle it to the ground, abolishing, for example, the Qualifications and Curriculum Authority and the Training and Development Authority, and formulating plans to move teacher training out of university departments and into schools. He is trying, however, to change the culture of a profession and the battle has hardly begun.

Why is it that the traditional educational values he wants to encourage in state education are the norm in most private schools?

Is it because the teachers employed in such schools are better qualified and more intellectually competent and less susceptible, therefore, to the progressive ideologies promoted by the Blob than their state counterparts? To an extent, yes. If a teacher does not understand the rules of English grammar or much about mathematics, he or she is likely to be attracted to a vision of education which emphasises the 'child as a learner' and the importance of 'learning skills'.

Most of the teachers who work at, let's say, Eton or Winchester, do understand the rules of English grammar. They have first class degrees from top universities and they are passionate enthusiasts for the subjects they teach. They are less likely to be seduced by theories that denigrate subject knowledge.

But this is not the whole story. In 1955, the economist Milton Friedman argued that the way to reform state education was for parents to be given a voucher to pay for the education of their children. They could use the voucher to send their children to a state or a fee paying school. If they chose the latter, then they may well have to top up the value of the voucher, but the initiative would nonetheless open up the possibility of private education to many who, without financial assistance, would not be able to afford it. The result would be that more suppliers of education would be attracted into the market, that parents would be empowered as consumers, and that there would be more competition between and amongst schools. Educational standards would, as a consequence, rise.

Friedman thought the voucher had another advantage, and a crucial one, at that. He knew that it would be a stake through the heart of the Blob. Fee paying schools have to listen to the expectations and aspirations of their customers. If they do not give the customer what the customer wants, they die. Parents as customers are more likely to argue for the kind of education Michael Gove believes in than are professors of education or quangocrats.

The current coalition Government is never going to contemplate an idea as radical as Friedman's voucher. The Blob will continue to squeeze the oxygen out of Gove's reforms. We have a Secretary of State who has a clear understanding of the enemy he is fighting, but who is hamstrung by the blobbiness of the Cabinet in which he serves.

***

In a voucher system, most parents would choose wisely

September 2012

My initial reaction on reading the following story about parents in Shanghai who had spent the best part of ten thousand pounds on a two week summer school for their children was to snigger.

The organisers of this summer school had convinced their customers that children who attended would be taught 'special powers' such as the ability to read a book in twenty seconds and to see answers in their heads to questions once they had skimmed an examination paper. They would be trained to tap into the right side of their brain, enabling them to detect 'waves' emanating from certain things, such as words on a page, and create a picture inside their mind.

Needless to say, none of the children developed these magical skills and the parents were demanding their money back.

Couldn't happen here, in England, I thought. Then I stopped sniggering. It is happening here in England. Teachers across the country are attending courses on how the latest developments in neurological research can transform classroom learning. Schools are competing one with another to embrace the next new initiative, happiness classes, student-centred learning, cross-curricular skills – whatever – provided it is glitzy and new. And, all too often, parents are taken in.

How many parents have chosen to send their children to an academy because they are impressed by the spanking new, architect-designed buildings? How many measure the quality of the teaching by the number of computers in the classroom? How many, conversely, have any clear sense of the kind of education they really want for their children?

It pains me to ask these questions. For years I have argued that the only way to raise standards in education is to remove the malign influence of politicians and their bureaucrats and to empower parents as consumers. I still think that this is true. Parents who pay the fees charged by independent schools may sometimes choose a school for the wrong reason, but I know from my own experience working within the sector that these parents are for the most part focused on what they want for their children and demanding in their expectations.

The problem in the state sector is that parents rarely have any real choice. State schools teach the same curriculum. They recruit their teachers from teacher training institutions which promote the same progressive teaching ideologies. Their headteachers attend government funded conferences which encourage the same lobotomised mindset. In the interests of 'fairness', they have to admit pupils of similar abilities. Everything conspires against any school developing a genuinely individual ethos.

The answer lies in less regulation and more free schools. It would help, too, if the Ofsted inspection regime were to offer parents a detailed critique of schools and if the examination system was made more rigorous so that parents could see which schools were really achieving top grades. To be meaningful, parental choice has to be an informed choice.

Within the political constraints of the coalition, Michael Gove is trying as best he can to achieve these reforms. If we want a market in education, what is really needed, however, is the introduction of a voucher system which allows parents to send their children to fee paying schools, topping up the voucher if necessary with their own money. Such a system would encourage competition between schools and, crucially, would result in new providers of education entering the market.

Some parents, like those in Shanghai, would no doubt be gullible enough to succumb to the blandishments of the snake oil merchants. I have little doubt, however, that if real choice was there, most would use it wisely.

***

Standards will not be raised without structural change

October 2012

Aged 11, or thereabouts, I used to line up with my fellow members of Carew House on one side of the playground. On the other side were the boys who had the misfortune to belong to Bridges House. We would spend our break times chanting 'Carew not Bridges', trying to drown out the opposition chant of, yes, you've guessed it, 'Bridges not Carew'. From time to time, somebody would scuttle into no-man's-land to shout some provocation too politically incorrect to print in the sanitized pages of a 21st century Sunday newspaper. It was great fun, and I enjoyed every minute.

I used to amuse myself with these playground memories when, in Tony Blair's first administration, I would sit in meetings in the Department for Education, listening to ministers and officials talking endlessly about 'standards not structures'. The alliterative zap of the phrase appeared to matter more than the sense or nonsense of its substance. It clearly gave them a political buzz which rivalled even my Carew House loyalties.

Now, Stephen Twigg, Shadow Education spokesman, has revived this 'standards not structures' mantra. It annoyed me back in the 1990s. It annoys me even more now. Does Twigg really think that Michael Gove is more interested in tinkering with the structure of English education than he is raising educational standards? Can he not see that the issue is not standards versus structure, but whether or not standards can ever be raised without radical structural change?

There are only two ways in which our children can be given a better deal in the classroom. The first is through the Secretary of State for Education issuing edicts and expecting 24,000 schools and nearly half a million teachers to jump to his command. The second is through freeing schools from state control, empowering parents as consumers who can influence the nature and quality of the service provided, and encouraging competition between schools in a market economy.

We know from the experience of the never-ending initiatives launched by Labour in the thirteen years in which they were in power that the former does not work. How could it ever work? The Secretary of State does not have the levers to pull, and never will have. The chain of command is too long and too fragile. The resistance of the teaching profession to politically inspired change is too strong, and, as I have witnessed time and again, when resistance to what the politician wants becomes too vociferous, the political will crumbles.

So Gove, who wants higher standards more genuinely and passionately than any Minister for Education I have known, has no option other than to pursue his free schools and academy programme. Whether this programme is radical enough to deliver the improvements we need is another question. I do not think that it is. I know, however, that if we want higher standards in our schools the structure of our educational system has to change.

***

Most comprehensives do not cater for very bright children

June 2013 *[Abridged]*

'They tread water. They waste time. They do stuff they've already done in primary school. They find work too easy and they are not being sufficiently challenged'.

On the evidence of my *Sunday Times* column, I imagine that these comments from Sir Michael Wilshaw, the Chief Inspector of Schools, introducing Ofsted's report on whether bright children are making sufficient progress in comprehensive schools, will have resonated with many readers. What to do when a bright child is clearly becoming more and more bored by the banality of what they experience every day in the classroom is one of the most regular questions I receive.

The Ofsted study, which was based upon evidence from 41 schools and 2,000 lessons, revealed that two thirds (65,000) of children who achieved level 5 in primary school mathematics and English failed to get an A* in both subjects at GCSE. The inspectors found that many schools do not track the progress their most academically gifted pupils are making 'sufficiently well'. Some do not even know which are the academically gifted.

Predictably enough, the teacher unions have reacted with their usual fury. Chris Keates of the NASUWT has dismissed the conclusions as untrue. She has questioned the size of the sample and the statistical analysis. In her opinion the whole thing is 'outrageous' and 'scandalous'. In particular, Wilshaw's suggestion that schools should stop pretending that mixed ability teaching works and set their pupils earlier and in more subjects according to ability has prompted widespread indignation.

It is always possible to raise methodological questions about educational research. A sample of 41 schools is not that large and Wilshaw's decision to base his argument on the progress made by students who achieved level 5 in their end of primary tests is probably shaky in that level 5 covers, in reality, a very wide range of ability. This does not negate the basic point. Our failure to inspire many of our brightest children is one of the greatest tragedies of the education system. We continue, rightly, to invest heavily in the education of the less able. It is time to think about the equally important needs of those very able children the system currently fails. Last week's Ofsted report was an extremely important wake up call.

***

Private schools have to be successful to survive

July 2013

His voice shaking, no doubt, with righteous indignation, Labour's spokesman on education, Stephen Twigg, told an audience last week that under Tory plans 'private firms could set up schools and then sell them on at a profit'.

The fact that a business can only be sold for a profit if it is a successful business seems to have eluded him. A successful school is one where the children make excellent progress because of the professionalism and commitment of their teachers, where the pastoral care supports every pupil as an individual, and where the range of extracurricular activities offered allows everyone to discover new interests and talents. This is the kind of school every parent wants for their child. If a for profit school fails to deliver this kind of excellence it will never be sold for a profit. It will go bust.

Michael Gove has indicated in the past that he is not ideologically opposed to the idea of allowing those who run academies and free schools to make a financial return. He recognises, presumably, that publishers, for example, make a profit from text books, that ICT in education is a massive industry, and that many support services have already been contracted out. Why shouldn't a Conservative government take the next step and allow private companies actually to run schools?

If the state monopoly had a track record of universal success then there would be no need to contemplate privatisation. In his speech, Twigg cited the fact that a company called JB Education, which had been educating ten thousand pupils in Sweden, had sold nineteen of its schools and closed four. I do not for one moment think that a market solution to education will provide universal success. Private companies can, of course, and do, fail. To pretend, however, that privatisation inevitably, to quote Twigg, 'results in chaos and a collapse of standards' is nonsensical; to ignore the failures of the state system and the failure of both Conservative and Labour administrations to achieve the radical reforms needed is disingenuous.

Charitable trust schools in the UK may not be run for profit but they compete one against the other in a market and to survive they must remain financially viable. Every year, some fail. But standards across the independent sector generally remain extremely high. They are high because they have to be high if they are to continue to attract the parents who pay their fees. The introduction of new systems of inspection and league tables in the 1990s certainly made state schools more accountable, but they do not face the same pressures. Indeed, while failure may result in a change of headteacher, it usually brings significant additional resources. The state coffers are inexhaustible and the profligacy with which they are used all too often sustains mediocrity.

Stephen Twigg and Nick Clegg appear to believe that education is a public good and must be both publicly funded and publicly managed. They think that the profit motive in some way must damage the quality of the service provided to pupils. Gove does not at present have the political power to pursue the possibilities of privatisation, but this ought to be a clear dividing line between the parties in the run-up to the 2015 election.

Equality of opportunity cannot be expected to produce equal outcomes

November 2013

There may, I suppose, have been vindictive comment in some obscure left-wing publication, but the mainstream media does not seem to have responded negatively to Boris Johnson's speech last week about the 'Thatcher legacy'. I am surprised. I would have thought that his comments on the sacred cow of equality and the linked, equally controversial issue of selective education would have seen buckets of ordure poured over his golden locks.

Boris told his audience that it was impossible to create total equality because people were 'already far from equal in raw ability'. Sixteen per cent of people, he observed, have an IQ below 85. Two per cent have a score of above 130. He proposed that the number of selective state schools should be expanded and that the assisted places scheme, which helped fund the education of poorer children in private schools, should be reintroduced in order to combat the growing anger at the lack of social mobility. Conservative MPs, he added, who opposed grammar schools whilst sending their own children to 'some of the most viciously selective schools in the country' were guilty of 'political madness'.

I do not see why any form of selection should be 'vicious', but Boris is obviously right to point to the intellectual hypocrisy. In a sane world his common-sense observation that men are not born equal and that no amount of utopian hope, financial investment and political tinkering are going to deliver a society where everybody is achieving high A level grades would be unremarkable.

But we do not live in a sane society. The chief executive of UCAS, Mary Curnock Cook, also gave a speech last week. Her argument was that the Government's attempts to make A levels more intellectually challenging were having a 'detrimental' effect on initiatives to increase the number of young people from disadvantaged backgrounds who go to university. Since 2004, she said, there has been an 'extraordinary growth' in the number of students following vocational courses. The percentage doing A levels has remained 'broadly flat' at 37 per cent, but entries for vocational qualifications have increased from 3 per cent to 15 per cent. Since candidates with vocational qualifications 'barely made an appearance' at top universities, Cook thinks that schools should steer students from disadvantaged backgrounds away from vocational qualifications so that they keep their academic options open.

She is right if we are talking about students who are genuinely academic. But her underlying assumption seems to be that a vocational qualification is inferior to an academic qualification and that students, to refer back to Boris's basic argument, are pretty equal and could be made more equal if we only abandoned divisive and elitist politics and policies.

Like Boris, I would say that we need, above all else in our approach to education, to be realistic. A few weeks ago, Michael Gove's special adviser, Dominic Cummings, published a very interesting paper in which he drew upon the work of Robert Plomin, who stresses the importance of IQ and the fact that our IQ score is heavily influenced, if not wholly determined by, nature rather than nurture.

To believe otherwise is the great myth of our time. We all want to believe that politicians can solve the miseries of man and create a society where equality of opportunity leads to far, far greater equality of outcome. It is a nice thought, but a banal hope.

***

Sorry, but children do vary greatly

July 2013

I wonder what DH Lawrence, if he were still alive, would have made of an article Danny Dorling, an academic and 'public intellectual' who is about to take up a prestigious chair at the University of Oxford, wrote in a national newspaper last week.

Professor Dorling thinks that there is 'a nasty little assumption' underpinning Michael Gove's new National Curriculum. This assumption is 'that children vary greatly in what they might be able to achieve, that some have far greater potential to do well than others, but all have only a fixed potential'. He interprets Gove's wish 'to allow teachers greater freedom to use their professionalism and expertise to help all children realise their potential' as an admission that the Government believes 'it would be foolish to try to help too many try to achieve more than we think they can manage'. The plan, as Dorling sees it, is to focus on the privileged whilst condemning the masses to a state of ignorance, thus entrenching the corrosive inequalities that blight our society.

It is almost a hundred years now since Lawrence wrote his essay, *The Education of the People*, in which he wrote these sentences: 'We have assumed that we could educate Jimmy Shepherd and make him a Shelley or an Isaac Newton. At the very least we were sure we could make him a highly intelligent being. And we're just beginning to find our mistake. We can't make a highly intelligent being out of Jimmy Shepherd. Why should we if the Lord created him only moderately intelligent? Why do we want always to go one better than the Creator?'

Why indeed? Lawrence points out what in a less egalitarian and sentimental world would be obvious to all. Children are not equally intelligent and some are not very intelligent at all. Why, he asked, pretend otherwise?

Last week's newspapers also carried reports of a study undertaken by Professor Robert Plomin, who works at the Institute of Psychiatry, Kings College, London. Plomin has conducted an analysis of a long term study of 11,000 twins born in the mid 1990s. His conclusions are that inherited intelligence may well account for almost 60% of a teenager's scores at GCSE.

The fact that 'children vary greatly in what they might be able to achieve' is not a nasty little assumption: it is a God given fact. I have spent a good deal of time and energy over the last thirty years arguing that expectations in our schools need to be higher. I know from my own experience as a teacher and, indeed, a child, that there is a good deal of truth in the theory of the 'self-fulfilling prophecy'. I had teachers who thought I was a fool and, looking back, it doesn't surprise me in the least that I behaved foolishly in their lessons. Conversely, there were teachers who thought I could do better than I was doing and, more often than not, I would rise to the challenge. Nothing used to depress me more when I was Chief Inspector than visiting schools where the teachers had written off their pupils because of the poverty of their home environment.

But unrealistic and utopian expectations can damage both the individual child and the entire education system. Parents and teachers who try to force a child to become somebody they are not can do that child incalculable damage. Similarly, when we have a politician who believes, as Lord Adonis believed when he was Education Minister, that there is 'no genetic or moral reason why the whole of society should not succeed to the degree that the children of the professional classes do today, virtually all getting five or more good GCSEs and staying on in education beyond 16', the inevitable consequence is that the system is going to be dumbed down to deliver the political dream.

Dorling, Adonis and their fellow travellers on the left want the Government to do more to level the playing field. They appear to believe that equality of opportunity can result in an equality of outcomes. We continue to subject young people who do not have real academic talent to a curriculum that is damaging and demeaning. As Lawrence said: 'Drag a lad who has no capacity for true learning or understanding through the processes of education, and what do you produce in him in the end? A profound contempt for education, and for all educated people'.

Lawrence would perhaps not be surprised to learn that the old utopian myths continue to run rampant. He would nonetheless have snorted with derision at Dorling's threadbare tissue of assertion.

***

Lowering entrance requirements is an admission of defeat

March 2015

Five grammar schools in Birmingham run by the King Edward VI Foundation have set a lower pass mark in their 11-plus test for disadvantaged children who have been eligible for free school meals during the past six years.

The education charity, the Sutton Trust, thinks this is a very good thing. All grammar schools, it believes, should give preference to disadvantaged children. The assumption underpinning this highly questionable argument is that there are significant numbers of children from disadvantaged homes who would have passed the 11-plus if they had had the advantages of a middle class home life and the teaching offered by a middle class primary school. I am not sure what the evidence is to support this idea, though it clearly resonates with the spirit of the times.

I do not for one moment deny that there are some such children, and I agree with the Sutton Trust that grammar schools should be doing more outreach work in primary schools to identify and support bright children who might have the potential to benefit from a grammar school education. They should also be working with primary school teachers to help these pupils understand the demands of the 11-plus test so that children from more affluent homes do not have the unfair advantage they possess at present.

What worries me is the argument that the playing field should be altered to give advantage to the disadvantaged. It is the same argument that has been used for some years now to encourage the acceptance of lower A level results so that students from poorer backgrounds are admitted to top universities. It is the argument that is used by advocates of positive discrimination generally. The accident of birth has denied some people the opportunity to fulfil their potential. We must change the rules so that they can make progress more easily.

There are two dangers. The first is that if the playing field is not level then everyone can come to feel resentment. Those who have benefited from positive discrimination will inevitably wonder whether it is their family background or the colour of their skin that has been more important than the incisiveness of their mind. Those who have missed out because of positive discrimination will experience a sense of unfairness and, quite possibly, bitterness.

Second, there is the fact that when the entry threshold is lowered the quality of the institution is damaged. It may be that students who are admitted to universities with lower A level grades catch up with their peers over the three years of the course, but university students ought to hit the ground running. If they have to catch up, then their presence in tutorials and seminars is bound to impact negatively on the level of academic discussion. So, too, with grammar schools. Do we really want to erode the quality of the institutions we, rightly, want the brightest disadvantaged students to attend?

There is a further point. If primary schools were doing their job properly, then their brightest pupils would be fulfilling their intellectual potential. This move to lower the entrance requirements to grammar schools is an admission of defeat. I have written before about the failure of state education to stretch the most able. We have here classic evidence of how we have come to accept that the problem is never going to be solved.

***

We should be careful what we wish for

June 2015

What does our collective preoccupation with social mobility tell us about the nation in which we live? It tells us that we have lost sight of everything that should matter most to us as human beings.

Whenever the Sutton Trust, a charity dedicated to the widening of access to top schools, elite universities and professions such as law and finance, publishes another report which rubs our noses in the unfairness of our society, whenever Alan Milburn, the social mobility tsar, climbs onto his soap box to berate schools, politicians and employers for failing to do enough to ensure that the disadvantaged can make it into the top echelons of society, I think of my grandfather, digging the vegetable patch in his Somerset garden.

He was a proud, independent and cantankerous old man, a skilled carpenter and a fanatical gardener. He would spend his days restoring antique furniture in his workshop and digging the vegetable patches and flowerbeds of his extensive garden.

The term 'social mobility' had not, of course, been invented when he was alive. If it had, I have no doubt that it would have prompted a sardonic riposte and a snort of derision. What mattered to this old man, who was something of a hero to me, was his individuality and independence. He would have rejected the idea that anybody would want to climb the social ladder in order to mingle with their supposed betters as a complete absurdity.

In the late 1960s when he died I was studying English at Bristol University. One of the writers who meant most to me was DH Lawrence. Lawrence, like my grandfather, despised anybody whose view of life was dominated by a sense of the importance of money or class.

Read Lawrence's letters from his time in Cornwall and you learn something of what it is to be genuinely alive and quick, alert to every emotional moment and to the beauty of the natural world. It is somewhere in one of those letters that Lawrence states that the first thing any genuine human being must do is free themselves from the treadmill of financial gain. There are more important things, he says, in life than the security of a steady job, and we should summon the courage to live for what really matters. Looking back, I wish I had found that courage.

It is squalid, this belief that what matters most is social mobility. I watched that BBC series on the *Tatler* magazine earlier this year, and switched off at the end of every episode wondering who on earth would want to be 'posh'. Posh, anyway, in the sense that you have a big house and a luxury car, and, if you've really made it, some polo ponies.

There is another kind of 'poshness', though. You do not have to be a millionaire to be an aristocrat of the spirit. Lawrence and my grandfather were true aristocrats. 'Cast a cold eye/On life, on death/Horseman, pass by'. Cast a cold eye, in particular, on the talk of social mobility which dominates our political and educational discourse.

***

The experts are determined to deny young children any intellectual stimulus

September 2013

My grandchildren spent the last week of their summer holidays with us in Wales. They swam in the river, scoured the fields for animal skulls, played hide-and-seek in the woods. When it rained there were plenty of books to read and adults to read to them. It was a privileged, middle class, *Swallows and Amazons* summer.

I thought of them when, rather reluctantly, I read a letter in a national newspaper last week from 127 'experts' on 'early childhood education'. I could not disagree with their opening statement that 'the early years of life are when children establish the values and mindsets that underpin their sense of self, their attitude to later learning and their communication skills and natural creativity', though I am not sure that this observation adds much to what the Jesuits have been telling us for centuries.

Chris with his daughter, Tamsin, and grandchildren, Elsa and Morva, in 2007.

Once I moved beyond this unexceptional truth, I began to wonder what these eminent authorities were trying to say. 'Early childhood', they wrote, 'is recognised worldwide as a crucial stage in its own right, (but) ministers in England persist in seeing it simply as a preparation for school'. A 'stage', by definition, is an interlude, a period which leads towards a further stage. If ministers want those responsible for the education of our youngest children to think about how what they are doing helps those children move forward in their learning so that they are properly prepared for the next stage in their lives, they are merely wanting what any sensible parent or teacher has always wanted.

They are horrified by the fact that: 'the role of play is being downvalued in England's nurseries'. Actually, it is not. Most of the nursery settings I know worship all too enthusiastically at the altar of the great god of play. Teachers and their assistants reach for the garlic at any possibility that they might be asked to teach young children anything. The inspectors and the bureaucrats in local authorities police adherence to the gospel of play. Over the years it has been clear that the experts in the field who have advised ministers have been equally resistant to the idea that there should be any element of instruction in the young child's day.

Was my daughter 'teaching' my three-year-old granddaughter to read when she encouraged her to start thinking about how the letters c-a-t represent the word cat? My granddaughter, who is desperate to learn to read like her older sisters, is clearly ready for the challenge. I fully accept that children should not be forced to clear hurdles they are not ready to clear, but I will fight in the ditch for the right of children who are ready to be taught new things by adults who know that while play is important young children can only benefit from sensitive interaction with parents and teachers who can help them master new knowledge and skills.

Whatever Professor Sir Al Aynsley-Green, the first person to occupy the Alice in Wonderland position of Children's Commissioner for England, Professor Lord Richard Layard, who has become the nation's leading guru on 'well-being', Professor Guy Claxton, co-director of the Centre for Real World Learning (sic) and Professor of the Learning Sciences (ditto) at the University of Winchester, and their co-signatories of this misguided letter might think, balance is as vital in the first stage of education as it is in any other.

They might also reflect on the fact that not every child benefits from supportive parents and *Swallows and Amazons* summers. It probably wouldn't make much difference to my grandchildren if they started school at seven rather than four, but the impact on the less advantaged would be catastrophic.

Examinations

Every summer when the A level and GCSE results came out, Chris Woodhead was asked to comment on the improvements in the award of top grades. It was not popular to say that there was no reason to celebrate, but he was not prepared to let ministers go unchallenged in their denial that the examinations had become easier over time. In these pieces he explains why.

First published in *The Sunday Times,* August 2007

Secretaries of State for Education might come and go but their clichés remain constant. A-levels? No, of course they have not been dumbed down. Our teachers are the best teachers we have ever had, our students are more intelligent and diligent than before and these wonderful results are a testament to the huge progress that has been made since Tony Blair promised us a world class education system in 1997.

To suggest otherwise is, wait for it, to 'insult' students and 'demoralise' their teachers. The nakedness of the emperor might be more and more obvious to more and more people but Ed Balls, like his predecessors, dismisses anyone who has the temerity to speak out as a disgruntled old reactionary interested only in spoiling the party.

What is there to celebrate? In the short term everyone is happy. This year's A-level candidates breathe an understandable sigh of relief. Parents bask in the achievements of their talented offspring and teachers congratulate themselves on another record crop of results. Ministers welcome an apparent good news story that may strengthen the Government's position in the polls. Everybody involved has a good reason to succumb to the temptation to shut up and drink up. Why rock the boat when the last thing you want to do is capsize?

That question is not rhetorical. The creak of vested interests might be painfully audible but the need for honesty is overpowering. An examination that fails to identify the brightest students and which, corrupted by the egalitarian zeal of politicians who think everyone can and must succeed, awards some sort of prize to almost every candidate, however ignorant they might be, is not fit for purpose. The A-level is such an examination.

The pass rate has improved each year for 25 years. This year 3% of candidates failed; 25% achieved an A grade. Top universities are now setting their own admissions tests. They have no alternative. Every candidate has three or four A grades so A-level results are useless. They are suspect, too, for research conducted over a number of years by Robert Coe of the University of Durham suggests that candidates of similar intellectual ability achieve higher grades today than they would have done in the past. A candidate who gained an A grade today, for example, would have been awarded a B in 1996 and a C in 1988.

Ministers and their officials have a standard defence against the accusation that the A-level examination has become easier. They argue that because the examination has changed so radically in terms of syllabuses and the nature of the assessment, it is impossible to make meaningful comparisons. This is nonsense. The whole point is that the examination has been changed. It is the nature of these changes that explains the loss of intellectual rigour.

In the mid-1990s, as Chief Inspector of Schools, I commissioned a report into the A-level examination that became known as Standards over Time. Subject specialists looked at the syllabuses and chief examiners' reports for a number of subjects. We would have liked to study examination scripts but it turned out that the examination boards had, somewhat surprisingly, destroyed this evidence. It was, however, possible to reach some strong conclusions.

In each subject the specialists remarked on the fact that intellectually tough topics had tended to drop off the syllabus to be replaced by easier material. They commented on the way that over the years the style of questions had changed. Older A-level papers asked open-ended questions requiring real thought. In the more recent examinations, questions tended to be broken into bite-sized chunks, designed to lead the candidate by the nose to the right answer. The specialists expressed concern at the increasing prominence of coursework with all its attendant problems.

In 2000 the Government decided that A-levels should be divided into modules or units and that candidates should be assessed when they had completed each module. This, predictably, damaged standards further. Does Balls really believe that an examination in which units of work are assessed as the course progresses and, worse, that allows candidates to retake units if they do not like their initial grade, is as demanding as one that tests the totality of a candidate's knowledge at the end of a two-year course?

He and his fellow ministers must know they are defending the indefensible. When Coe's latest research was released a couple of months ago, Jim Knight, the Schools Minister, failed to muster a coherent response on the *Today* programme. Last week he was telling us complacently that the number of students taking 'harder' A-levels such as mathematics, science and foreign languages had increased this year. True, 14% more students sat mathematics A-level this year than last. What he failed to say was that 10.4% more students took the examination in 2000. In the same period the numbers taking French and German have fallen by 20.5% and 27.5% respectively. Numbers taking media studies, physical education and ICT continue to rise.

Knight also forgot to mention the fact that the supposed improvement in A-level grades has been driven almost entirely by independent and grammar schools. Comprehensive schools have by and large failed to improve their performance. Note that what we are talking about here is the rate of improvement. A selective school ought, as the teacher unions have been quick to point out, to do better in absolute terms than a non-selective school. Why, though, should the former raise standards each year while the latter achieves little or no improvement? The answer is that selective schools work and that independent schools benefit from their independence, truths that Knight would prefer to keep firmly under wraps.

The Liberal Democrats are calling for a review of the A-level examination. The truth, I am afraid, is obvious. This is an examination that was once admired across the world. It has been destroyed by a Government determined to expand higher education and desperate to demonstrate a supposed rise in educational standards.

What is to be done? The first and most fundamental need is to rescue public examinations from politicians, irrespective of party, who inevitably succumb to the temptation to dumb down examinations to secure apparent improvements in standards and therefore, hopefully, electoral advantage. Top universities should be invited to collaborate with the highest achieving state and independent schools to create a new A-level system with sufficient intellectual rigour to challenge and identify the most able. This new examination should be independent of ministers and their officials. It will be an examination that can be failed, and many will fail. In other words, a real examination.

Each year a fixed percentage of candidates should be awarded each grade. The top 10% could, for example, be awarded the A grade, and that would be that. The best students would be identified, as they were in the past, and universities would know which candidates deserved a place.

Its focus should be explicitly and unashamedly academic. Sir Mike Tomlinson's 2002 review of examinations concluded that there should be a British baccalaureate that required everyone to do a bit of everything. A module of Greek, perhaps, followed by a week or two of bricklaying, according to personal whim. This would be disastrous. If we want a proper academic examination, then we have to recognise that real study means submitting oneself to the body of knowledge one wants to master. Learning cannot be 'personalised'.

It is the debased practice of A-levels that is wrong, not the concept. A course that gives intellectually able 16 to 18-year-olds the chance to study three subjects that interest them in depth is an ideal preparation for university. Other students may prefer the broader curriculum of the international baccalaureate. Fine, let them go down this route. The danger now is that the crisis that has engulfed A-levels will lead to the introduction of a debased baccalaureate along the lines that Tomlinson proposed.

If this were to happen, nobody would learn much but everyone, I suppose, would continue to feel valued and the party, at least in the short term, would continue.

***

First published in *The Sunday Times,* August 2009

Forty-seven years ago I cycled the dozen or so miles from my home in south Croydon to Wallington Grammar School in a state of hyperventilating panic. It was O-levels rather than GCSEs in those days and, if you wanted immediate information, you had to go to the school to learn your fate. The nerve-racking tension in the run-up to the publication of results was the same. Anxious to avoid public humiliation, I set out early in case my grades were really bad. In the event, I scraped through the lot. I even managed a grade 6 in maths. The realisation that I'd never have to struggle with another quadratic equation remains one of the most ecstatic moments of my life.

Next week A-level hopefuls are going to experience the agony or the ecstasy. The week after it is the turn of this year's GCSE candidates. Two things are certain. One, that results in both GCSE and A-level exams will continue to improve with even more candidates achieving top grades; two, that girls will continue, because exams now depend so much on coursework, to outperform boys.

In 1962 there were some pretty bright boys in my O-level class. Half a dozen went on to win awards at Oxford and Cambridge. Virtually everybody ended up at a top university. Few, if any, achieved 10 grade As at O-level. Today, anyone who goes to an academic school and doesn't get that many A*s at GCSE might as well become an apprentice dustman or, worse, sign up for one of the Government's new diplomas. Tuck into your bacon and eggs and thank your lucky stars that you are not 16 and struggling in a world where academic standards have improved so radically.

This is not a wholly ironical observation. I talk to bright GCSE and A-level students and I am horrified by the treadmill of their classroom existence. They are taught the 'right' answer as prescribed by the examiner and warned against any independent thought. One tedious coursework assignment is completed and another immediately looms. Above all, these students realise that it is a farce. They know that the intellectual challenge is pathetic, and, because everybody will win it, the prize (10 A*s at GCSE, three or four A grades at A-level), meaningless.

You either believe that every generation of students is brighter and more diligent than the last and that teachers today are more competent than the nincompoops who struggled to teach me in the early sixties, or you don't. I don't. I know that I had some wonderful teachers, and I thank them for all that they did for me.

Ministers might fulminate against anyone who questions, to quote the threadbare defence that has been dragged out every summer in recent years, 'the achievements of hardworking students and their deeply committed teachers'. However, the evidence speaks for itself: more students are now awarded top grades at GCSE and A-level because the exams they sit have become progressively easier.

Take the GCSE in my own subject, English. The Headmaster of Harrow School, Barnaby Lenon, makes his sixth-formers take a literacy test that assesses their ability to use full stops and capital letters and spell words such as 'committed' and 'accommodation'. Those who make more than 20 mistakes are given extra tuition until they pass. Harrow is a top public school whose sixth-formers are likely to have an A* grade in GCSE English. If its headmaster has these concerns about the basic literacy of his students, and has gone to the extent of devising such a test, what does it say about GCSE English standards generally?

The truth, however vigorously ministers might pontificate to the contrary, is that it is perfectly possible to pass GCSE English with a good grade and be weak at spelling and punctuation. Today's GCSE English exam bears no resemblance to the O-level I took in 1962. We had to write an essay of 450 words, answer comprehensive questions on a lengthy and quite complex passage, and reduce a second passage of 500 words to 150. The latter task, the infamous precis, went years ago. So, too, did clause analysis along with any explicit questions on grammar. The intellectual demand of the comprehension passages and the sophistication of the questions have been gradually reduced. I would say, having dusted down some old exercise books, that today's English GCSE roughly equates to the work we were doing at 13 or 14.

At some point next year there will be a general election. If Labour wins, the rot will bite deeper. The latest ministerial wheeze is to 'modularise' GCSEs. This means that each subject syllabus will be divided up into a number of units and that candidates will be tested on each unit as it is completed, as has already happened with A-levels. If students fail a module they will be allowed to retake it. Kathleen Tattersall, the Chairwoman of Ofqual, the body created to regulate exam standards, has insisted that 'GCSE standards will be maintained'.

She did not, however, explain how an exam where candidates are tested on small parts of the syllabus (and can retake each test if they do not like the mark they achieve) can be compared with a traditional end-of-course assessment in which they have just one chance to demonstrate their grip on the totality of the syllabus. You might not like the stress involved in the latter kind of exam, but you cannot pretend that the modular version is as demanding. Unless, that is, you are the chairman of the body responsible for defending educational standards.

This debacle is typical of what Labour has done to public exams. Michael Gove, the Conservative spokesman on education, has said that a future Conservative government would restore credibility to the exam system. He has not yet spelt out what this means. He should, and quickly. No issue in education is more important. What he says could decide how a good many people cast their vote.

***

June 2012

I have never, in my whole life, felt the slightest desire to hug a politician, but, listening to the news last Thursday morning, I was swept by an overwhelming sense of gratitude towards Michael Gove.

The man is a hero. In a cabinet of political pygmies, he has the intellect and courage to challenge an educational and political establishment which has betrayed generations of young people. If he can abolish GCSE examinations and restore the traditional O level, he will have achieved more than any other Secretary of State for Education in the last quarter of a century.

For years, anyone who has dared to suggest that the explanation for the never ending improvements in GCSE grades might be that the examinations have been dumbed down has been accused of undermining the achievements of hardworking teachers and their ever more intelligent students. Parents, teachers and politicians have all colluded in establishing an Alice in Wonderland world of grade inflation.

Now, Gove has admitted it. The GCSE examination is broken beyond repair.

When I took my O levels in 1962, the English paper required me to analyse sentences into clauses and to state the grammatical function of each clause. I had to summarise a complex passage of 500 words into 150 of my own words. I had to answer a demanding set of comprehension questions and I lost marks, of course, for any mistakes in grammar, spelling or punctuation.

I struggled with a physics question which asked me to 'describe an experiment to obtain a series of corresponding angles of incidence and reflection for rays of light reflected from the surface of a plain mirror' and to 'indicate the relationship between these pairs of angles'.

Compare this to the following question from a recent GCSE science paper:

> Residents have a variety of thoughts concerning the siting of the new power station. The two views are: i. the nuclear power station will provide more employment in the area; ii. any release of radioactive material would be very dangerous. Which statements are arguments in favour of siting the nuclear power station here – i. only, ii. only, both i. and ii., neither?

The rubric for the 1972 London French O level stated: 'You must take special care to write correct, grammatical French which fully answers the question asked'. In 2008, modern foreign languages GCSE candidates were told that: 'The important thing is to convey the message' and that they did 'not have to write in full sentences'. It added that their 'answers would not be marked for the accuracy of the language'.

Michael Gove is right. The intellectual demand of today's GCSEs does not compare to that of the traditional O level. Syllabuses have been divided into bite sized chunks, or modules. Coursework has eased the trauma of terminal examinations. Year by year, the percentage of marks required to achieve different grades has been reduced. Nobody who studies the evidence can come to any other conclusion.

But the evidence does not appear to matter to his critics. Shadow Education Minister, Kevin Brennan, for example, agrees that GCSEs may need improving, but accuses Gove of introducing a 'two-tier system which divides children into winners and losers at 14'.

I know, from my experience as a teacher and from the thousands of lessons I have watched as an inspector, that the attempt to prepare all students for the same, essentially academic, examinations is doomed to fail. Fourteen year olds are different. Some are going to win scholarships to colleges at Oxford and Cambridge; others will leave school to become hairdressers or car mechanics.

It is absurd to pretend that all have the same academic potential and wish fulfilment to believe that one examination can possibly challenge the most able whilst allowing others to demonstrate some minimum competence. This is where the politicians went wrong in 1988 when the GCSE was brought in to replace the old O levels and CSEs.

We have been tinkering with the GCSE ever since, to try to make it work. Now Gove has recognised the impossibility of the task.

I was fortunate to grow up in the 1950s and 60s, when England was a genuinely meritocratic society. There were O levels and there were CSEs. There were A levels and there were apprenticeships. There were, though Mr Gove will not want to be reminded of the fact, grammar schools and secondary modern schools. Able students, irrespective of their family background, had the opportunity to go to top universities, and many did. The stranglehold of public schools on the professions was under serious threat.

Michael Gove's cabinet colleagues talk endlessly about social mobility. In restoring O levels, he is taking a dramatic step towards the restoration of the meritocracy which the pursuit of egalitarian ideals has undermined so tragically.

***

From his weekly blogs for *The Sunday Times*

Restoring intellectual rigour to A level and GCSE will take courage

March 2011

If I were to write that I did not experience a frisson of bitter sweet satisfaction as I read the latest education report from the Organisation for Economic Cooperation and Development (OECD), I would be lying. But my 'told you so' moment quickly evaporated. Once again I found myself asking the question I have been asking for the last fifteen years. How could those responsible for educational standards have been so stupid?

The OECD report tells us two things. First, that the inexorable rise in examination standards means nothing. Each year, the number of students achieving top A level grades increases. The scores they achieve, however, on an independent cognitive test do not reflect this surge in A level performance. Today's students are not brighter, better taught or more hard working than their peers twenty years ago. The explanation for the improved grades is that the examinations are easier.

Second, this smoke and mirrors charade has been played out against the backdrop of a doubling in educational expenditure under the last Labour Government. Gordon Brown used to refer to it as 'investment' and education minister after minister would preen themselves in front of the cameras as they announced how much more money was being spent and how much more our young people were achieving at school.

The truth, as the OECD report shows, is that standards of educational achievement have at best remained static in recent years. The additional spending has had little or no impact and, in particular, there has been no improvement in the educational success of children from disadvantaged backgrounds.

I do not blame teachers or parents. Few schools are going to complain about an examination system which shows them to be doing better and better every summer; few parents are going to stand up and denigrate the A grades their sons and daughters have just been awarded. It is the politicians and the education bureaucrats who have danced to the ministerial tune who are responsible.

Some Labour ministers probably did believe that all was well and getting better. They did not have the intelligence or educational understanding to see the truth. Others, however, like Blair and Andrew Adonis, must have known the sham they were promoting. They stood there and they told us that these apparent improvements in examination grades demonstrated the success of their policies. Behind the closed doors of Number 10, they must either have laughed at the nation's credulity or asked themselves how long they were going to get away with it.

For grade inflation in examinations, like any other kind of inflation, sooner or later rears up to bite the political hand that feeds it. In the end, the pretence has to be acknowledged. The complaints of university admissions tutors and employers have to be listened to. Somebody has to have the courage to stand up and say that the emperor has no clothes.

To his credit, Michael Gove has stated what the OECD report is now telling us. But this is the easy part politically. Indeed, he has to expose the failures and corruption of the previous regime in order to implement the reforms he wishes to implement. The hard challenge begins when the detailed reform of the examination system begins. Will this new administration have the courage to restore intellectual rigour to our dumbed down GCSEs and A levels?

If it does, then there will be fewer A grades. More students will fail. The performance of schools will appear to deteriorate. Labour politicians will dance joyously on the sidelines, shouting that this collapse in standards is evidence of the failure of the coalition's education policies.

It is going to take courage to remain resolute. Let us hope Michael Gove has that courage.

***

More evidence that the examining system needs reform

November 2012

Sometimes I wonder just a little about the intelligence of those responsible for managing the Government's business.

I am typing this having just listened to the news on the *Today* programme. The GCSE English debacle and the qualifications watchdog, Ofqual, have once again hit the headlines. Ofqual is now, apparently, arguing that many teachers deliberately overmarked coursework and that this is a major reason why the grades had to be made tougher in the summer examinations. The teacher unions are, predictably, outraged at this scandalous attempt to shift the blame. As, in fact, am I, because if this is the real reason the grade boundaries were shifted it means that the students of any teacher not guilty of this overmarking will have been unfairly penalised.

It was clear from the day this story broke that it would run and run. The sensible thing would have been to admit that something had gone wrong and that the playing field should not have been altered during the course of the year. The alleged injustice to candidates could have been corrected, as it has been in Wales, and the story would have died down. As it is, the unions, acting on behalf of schools desperate to maintain their position in the league tables, have now taken legal action and the sorry saga will wend its way through the courts with, no doubt, extensive and, for Ofqual and the Government, embarrassing media coverage.

Such a strategy could have been used by Michael Gove as further justification for his radical and speedy reform of a broken examination system which he had inherited from the previous government.

That reform goes ahead, but when the news headlines are not dominated by spats between Ofqual and the teacher unions, they are full of stories about how the great and the good in the world of education are uniting to condemn the Secretary of State for the reckless timetable he has set to introduce his new examinations. Last week, it was Mary Curnock Cook, the Chief Executive of the University and Colleges Admissions Service (UCAS), who popped up to tell the world that this timetable was 'highly risky'. She went on to ask whether people had forgotten that 'if you make A levels tougher, you will depress participation and you will depress achievement'.

Her audience at a conference on higher education no doubt clapped this extraordinary remark enthusiastically. The whole point of Gove's reforms is to stop the rot of inflated grades which have, over the years, allowed mediocrity to masquerade as excellence. What appears to matter to the Chief Executive of UCAS is the number of students applying to university, not the reality of their academic achievement.

Her statement exemplifies the huge resistance Gove faces in trying to develop an examination system that has real academic demand and which rewards genuine excellence. He cannot afford to become mired down in unwinnable news stories which deflect attention and sap political strength. If his reforms are meaningful, they will, inevitably, result in a significant reduction in A grades and pass rates. The opposition will, equally inevitably, seize upon this fact as evidence of his political failure. He needs the best possible political brains to cover his increasingly exposed back.

***

Warm words ignore the reality that new research is showing us

November 2012

'In this country, the quality of teaching has risen dramatically. It annoys me intensely that we don't give credibility for that, and one of the consequences of that is young people working harder, with support from their schools, parents and communities, to achieve as high as possible'. Thus spoke Sir Mike Tomlinson, ex Chief Inspector of Schools, last week at a conference of the Independent Academies Association, the intensity of his irritation rather obfuscating the clarity of his meaning.

I have in front of me new research from the educational software company, Renaissance Learning, which has found that GCSE students' reading age lags, on average, five years behind examination material.

The researchers assessed the reading ages of 24,795 children in GCSE years 10 and 11 across the UK. They also assessed the reading age of the exam materials. The latter was found to be 15 years and 7 months, the correct age for GCSE age pupils. The students' actual reading age was found to be, on average, just 10 years and 7 months.

When I was Chief Inspector, the Director of Education in Birmingham, Tim Brighouse, complained repeatedly that I was a 'glass half empty' man. I should, he told me, be celebrating the progress that was being made in order to talk up morale. That was fifteen years ago. My view, then and now, is that we are never going to solve the problem of underachievement in state schools unless everybody involved in state education faces up to the facts.

Yes, GCSE results have improved every year since GCSE was introduced in the late 1980s. Does this mean standards are now higher? How can they be higher, when the research published today indicates such huge problems in reading ability? How can they be higher when the business community makes it so clear that standards of numeracy and literacy are so unacceptably low that they find it difficult to recruit new employees? When admissions tutors in even the better universities tell us that students need support to cope with the demands of undergraduate study?

I recognise, of course, that there are times when a dire situation has to be talked up in order to win through. Equally, I am convinced that the current Secretary of State, Michael Gove, is absolutely right to speak out honestly about the crisis in our schools and the need for radical reform.

Tomlinson has no evidence at all to back up his assertion that the quality of teaching has risen dramatically. How on earth does he know that today's 15 and 16 year olds are working harder than I did in 1962 when I took my O levels?

It is easy to stand in front of an audience of headteachers and secure a round of rousing applause. The great and the good in the world of education do it all the time, their warm words contributing to the depth of the educational malaise. We should celebrate real achievement in individual schools, whilst recognising, as Michael Gove has recognised, that we have basked in the warm glow of worthless examination results for far too many years.

Look at what the critics of A level reform are saying

January 2013

There are two kinds of politician. The first enjoys the trappings of power too much ever to take controversial decisions and, hiding behind the old adage that politics is the art of the possible, does nothing. The second knows that their time in office is inevitably limited and, showing real courage, does everything in their power to remedy problems.

Michael Gove, who is showing himself to be a genuine reformer, is the one minister in this coalition Government who sits firmly in the latter category. His initiatives have always provoked hostility from many in education. The changes to A levels he proposed last week have earned him pretty well universal condemnation. So be it. He is right to ignore the squeals of pain and indignation and to push through the examination he wants with all possible speed.

Here is a sample of what the critics have been saying. Brian Lightman, General Secretary of the Association of School and College Leaders, dismisses his proposed reforms as 'a classic case of fixing something that isn't broken'. Chris Keates, of the NASUWT, reprimands the Secretary of State for 'recycling the incoherent grumblings of a few isolated and unrepresentative academics' and suggests that he should 'take note of the fact that there has been no clamour for reform'. Pam Tatlow, who works for the Million+ university think tank, believes that 'these proposals risk creating a two-tier A level system'. Even HMC, the body which represents leading independent schools, has gone on record to condemn Mr Gove's plans as 'rushed and incoherent'.

A few isolated and unrepresentative academics? Hardly. I cannot think of one academic I know at Oxford or Cambridge who believes that the current A level examination is of any assistance in helping them to identify the most deserving candidates. How could it be, when a quarter or more of candidates now achieve an A grade? Neither, my friends tell me, does it constitute an adequate preparation for serious academic work. Students who have had to endure a curriculum which has been emptied of much intellectual challenge and who have cruised their way through an assessment procedure which tests them on bite sized chunks of knowledge are unlikely to begin undergraduate study with the experience and understanding they need.

It makes complete sense to do away with modularity. The first year sixth should be what it always was: a period in a young person's life when they can read and think freely rather than prepare for the next examination. A terminal examination requires students to reflect upon and make links between different aspects of the syllabus they have covered. This is what an A level examination should demand, not the ability to memorise a term's work and churn out a few well-rehearsed answers (with re-sits available if you cock it up).

Neither is there any reason not to applaud Gove's decision to de-couple the AS examination taken at the end of the first year sixth from the current A2 qualification. The University of Cambridge admissions department has complained bitterly that this change will undermine their efforts to widen access because, they allege, the results students achieve in the AS are the best predictor of success at degree level. Surely, GCSE results combined with A level predictions and school references give enough information, particularly if the final examination which students are now to sit is tough enough to ensure that far fewer candidates achieve top grades?

What really sticks in my throat is the cant. These people, or at least the organisations they represent, were delighted with Sir Mike Tomlinson's proposals in 2004 to replace A level with a baccalaureate type qualification. They loved the fact that his diploma was stuffed full of thinking skills and people skills and creativity skills and every other skill you could possibly want. They were beside themselves at the fact that the elitist A level examination was going to be replaced by a rag bag of quasi academic and half-baked vocational study. They could not wait to see the back of this hated dinosaur of a qualification.

Now, because Gove wants to make the A level more rigorous, more, in their language, 'elitist', the A level suddenly, miraculously, becomes the qualification that must be defended in its current dumbed down state against any reform which tries to make it, once again, fit for purpose.

Those who care about the future of our education system should back our courageous Secretary of State to the hilt. The establishment education lackeys should hang their heads in shame.

***

The art of the possible

February 2013 *[Abridged]*

Personally, I do not care what the examination students take at 16 is called. EBacc, GCSE, O level: does it really matter? I cannot get very excited about Michael Gove's supposed concessions to the hysteria of the arts world at the exclusion of arts subjects from his EBacc. I think that the decision not to proceed with an arrangement whereby each examination board took responsibility for one of the core subjects is a very good thing because I am convinced that the only way to ensure more rigorous examinations is through competition amongst the exam boards. The only thing that really concerns me is whether the Secretary of State is sticking firm to his determination to make these examinations more rigorous.

He has not given an inch on this fundamental point. The new qualification will have a terminal examination. Modularity will be a thing of the past. We are no longer going to have questions which guide the candidate by the nose to a half satisfactory answer. The content of syllabuses will be intellectually more demanding. Coursework will be abolished. All this is good and remains very much on Gove's agenda.

The press coverage of his Commons statement gave a frightening example of what Michael Gove is up against. The headline in virtually every paper focused on his 'humiliating' climbdown; the leader columns sometimes praised him for his willingness to confess to his mistakes, but they have also emphasised the fact that he should proceed more carefully and listen more sensitively to those who really understand education, like the general secretaries of the teacher unions.

What explains this predominantly negative reaction? The answer is that Gove is challenging two of the fundamental tenets of the left-leaning educational orthodoxies which have dominated policy making and classroom practice for so long. In his examination and curriculum reforms, he is stressing the intrinsic importance of teaching children the knowledge they need if they are ever to understand the world in which they live. His predecessors have taken a utilitarian approach which elevates relevance, practicality and skills over this traditional liberal view. And, second, he has a tough-minded recognition that the most able must be challenged. He is not prepared to preside over an examination system or a National Curriculum which his sentimental predecessors have dumbed down to the lowest common denominator so that every student can win the prize they supposedly deserve.

But I have put this last point too strongly. I have no idea what Gove really believes, but, like everybody else, I have watched him twist and turn in the political wind since the story broke last year that he wanted to restore O levels for the more able and introduce a successor to the old CSE for those who were not academically able. Nick Clegg erupted in fury at the possibility of turning the clock back in this distinctly 'unprogressive' way. So, too, did all the egalitarian great and good of the teaching profession. So the idea of O level was dropped and now we seem to have returned to the belief that somehow or other the GCSE can test the most able whilst simultaneously offering the least able some chance of demonstrating that they know something.

It cannot be done. This is obvious to anybody who looks objectively at the evidence of what has happened to examinations since the GCSE was introduced in the late 80s. If Gove really believes that it is possible, then he is a fool. I do not think that he is a fool, and I believe, therefore, that he is attempting the impossible because of the political necessity. I sympathise, but, whilst I applaud his continued attempts to rescue the 16+ examination from the swamp into which it has sunk, I fear that this whole initiative could well end in tears.

***

Public sector accountability never has real teeth

March 2013

Andrew Hall is the Chief Executive of AQA, one of the three examination boards responsible for GCSE examinations. Last week he appeared before the Education Select Committee. He said that he did not think that teachers were 'cheating' in the way they marked the 'controlled assessment modules' completed by their students, but he did think that 'their judgements were influenced by the pressures of the accountability system'. Reading press reports of his appearance, I wondered whether he had managed to keep a straight face when he uttered this statement.

When I was in the third form at school I was caned for cheating in a Latin test. I suppose I could have argued that I wasn't really cheating and that the school was at fault for putting me under such pressure that my judgement as to what was right and wrong was affected by the situation in which I found myself. Somehow, I don't think that my headmaster would have been persuaded. The Select Committee does not seem to have batted an eyelid. Mr Hall's comment, which was not so much economical with the truth as transparent in its disingenuousness, went unremarked by any of the MPs on the committee. But, then, the Education Select Committee never has been much good at asking the right question at the right time.

Teachers control 60 per cent of the marks in some GCSE examinations. Graham Stuart, the Chairman of the Committee, observed during the hearing that when the penny dropped that all they had to do was to find two more marks and a D grade would magically become a C it was not surprising that some papers may have been overmarked. Mr Hall agreed.

These 'controlled assessments', which were brought in to replace coursework, are clearly a nonsense and the Secretary of State is absolutely right to want to see the end of them. The only way in which we can guarantee a reliable examination system is to have the examinations set and marked externally. It has taken an awful long time for this particular penny to drop, but, thankfully, reform is coming.

The real question concerns the possibility of making public services accountable. In the aftermath of recent scandals in the NHS, the Government has announced a new inspection regime for all hospitals. There is much angst about the behaviour of some policemen. And we continue, of course, to beat our breasts about the performance of too many schools in the state education system.

When a new school inspection regime was introduced in the early 1990s and the decision was simultaneously taken to make test and examination results public on a school by school basis, I thought that the system would be improved. I could understand the shock and horror expressed by many within the profession. Teachers had never before had their successes and failures exposed to public scrutiny. But I believed that over time this public accountability would come to be accepted as both inevitable and right. It has not.

The teacher unions continue to whinge about the brutality and unfairness of school inspections and the fact, as they see it, that league tables do not tell the truth about school performance. This, I suppose, is what unions are paid to do. If it were only the unions, then maybe we would have seen progress with regard to the acceptability of accountability within education. But it is not. If anything, the pendulum of media and possibly public opinion has swung over the last decade away from the idea of shining the spotlight of accountability into the murky depths of underperforming schools. Teachers are seen as the victims of an unfair system. Andrew Hall's comment to the Education Committee is but the latest example of this trend.

I do not think that a new inspection service for hospitals will achieve very much. There will be much lamentation when the inspectorate publishes critical reports. The media will move on. There may be some minor improvements, but life will continue much as it did before. Just, in fact, as has been the case in schools.

On the one hand, the problem is that we live in a society which deep down wants to believe that all public servants are doing a good job; on the other, it is that public sector accountability never has real teeth.

Some individual teachers and headteachers have, of course, been sacked following poor inspections, but not, in the great scheme of things, that many. Taxpayers' money rolls inexorably into the state coffers, public services have to be delivered, the machine grinds on. In the private sector, a company which fails to satisfy its customers goes to the wall. It is not like that in the public sector. Market forces do not work and, until they do, the publication of examination results and inspection reports will never trigger radical reform.

***

Was I naive?

August 2013

Last week Ofqual, the body responsible for keeping an eye on examination standards, confirmed what everybody involved in education already knew: so as to achieve the best possible results, more and more schools are entering their students for GCSE examinations with two or more boards. Last year, 15 per cent of pupils taking mathematics were multiple entries. Almost a quarter of pupils taking mathematics this year were under 16. This may mean, of course, that their teachers judged them to be ready for the examination a year early, but, equally, and perhaps more likely, they were doing this because it gave the youngsters two bites at the cherry.

Christine Blower, leader of the National Union of Teachers, responded to the Ofqual news with this statement: 'When accusations fly that schools are somehow gaming the system, it is often the case that a blind eye is turned to the malign influence of Ofsted benchmarks and ever changing floor targets from government'.

For once, I think Ms Blower may have a point. A lot now rides on the examination results a school achieves and it is perhaps hardly surprising that schools will, therefore, do everything in their power to bolster their position in the league tables.

Ms Blower appears to believe that the problem is entirely systemic. She does not seem to think that teachers should do everything in their power to behave as professionals and that wasting public money on multiple examination entries and forcing students to sit two or more examinations in the same subject might well not be a very professional thing to do. I was involved in the introduction of the reforms to school inspection in the 1990s which saw reports published. I have long been an advocate for the publication of test and examination data. How can problems in schools ever be solved if those problems are not dragged into the open, however tough this may be for a school and its teachers? How can we talk about parental choice in any meaningful way if parents do not have basic information about the success of the school their child attends or might attend?

I hoped and expected a quarter of a century ago that the teaching profession would adjust to the spotlight of accountability and that the initial hysteria and resentment would subside. It has not happened. If anything, the resentment has intensified over the years.

So I have to ask myself two questions. One, was I naive? Two, is Christine Blower right in asserting that the influence of Ofsted and league tables is inevitably 'malign'?

Given the realities of human nature and the fact that we have 24,000 odd schools in this country, I think I was probably naive in believing that the profession as a whole would grow into an acceptance of accountability. Good teachers and good schools take examinations and inspections in their stride. They have the confidence to do what is best for their students in the knowledge that nothing of any real educational benefit is achieved by obsessing about league tables or gaming the system. The truth is, we still do not have enough such teachers and schools. We never will have if Ms Blower's words are heeded and the pressures of accountability lifted. However difficult the situation is at this point in time, there can be no turning back.

***

The changes need to be harder and faster

August 2013

As with the economy, so with education. The Government's attempts to reduce the level of public spending have had, given the magnitude of the problem we face, precious little impact. Michael Gove, rightly, wants to stop the rot of grade inflation in GCSEs, but the statistics published last week show that there is an awful long way still to go before we have any meaningful improvements.

The proportion of candidates achieving A* to C grades in at least five subjects has fallen from 69.4% last year to 68.1%. A reduction of just 1.3%. The number awarded an A* or an A grade fell from 22.4% to

21.3%. The proportion getting A* grades fell by 0.5%. There was a 0.5% decline in candidates achieving an A* to C grade in English and a 0.8% decline in mathematics. The tanker has perhaps begun to turn, but if this is the speed of progress it will take many years for credibility to be restored to GCSE examinations.

It is not, in fact, clear whether these changes are, in subjects other than science, down to any toughening of the examination. In science, there was a drop of 7.6% in A* to C grades following the introduction of revised examinations. This figure is significant. In other subjects, particularly mathematics, it may well be that the ridiculous practice of schools entering students early for the GCSE so that they have more than one bite at the cherry is the real reason why the examinations appear to be becoming more rigorous.

Given the political risks inevitably involved in examination reform, Gove is to be congratulated on the start he has made. Brian Lightman of the Association of School and College Leaders is, nonetheless, right to say that 'a constantly changing and turbulent (examination) environment' is not in anybody's interests. The Secretary of State must, however anguished the squeals of opposition from the educational establishment, press on harder and faster with the changes that have to be made. The medicine has to be taken and it needs to be swallowed in one gulp.

***

There is no hope of returning to the standards expected in the past

August 2014

'The results in English have brought to an end years of steady improvement'. Well, yes, that's true if you believe that twenty years of improving GCSE English statistics bear any resemblance to the ability of 16 year olds to express themselves in the English language.

One newspaper report last week carried comments from examiners confronted by 'stream of consciousness' answers that had no paragraphing, punctuation or grammar. The spelling was apparently pretty wonky, too, though the indecipherability of the handwriting made it difficult for these examiners to come to a clear view on this weakness.

How can anybody believe that there was 'steady improvement' in any meaningful sense, when year after year employers' organisations such as the CBI and the IoD complain that graduates, let alone 16 year olds, are incapable of writing a half decent job application?

We have the examination system we deserve. Students, understandably enough, want to be awarded the highest possible grades. Their parents want, equally understandably, to bathe in their success. The reputation of their teachers and the school they attend depends upon their academic achievements. Politicians like to be able to preen themselves on results day and welcome, therefore, every improvement in the examination statistics.

Nobody in my professional lifetime, until Michael Gove, has had the courage and the determination to attempt to puncture this collective delusion. Last Thursday, predictably enough, he was held personally responsible for every failure, pupils and schools alike, to achieve the results they wanted. Some bright wag posted his picture on the Internet encouraging viewers to give him an interactive slap. In a matter of hours, he had apparently been assaulted more than 38 million times.

In fact, this year's results are not very different from those in previous years. The overall pass rate actually improved slightly. There was a marginal drop in the percentage of candidates awarded A* grades, and there was no change to the percentage awarded an A grade. Even in English, the drop was only 1.9 per cent to 61.7 per cent.

We can ignore the fury of headteachers' unions, who, incensed by the way so many students have been turned into 'victims', are threatening an investigation into these unacceptably 'volatile' results. The truth is that the status quo has been more or less maintained.

The real question is why the impact has not been greater. Gove ended the early entry regime which allowed schools to game the system, using the best grade their students achieved after multiple bites at the cherry. He cut back on modularity and coursework. He set in train the introduction of more intellectually rigorous syllabuses. All this, and minimal impact. How can this be?

The answer is that, however determined a Secretary of State might be to make the examination system more rigorous, it is in the end the examination boards who determine the standards each year through the grade boundaries they set. A grade boundary is the minimum mark needed for a candidate to be awarded a particular grade, and the decision as to what this minimum mark should be is decided by the chief examiner in the light of how difficult the paper has proved to be. Crucially, the examination boards are expected to ensure that the standard of work required for a particular grade is maintained year on year.

There is no hope of a return to anything like the standards expected by the old O level examination until this changes. But in the foreseeable future it never will change. The spirit of the times is one in which examinations are meant to give everyone the opportunity to demonstrate what they know rather than a mechanism to identify what they do not know. Everyone, in Melanie Phillips' famous phrase, must have a prize.

We prefer to wallow in a soggy, feel good, egalitarian mess than to rediscover an education and examination system rooted in a spirit of genuine meritocracy.

***

Circles cannot be squared

May 2015

Just six school weeks before schools have to start teaching the new GCSE maths syllabuses, the exams regulator, Ofqual, has told the examination boards that they must reconsider the level of difficulty of the questions they are asking. A research exercise has, apparently, shown that three of the four main boards are asking questions which are too hard and one is asking questions which are too easy.

If I were in charge of a mathematics department, I would be pulling out what remains of my hair. Glenys Stacey, the chief executive of Ofqual, thinks that there isn't a problem. I doubt that there is a mathematics teacher in the country who agrees with her. I imagine that parents must be wondering why the DfE and Ofqual have failed so abysmally to introduce this new GCSE in a timely fashion so that schools are properly prepared to teach their students when the new school year starts in September.

But this latest debacle is not simply a matter of administrative incompetence. When Michael Gove first announced his intention to make the GCSE examination more rigorous so that it was a better preparation for the A level, there were newspaper reports that he wanted to return to the old system where there were O level examinations for the academically able and a different examination, the certificate in secondary education (CSE), for the less able.

It was said at the time that Nick Clegg thought this proposal elitist and anachronistic and stamped his deputy prime ministerial foot. Whatever the dynamics of this coalition spat, Gove backed down and those responsible for the implementation of the new examinations have had to struggle with the impossible task of creating a more intellectually demanding GCSE which both challenges the most able and gives the least able some opportunity to demonstrate what they know.

Circles cannot be squared. Nobody can devise an examination which caters for every level of ability. In offering a two tiered examination in mathematics (a more difficult exam for the more able and a 'foundation' level paper for the less able), the Government has in effect recognised this. Nonetheless, the problems remain.

Was the old O level/CSE really so anachronistic and elitist? In my view, it simply recognised the truth that our system of public examinations had to recognise the fact that there is a huge range of ability amongst secondary school students. I have never understood how the civil servants managed to persuade the highly intelligent Sir (later Lord) Keith Joseph, who was Secretary of State for Education at the time the GCSE was introduced, to accept their pie-eyed, egalitarian proposals.

What is clear is that the soothsayers at the DfE have spotted trouble down the line. If the exam boards had been allowed to set papers that were really challenging, Nicky Morgan, or whoever is Secretary of State for Education in two years time, would have to explain to the electorate why so many more children were failing to achieve a good grade in this key subject.

On the one hand, our soggy egalitarian ideals; on the other, the political realities when it comes to examination results. What a mess it all is.

English teaching and the importance of literature

From his weekly blogs for *The Sunday Times*

Why literature is important

March 2011

I have no recollection of being taught to read. I can't recall my parents reading stories to me, though I am sure they did, and I have no memory of sitting in a primary school classroom learning, parrot fashion, the letters of the alphabet, though I am sure I did.

Somehow, sometime, the miracle just seems to have happened. The impenetrable hieroglyphics on the page in front of me suddenly began to make sense and a new, alternative universe began to open up.

What I can remember is walking up Old Farleigh Road most Saturday afternoons with my parents. It was a family ritual, the weekly visit to Selsdon library, and I can still see myself trudging along, holding my father's hand, eager to get home to start thumbing the pages of the new acquisition.

It was in my mid teens that I started to haunt second hand bookshops. There used to be a number of junk shops on the Brighton Road between Croydon and Purley with a couple of rooms full of books. I have still got some of the prizes I picked up in these shops, inscribed in my adolescent hand with my name and the date of purchase. I still have a Nonesuch edition of Blake's *Collected Poems*, bought while on holiday with my parents from a bookshop in Rye in the early 60s. It cost 18 shillings and sixpence, which was a fortune. It was and is one of my most prized possessions.

A little later, I discovered the joys of Cecil Court and the Charing Cross Road. What was it about these second hand bookshops? I say 'was it' because the second hand bookshop has, of course, disappeared from most high streets. Buying what you want off the Internet is convenient, but we have lost so much. The dusty smell, the excitement of scanning the next shelf, the peace and the quiet: many of my happiest hours have been spent rooting around looking for nothing in particular, but, more often than not, leaving the junk shop or bookshop with a new volume and a new author to read and explore.

In fits and starts, the alternative universe opened up. I moved from Biggles to Baudelaire, via, one Damascene day in the summer holidays before I started the sixth form at Wallington Grammar School, Emily Bronte's *Wuthering Heights*. For some reason, I had convinced myself that the latter was going to be a boring novel to read. I set out on what was going to be a day's cycle ride. By the time I had got to Sevenoaks, I was drenched. I stood in a church porch somewhere on the Sevenoaks Weald and said to myself that there was no alternative to peddling home and starting the wretched book.

Two pages in, I was, of course, captivated. Literature doesn't make you a better person, but it does tell you what it is to be a human being. Wallington was an all boys school and my experience of the opposite sex was limited to the nervous and frustrated perusal of inaccessible beauty at the occasional dance I forced myself to attend. Here, in *Wuthering Heights*, was a world of volcanic passion in which human beings were caught in the inescapable hand of fate. I had no idea whether it was true or not. I still don't, actually, but, having read and re-read Iris Murdoch over the years, I suspect it is. What I did come to see that wet summer afternoon was that books furnished not just a room, but a life.

Without literature my life would have been very different. It would have been bleakly impoverished. I was lucky. I had the parents who took me to the local library. I had teachers who introduced me to the great books. I had second hand bookshops in which I could spend my hard earned pocket money.

Today, the libraries are closing and the school literature syllabuses amount to little more than a collection of excerpts from fiction deemed 'relevant' to stunted adolescent minds. The second hand bookshops have all shut. We seem as a nation to think that if we invest billions in laptops for every child all is going to be well. It isn't. The child who leaves school unaware of what books can offer is a child we have failed.

***

Lifelong learning can happen, but not because of education policy

September 2011

I used to laugh at David Blunkett's obsession with Lifelong Learning. Children were leaving primary school illiterate and innumerate. Tens of thousands of 16 year olds were departing into a world of adult unemployment with few, if any, qualifications to show for their eleven years of compulsory schooling. Blunkett sat in his Whitehall ivory tower extolling the virtues of a lifetime dedicated to the pursuit of new knowledge and skills. Departments of Lifelong Learning sprang up in universities and local authorities. Billions of pounds of public money were wasted in the pursuit of yet another utopian fantasy.

And yet, learning should go on through one's lifetime, and if it does not there is not much point in being alive. A year or two ago, the poet Geoffrey Hill asked me what I thought about the New Zealand poet, James Baxter. I had never heard of Baxter, let alone read any poem he had written. He is now, thanks to Hill's casual mention, one of my favourite poets.

'It's a long time now/since the great ikons fell down,/God, Mary, home, sex, poetry,/whatever one uses as a bridge/to cross the river that only has one beach'. Those lines are from his poem, *The Ikons*. It was a dozen or so years ago, when I was Chief Inspector, that my 'ikons' started to fall down. My belief in the power of political action to transform the world, my deep-rooted sense that progress was possible, that education was a means of liberating the young from the intellectual and social confines of their childhood. It was not a dramatic, immediate collapse. More a gradual thing, a dawning realisation that David Blunkett's hope that Lifelong Learning would create a better Britain was just one more threadbare example of the gap between human hope and the intransigent reality of the world in which one lives.

So, what does one do? Baxter went looking for mushrooms. 'I go on looking', he writes in the last three lines of his poem, 'for mushrooms in the field, and the fist of longing/punches my heart, until it is too dark to see'.

Forty years ago, an enthusiastic, young English teacher, if I had come across that poem and had been moved by it as I am now, I would have wanted to teach it to my students. The idea that literature can be taught and lives enriched is an 'ikon' that has carried me through my professional life. Now I wonder. A love of literature, like a commitment to lifelong learning, is something I suspect that comes from within, and which cannot be cultivated by a government, however millennial it might be in its aspiration and profligate in its spending.

***

The demise of bookshops

December 2012 *[Abridged]*

I want it to be known that I am not a complete Luddite. We might live half way up a mountain, buried in mud. The water supply comes from a stream, but we do have electricity most of the time and, when I am not listening to the wireless, I spend a good part of the day sitting in front of the computer screen. Indeed, I am feeling very anxious today because if the world ends tomorrow I will be denied the last episode of *Homeland*, which would be a personal tragedy of some magnitude.

Across the room from where I am sitting there is a bookshelf full of Penguin classics and modern classics. I bought most of them in the early sixties when I was a sixth former. To tell you the truth, there are some books on the shelves which, fifty years on, I still haven't read. But there are others, like *War and Peace* and John Cowper Powys's neglected masterpiece, *Wolf Solent*, which I have read and re-read.

Last week, the National Literacy Trust published a report saying that a third of dads never picked up a book. The Selsdon library I visited has been demolished. The junk shops with their back rooms piled high with mouldy treasures have no doubt long disappeared from the Brighton Road in south Croydon. The wonderful bookshop at the top of the high street in Guildford shut its doors years ago. Tunbridge Wells still has a marvellous second hand bookshop on the corner in the Pantiles, but every time I re-visit I wonder if it will still be there.

To state the obvious, it is a different world, isn't it? Once there were books and wirelesses. Then everybody plonked themselves down in front of the television. Now we peer in solitary isolation at our computer screens and iPads and seek instant and constant excitement from the latest interactive game.

As I say, I am not a complete Luddite. I have watched every episode of *The Killing* on iPlayer and, like everyone else, I have been totally gripped (though, I have to say I thought the ending was out of character and pathetic). A good number of recent television dramas have had plots which draw you to the front of your seat, and a few have had characters whose emotions and motivation have some intrigue. But, compared to *Wolf Solent*, the gratification is instant and the intellectual and emotional effort needed minimal. Many of us, it seems, are no longer prepared to make the effort.

***

Great literature does not have populist appeal ....

November 2013

Everyone these days seems to have jumped onto the bandwagon. Phone as many friends as you can, persuade them to sign a letter attacking Michael Gove, send it to a national newspaper and bathe in the publicity it generates.

First, there was the criticism of his proposals for a new National Curriculum for history as reactionary, jingoistic and unteachable. Then there were the experts in early childhood education, who alleged that he was destroying childhood and would cause untold emotional and psychological problems. Most recently, his decision to consult on a new GCSE syllabus for English which would introduce an optional literature examination and focus the main English paper on the ability to spell, punctuate and write grammatically sparked a furious response from two hundred writers and academics. There may well have been other examples of this anti-Gove hate mail. It is hard to keep up.

I very much doubt if many of those criticising the idea that not everybody should study English literature have tried to teach a

Shakespeare play to a class of 16 year olds who can barely read and write. I have. 'Reluctant readers', they were called in my day, and I can well remember my highly unprofessional relief when, ten minutes into the lesson, I realised that the least motivated of them had decided to bunk off. The theory was that you would hook a reluctant reader on a short novel written in simple sentences and rooted in their immediate adolescent experience. These books were called 'Topliners'. Entranced by the magic of narrative, the reluctant reader would progress inexorably, it was argued, from the Topliner to Tolstoy.

I am sad to say that, in my experience at least, it rarely happened. I simply do not believe that great literature is for everybody. Why should it be?

'Simple fictions are the opium of the people', as the literary critic, Frank Kermode, once observed. A romance ensues and the vicissitudes of fate drive them apart. All is resolved in the final pages. They meet unexpectedly and scoot off into the sunset to live happily ever after.

Life is not like this, and neither is great literature. Great literature forces its readers to question their beliefs and prejudices and to scrutinise their expectations. It can lift the soul, but it can shock and depress. It strips away the veil of pretence and not everybody wants to stand shivering and naked.

Rose Hilton, widow of the painter Roger Hilton, mentions in an introduction to *Night Letters*, the wonderful collection of his thoughts on art, his instructions to Rose as to what she should buy to tickle his palate and his marvellously quirky drawings, that in the last months of his life, as he lay bedridden and insomniac in his cottage on the north coast of Cornwall near Land's End, he became obsessed with *King Lear*.

I have been in hospital this last week and I, too, have been thinking a lot about *Lear*. Lines like: 'Men must endure/Their going hence, even as their coming hither:/Ripeness is all'; 'Unaccommodated man is no more but such a poor,/Bare, forked animal as thou art'; 'As flies to wanton boys are we to the gods,/They kill us for their sport'. Nothing in *Lear* consoles. A man struggles to live with his past and flails towards his future. I woke last night thinking that the impact is a bit like the experience of lying in an MRI scanner.

The play explains nothing and allows, unless you believe that Lear dies thinking Cordelia is still alive, no hope.

Great literature does not have populist appeal. Those who want to explore its mysteries should, of course, have the opportunity to do so. Under Gove's proposals, they will.

***

… but we should not underestimate its power to enrich our lives

March 2014

There are many marvellous things in George Eliot's novel, *Middlemarch*, but one of the most marvellous of all is this poignant aside: 'If we had a keen vision and feeling of all ordinary human life, it would be like hearing the grass grow and the squirrel's heart beat and we should die of that roar which lies on the other side of silence. As it is, the quickest of us walk about well wadded with stupidity'.

For Eliot, it is a fact of human life: 'the coarse emotion of mankind' protects us from an excess of sensitivity which would render our existence intolerable.

I sometimes wonder what this great Victorian novelist would make of the utopianism which drives so much current thinking about education. It is assumed that schools can deliver 'well-being' and a happy adult life. We believe that we can teach our children to be more sensitive, more empathetic, more emotionally intelligent.

Some virtues can be taught. A school which insists upon punctuality and politeness, for example, can probably have an impact on the majority at least of its pupils. But fundamental aspects of personality are a different matter and there is something comically naive in the determination of so many educationalists and politicians to believe that what happens in the classrooms and playing fields of schools can rid us of our self-protective stupidity.

Great literature like *Middlemarch* cannot make anyone a better person. When I taught English I used to think that it could and, indeed, that the whole point of English as a subject was somehow to quicken emotional intelligence and deepen moral sensitivity. I have come to realise that, sadly, it isn't so. The intellectual and emotional perception which can be prompted by reading does not necessarily translate into everyday action. What, in my experience at least, does happen is that one's understanding of the frailty of the human agent, the power of coincidence and fate and the imperfectability of man generally is deepened.

It would be good if those who believe that schools can achieve the impossible and who take such delight in sneering at Michael Gove's efforts to restore academic integrity to the curriculum understood what the pages of *Middlemarch* demonstrate so clearly.

We can and we should teach our children to read and to add up. We should do everything in our power to enrich their lives by developing their understanding of history and geography, literature and art, music and mathematics. To denigrate these immensely important and achievable goals because they do not live up to quasi therapeutic, utopian aspirations is simply to ensure that generations of children continue to languish in a state of ignorance.

***

Talking through concepts is the way to develop eloquent speaking

April 2014

Why do teenagers grunt?

Peter Hyman, who was once one of Blair's speechwriters and who now runs a free school in East London, thinks that it is because schools place too much emphasis on reading and writing and pay too little attention to teaching children 'to speak eloquently'.

Reflecting on my own adolescence, and my experience as a teacher and a parent, I have to say that I disagree. Teenagers grunt because they can't be bothered to reply, they are tongue-tied and embarrassed, they are pig ignorant but convinced of their own unassailable superiority, they are sullen, recalcitrant, half asleep, or didn't hear the question because of the volume of the music playing through their headphones. Perm any combination of the above and you have an explanation for their tedious indifference to the norms of ordinary human conversation.

For Hyman: 'Speaking eloquently is a moral issue, because to find your own voice, both literally and metaphorically and be able to communicate your ideas and your passions is crucial to how (young people) are going to be a success in the world. If you can speak and articulate yourself properly, that will happen'.

It is obviously true that the ability to explain yourself and engage with other people's ideas is important. Teachers have known this for as long as I have been involved in education. I remember attending courses as a young teacher on what was in those days called 'oracy'. Nobody then used Hyman's odd phrase of us needing to 'articulate ourselves', but the idea was the same. He gives it a new spin by proclaiming that he has discovered a 'moral issue', but contemporary educationalists love to pontificate on the deep morality of every aspect of their pedagogic task. This is about it. Nothing else he says is new.

He is confused, too. Does 'speaking eloquently' equate to being able to function effectively in the world of work? No, of course it does not. The truth is that not many of us are or can be eloquent, though a lot of us, if we tried harder and thought more clearly, could engage others more effectively. Is the ability to communicate predominantly a matter of being able to explain 'your ideas and your passions', as he thinks? Again, this exemplifies a current and very damaging obsession within the world of education. What matters in today's classrooms is the expression of opinion, however half-baked that opinion might be. What employers in fact want is young people who can listen and respond and forget for a moment their own gobby self-importance.

Hyman criticises the examinations watchdog, Ofqual, because it has removed the speaking and listening element from GCSE English. It did this because it was virtually impossible to guarantee the reliability of these assessments, and it does not matter a jot. Good schools will continue to offer their students practical experience of interviews and the different demands of the world of work.

More fundamentally, they will ensure that there are opportunities across the curriculum for children to discuss ideas. Talking through concepts is one of the ways in which human beings master new learning. It is not that, as Hyman would have us believe, 'the silent classroom .... is the death of learning', for there are often very good reasons to demand the silence upon which true concentration depends. But he is right to say that 'high quality talk.... ...should be built into the DNA of the school'. That is exactly what I was taught when I did my Post Graduate Certificate of Education in 1968.

***

Literature is more than a text on which to hone skills and explore emotions

October 2014

Why do we read stories and poems to children? Why do we teach them history and geography, or, for that matter, any of the other subjects that fill the school timetable?

I was interested to read some comments last week by the children's author, Frank Cottrell Boyce, who is to give the annual David Fickling Lecture in Oxford. Reflecting on his experiences visiting schools to read his stories to children, he has come to the conclusion that the way we teach literature in schools makes any engagement with and enjoyment of literature impossible.

He quotes the teacher who popped up immediately after he had finished reading a story to say to the class: 'We're going to use our listening skills to spot his wow words and his connectives so that we can appreciate how he builds the story'.

This, I am afraid, is typical. It was typical forty years ago when I wrote an article for the *Times Educational Supplement* complaining about the way English teachers either turned a poem into a crossword puzzle with questions about the meaning of difficult words and interesting images or used it as a kind of therapeutic stimulus to encourage their students to explore their own emotions. Would that things had changed. If anything, the situation has become worse.

It is not only English. History teachers are more interested in the empathetic engagement of their pupils than they are in involving them in the complexities and excitement of the historical event. History is a resource to be plundered for its relevance to our 21st century world, not for its intrinsic intellectual interest. Science is more often than not taught thematically, the individual scientific fact subsumed into the topic of the day, be it climate change or the evils of the motor car or whatever. And our obsession with the teaching of skills such as 'critical thinking' and 'learnacy' (the ability of the child to find out things for themselves) grinds any concern for the knowledge different subjects embody into the pedagogic dust.

Boyce is right. When you encounter a new piece of literature you need time to sit still and think. You do not want somebody asking you a load of trivial and irrelevant questions designed to hone your listening skills. It is the same with every other subject. Teachers have a responsibility to engage and inspire, but they need to rediscover the virtues of patience and silence. They should stop using the subject disciplines which ought to be at the heart of the educational enterprise as a vehicle for the teaching of skills, a medium for the discussion of current social and political preoccupations, and a quasi therapeutic tool for the exploration of feelings.

Universities

Chris Woodhead was convinced that the only sound way to ensure that more disadvantaged pupils win places at top universities is to improve teaching so that their achievements do justice to their potential at primary and secondary school. Schemes to lower entrance requirements would in the long run only destroy the academic status of the universities. Here he summarised his remarks to the Oxford Union on intentions announced by the Labour Government in 2004.

First published in *The Sunday Times,* June 2004

The conundrum is this. In 1997 the Prime Minister informed us that his priority was education. Since then he has promised to deliver a 'world-class education system'.

Having failed to achieve, despite the investment of billions of pounds of taxpayers' money, much in the way of improvement to schools, he has now turned his attention to higher education.

His ambition? To dumb down, it seems, the genuinely world-class universities that have survived, miraculously, into the 21st century. Is he stupid, mad, or simply, poor man, misguided? We can quibble about the precise ranking, but Oxford is one of the top five universities in the world. In 2010, its academic heart impaled on Blair's egalitarian stake, it will be lucky to be in the top 30.

Oxford must, the Government says, become more 'socially diverse'. It must admit more students from bog-standard comprehensive schools, and, though the corollary is never, in public at least, spelt out, fewer public school toffs who slide from one quad to another on wheels greased by the depths of their daddies' pockets.

Last week, I visited a bog-standard public school. Not high in the league tables, not famed for Rolls-Royces littering the drive. Many of its parents scrimp and save to buy their children an education they wish the state provided.

The talk in the staff room was of Oxbridge candidates who a few years ago would have been certain to succeed. Outstanding students with a string of predicted As and a wide range of other achievements. Everything an admissions tutor could desire. Not, apparently, this year. Rejection letters were arriving with depressing regularity.

This, I suppose, is what the Prime Minister wants. This is equality of opportunity in action. The public school candidates have benefited from expert teaching; their state school peers have suffered years of miseducation. Our top universities have finally understood that they must take the background of the candidate into consideration and give the benefit of the doubt to the student who comes from the wrong side of the tracks.

'We are wasting,' Blair said in the run up to the last election, 'too much of the talents of too many of the people. The mission of any second term must be to break down the barriers that hold people back, to create a society that is based on merit and the equal worth of all.'

It was a vision to warm the socially inclusive cockles of any floating voter's heart. Now, as another election draws near, we know the truth. The barriers have not been broken down. All that has happened is that the Government has threatened universities with dire penalties if they don't contribute to this new meritocratic society.

And, sadly, shamefully, many top universities, to an extent perhaps even Oxford, have capitulated, salivating gratefully at the prospect of the pathetically inadequate £3,000 top up fee.

The admissions statistics at Oxford are interesting. For several years the number of entrants from state schools was fairly steady, at between 46% and 48%. In 2000, at around the time the Government started banging the admissions drum, a noticeable increase began, leading to 54.3% state school entrants in 2002. The official explanation for this is that more state school pupils have been encouraged to apply and therefore more are successful. Last year, however, saw a drop to 51.7%, despite the fact applications remained high.

The public explanation is that there was a surge in applications from independent school students and, though this sits uneasily with rises in earlier years, because state school pupils are less likely to get the A-level grades needed.

As to the future, who knows? The percentage of state school students may rise still further because more who deserve a place apply, which is, of course, fine. The tragedy is that the Government's posturing has created a climate of doubt that is good for neither students nor the university.

Those on the left, who like to occupy the moral high ground, will dismiss what I have said thus far as a shameful defence of privilege. Not so. I spent 30 years trying to improve state education. My main motivation as Chief Inspector of Schools was the plight of the bright child from a disadvantaged background who could, if they had access to a decent school, have made it to Oxford or Cambridge.

But the answer is, or ought to be, obvious. It is not to fiddle with university admissions criteria, but to challenge the child-centred ideologies which result in thousands of children leaving primary school illiterate, to raise expectations in inner-city schools, to ensure that the child from the council estate has the same educational opportunity as his peer from the suburbs.

Why not? It can be done, and in a minority of schools it is already happening. Yes, of course, it is a slow process. But think for a moment about the reality of the quick fix Blair is proposing. It is not the unfairness on the candidate from the public school, bad though this is, that really angers me. It is the stupidity of the politician who cannot see that social engineering will destroy the excellence of universities that are pusillanimous enough to conform, and, ironically, render the prize that is being offered to the student from the disadvantaged home worthless.

The government wants 50% of 18 to 30-year-olds to get a degree. We do not as a nation need 50% of the population qualified to degree status. Many graduates are, of course, finding it difficult to obtain a job that makes real use of the knowledge and skills they have mastered. The reality is that thousands of youngsters would be better off studying for vocational qualifications or undertaking apprenticeships that lead to a worthwhile job and a lucrative income.

And why should a university be socially diverse? If the best-qualified candidates are white, male and from public schools, then they should be given places. So, too, if they are black, female and from a comprehensive. We cannot afford to move away from an exclusive focus on academic achievement and potential. If we do, Oxford as an elite university is finished.

Social diversity is a desirable characteristic. As a goal, it is fatal. Oxford must remain a university where the brightest young people know that they will spend three years mixing with their equally bright peers. Start to water the entrance criteria down and the whole point of Oxford will be lost.

What, moreover, is the justification for a policy of positive discrimination which leaves those admitted on less stringent criteria truculently defensive? You only have to read Allan Bloom's *The Closing of the American Mind* to see that similar initiatives in the States have proved disastrous. Nothing, in Bloom's view, has damaged race relations more. The prize, if it is a dumbed down version of what it once was, is not worth having.

It is vitally important for Oxford to reach out to comprehensive schools that might never have encouraged their students to apply for a place. Undergraduates should visit state schools to explain what the experience of studying there could mean to pupils. Those same pupils should be invited to summer schools to see for themselves. In interviewing such candidates dons should, of course, exercise discretion. Most always have.

To return to my opening conundrum, Blair must know this. He is neither mad nor, given his profession, particularly stupid. He is, however, misguided. If he thinks a little anti-elitist rhetoric will pacify the class warriors massing on his back benches, he is wrong. They want action and he is merely raising their expectations.

If he hopes that his policies will play well with the electorate, then he misjudges the growing anger of middle-class parents who know that the real problem is the failure of state education. If he really believes that Oxford will be a better place when the children of the rich few have been kicked out to admit those of the socially deserving many, well, I take back what I have just said. He must be mad.

***

From his weekly blogs for *The Sunday Times*

We do fail bright children from poor homes, but the place to address that is schools, not universities

November 2010 *[Abridged]*

When the New Zealand Prime Minister, Helen Clark, came to England a few years ago she remarked that there were two kinds of politician: those that sought power because they wanted to change things and those that wanted to glue their backsides to the plushest ministerial seat possible. She is right.

We are all too quick to take refuge in the cliché that politics is the art of the possible. It is, of course, but there is a world of difference between the principled judgment about what can be done which is driven by a desire to improve upon the current situation and the shoddy compromise which amounts to little more than the need to cobble some solution together in the interests of political expediency.

I do not see how any Liberal Democrat politician can live with their conscience. Yes, of course, Vince Cable was right when he muttered rather shamefacedly that the decision to join a coalition Government meant that previous policy commitments might have to be jettisoned. But the Lib Dem pledge to abolish tuition fees was central to their whole election campaign. It is, or was, totemic: an icon of political faith. Now it is gone, sacrificed on the altar of coalition politics. Is anybody surprised that the popularity of the Liberal Democratic Party has collapsed so catastrophically? We want politicians who believe in something and come the next election will without doubt punish those who have abandoned everything in the pursuit of power.

Michael Gove, rightly, has emphasised how much he wants to liberate schools from bureaucratic state control. His most imaginative and radical policy is the 'Free Schools' initiative. When it comes to universities the commitment to institutional freedom evaporates. Yes, the cap on tuition fees will be lifted for some institutions to £9,000. But only if these institutions commit themselves to access policies agreed with the Office for Fair Access (OFFA). In part this is, of course, a Conservative sop to the Liberal Democrats. But I suspect that Cameron himself approves. Either because he believes that politics is the art of the possible or because in the misguided, illogical depths of his compassionate Conservatism, he thinks that forcing universities to admit more students from disadvantaged homes and failing state schools is going to make England a better place.

It will not, of course. Top universities admit more students from independent and grammar schools than they do students from failing comprehensive schools because these students have demonstrated their academic ability and potential. I have written for years about how as a nation we continue to fail bright children from poor homes. This was my greatest concern when I was Chief Inspector. But the solution to the problem lies in our schools, not in our universities. To force top universities to lower their academic expectations in the interests of social engineering will result in nothing other than damage to the academic achievements of these universities.

This, however, is what our coalition Government has set out to do. Intellectually, Cameron and Clegg must see the absurdity; politically they no doubt lean back in their comfortable Ministerial chairs and sigh to themselves that politics is, after all, the art of the possible.

***

Buckingham is a success story for the private sector in higher education

June 2011

The conventional wisdom is that only the Republicans could have done a deal with the communists. It would have been politically impossible for a Democrat administration to have flirted so dangerously with the devil. In the euphoric months following his 1997 election victory, Tony Blair's Labour Government could certainly have dented the state monopoly in the provision of public services. As we all know, he did nothing and, for the remainder of his premiership he did nothing, although he talked a lot about what he was going to do.

David Cameron would find it hard, even if he were not saddled with his Lib Dem partners. The public sector unions are implacably hostile to both a Conservative government and to any talk of privatisation of public services. Cameron has, however, a very real problem. Anyone who thinks for half a minute about the flagship free schools policy and reflects upon the experience in Sweden, where the success of the initiative quite clearly depended upon the involvement of the private sector, can see that if the Government is not going to allow for profit companies to run free schools the initiative is never going to gather sufficient momentum to challenge the status quo.

I cannot really think that Michael Gove believes what he is saying, but he is saying it. We don't need a for profit culture, he announced recently, in the state sector. His colleague, David Willets, the Minister responsible for universities, appears, however, to recognise that we do and has been talking to private companies which run universities in the States.

Inevitably, he has been castigated for his efforts. Labour's Higher Education spokesman immediately clambered up onto his soap box to declaim that: 'the potential damage to our higher education system is too dangerous to risk allowing the profiteers in'. Sally Hunt, leader of the UCU lecturers' union, is banging the same drum. She thinks that private providers of higher education are not accountable to the public and do not deserve to be classed as universities.

I started the education department at Britain's first private university, Buckingham, and should, therefore, declare an interest. But, I have to say that comments such as these make me wonder how it is that anyone can talk such nonsense, and, more to the point, have anyone believe them. Buckingham has consistently topped the league tables for student satisfaction. It would not have survived in a highly competitive market place if it had not delivered what its fee paying customers wanted. So, too, with my own department. We began in 2003 with 13 students. This year we are likely to have 200. Do these union spokespersons and Labour MPs really think that so many people are so stupid that they pay money in ever increasing numbers to be ripped off?

***

Don't let the facts get in the way of the message

August 2012

I have to confess that until last week I had never heard of the Independent Commission on Fees, a supposedly independent body funded by Sir Peter Lampl's Sutton Trust and chaired by Will Hutton, Principal of Hertford College, Oxford, and Chair of the Big Innovation Centre (another body about which I am blissfully ignorant).

Checking out the Independent Commission's website, I came across this disarmingly humble statement from Mr Hutton: 'It is incredibly important that we provide an independent check on the biggest reforms for higher education in a generation'.

Is it really so important? The information communicated in the Commission's first report (that there has been an 8.8% reduction in applications to university this year compared to last) is already available in the public domain. Neither does the Commission appear to be that independent. Sir Peter, writing in *The Times*, tells us that 'the decision to allow English universities to treble tuition fees to £9,000' constitutes 'an even more ominous barrier to opportunity' than the obstacles allegedly encountered by would be Olympic athletes from poor homes. In other words, the agenda is clear and the fact that the data tells us that there has been no disproportionate drop in applications from students from disadvantaged backgrounds is not going to get in the way of the Sutton Trust's message.

The Commission, like the Government and, of course, the higher education sector as a whole, takes it for granted that a fall in the number of students applying to university is a bad thing.

It is not. I believe people are finally coming to their senses. We know that in some institutions more than 30% of undergraduates drop out before they complete their course. We know that unemployment rates for recently qualified graduates (roughly 25%) are higher than unemployment rates for young people who leave school with A levels at 18. We know that many graduates find it desperately difficult to find graduate status work which might justify the debts they have accumulated.

We also know that more and more employers are seeking to recruit students at 18 in order to train them on the job. It is disingenuous in the extreme to ignore the growing popularity of apprenticeships in order to bang the drum for the importance of university study. The truth is that many young people who, stuck on the conveyor belt of conventional educational expectation, end up doing degrees which have no intellectual integrity or real vocational relevance, would be better off leaving school at 18 to find a job with apprenticeship type training.

I can understand why spokesmen for higher education do not want to face up to the fact that the introduction of higher tuition fees has encouraged potential applicants to ask themselves whether they really do need a degree. I can understand why politicians, keen to convince the electorate that they are encouraging social mobility, continue to argue that a university education is essential to any kind of fulfilled life.

An independent commission is, or ought to be, different. It needs to be both independent and original in its thinking. This commission appears to be neither.

***

We have encouraged too many sixth formers to think that university is their only option

August 2013

Are market forces starting to correct twenty-five years of political folly?

We learnt last week that up to 35 school leavers are competing for every job vacancy. An apprenticeship post typically receives eleven or more applications. We already knew that for the first time ever many top universities have used Clearing this year to fill empty places.

The competition for jobs amongst school leavers in part, of course, reflects the continuing woes of the economy. But the increased interest in apprenticeships also suggests that increasing numbers of school leavers are questioning the value of a university degree.

For years now politicians have been telling us that it is imperative, for reasons of social equality and economic competitiveness, that more and more young people study for a degree. When Tony Blair made his famous statement in the late 1990s that he wanted 50 per cent plus of 18 to 30 year olds to gain a degree, he and his ministers deployed two arguments. The first was that access to university had to be widened because too few students from disadvantaged homes were applying to university; the second was that technological advances demanded a workforce that had high level educational qualifications.

I have always argued that as a nation we need to do far more to ensure that no student who has the intellectual capacity to benefit from a university course should be denied that opportunity because of their family background or the poverty of their educational experience. This is not to say that access per se should be widened. The truth is that we have encouraged too many sixth formers to think that university is their only option. The result is that drop out rates at some universities now top 40 per cent and when it comes to getting a job unacceptable numbers of graduates find it impossible to secure employment which utilises the knowledge and skills they have developed over the three years of their university course. They are saddled, moreover, with a debt to the state that a recent estimate put at typically over £40,000. These are the actual results of the misguided drive to achieve greater social equality through widened access.

The argument that the economy needs employees with more advanced qualifications is equally suspect. You do not need a degree or, quite possibly, a post graduate degree to serve coffee in Starbucks. The inevitable consequence of increasing graduate numbers has been for employers to raise the qualification level they demand. There has been no real increase in the intellectual demand of many of the posts they can offer. What the economy really needs, as employers' organisations keep telling us, are school leavers who have a good command of literacy and numeracy and who understand the importance of qualities such as punctuality, commitment and politeness to customers.

The increased interest in apprenticeships, the fact that more companies, large and small alike, are recognising that it makes business sense to recruit new staff straight from school, and the impact of tuition fees are perhaps combining to halt what once seemed an inexorable movement towards Mr Blair's ludicrous target.

***

A welcome message on the need to improve the teaching of undergraduates

November 2013

Michael Arthur, President and Provost of University College London, deserves a standing ovation from everyone who is concerned about the future of higher education in this country.

In his inaugural lecture last week, Professor Arthur told UCL's academics that the quality of their teaching must rise. Everyone, he said, from star professors to PhD students should be involved in the teaching of undergraduates.

For years now the obsession with ranking academics and universities in terms of their research activities has helped undermine undergraduate provision. In my column in the main paper this week, there is a letter from a parent complaining that a top university had failed to provide proper teaching for his daughter. Hardly a week goes by without my postbag including a similar despairing comment. It is not only universities at the bottom of the league table that are attracting this kind of criticism. Top institutions, such as, sadly, the University of Bristol, which I attended as a student, are also attracting a good deal of criticism about the undergraduate teaching they are offering.

I cannot speak for research in the sciences, but I know that much of the research activity in the humanities and, in particular, in education is a farcical waste of time. Some years ago I commissioned a review of education research published in the major journals. Typical was a paper summarising an investigation into the experiences of a lesbian PE teacher in her first year of teaching. This week the press reported research undertaken by the National Literacy Trust which concluded that boys are twice as likely as girls to say that they do not like writing. Surprise, surprise! It was ever thus, and yet money continues to be spent year after year on rediscovering the obvious.

What ambitious young academics need to progress in their careers is the publication of paper after paper. The more times a paper they have written is cited by other researchers, the better it is for them. Inevitably, the result is that there is a great deal of mutual back-scratching. It is a self-obsessed and self-congratulatory world which contributes little or nothing to the discovery of worthwhile new knowledge and nothing, of course, to the teaching of undergraduates.

Three cheers, then, for Michael Arthur. In *The Closing of the American Mind,* Allan Bloom wrote that the university should be 'a place where inquiry and philosophical openness come into their own. It is intended to encourage the non-instrumental use of reason for its own sake, to provide the atmosphere where the moral and physical superiority of the dominant will not intimidate philosophical doubt. And it preserves the treasury of great deeds, great men and great thoughts required to nourish that doubt'.

We need more top ranking research institutions like UCL to commit themselves to a culture in which every academic engages their students as a core part of their professional responsibility.

***

There is certainly grade inflation in the awarding of university degrees

January 2014

Some years ago I was asked by the BBC to comment on a film shot secretly by a university lecturer during a meeting to decide the grades students should be awarded for their final degree. She argued that many should fail. Their work, she said, was factually weak, poorly argued and, on occasion, scarcely literate. Some was barely worth a GCSE pass. Her colleagues were seen gazing at her incredulously. The view of her head of department was that she was living in cloud cuckoo land.

They all have to pass, he smiled, and preferably with a decent grade. If we do not pass them we are going to get a barrage of complaints from the students themselves and the Dean is going to be on our back asking why we are torpedoing the university's league table position. We will simply have to come back during the summer holidays and change our grades.

The programme caused a bit of a stir at the time and was then forgotten. I had forgotten about it myself until I read last week about a study from Lancaster University which had concluded that there is no evidence of grade inflation in the awarding of university degrees.

In 2012/13, 19% of undergraduates achieved a first class degree, 51% an upper second, 25% a lower second and 5% a third. In 2004/05, 11% of undergraduates were awarded a first class degree. In the early 1990s the figure was 8%. When I graduated from Bristol University in 1968 in English, the department had given nobody a first for thirteen years.

Chris graduating from Bristol University in 1968 with his mother.

In the 1960s, around 7% of eighteen year olds went to university. In the last couple of decades the figure has risen inexorably towards Mr Blair's infamous target of 50%. So we have a situation in which vastly greater numbers of less academically able students have been admitted to university while simultaneously the percentage of top degrees awarded each year has increased hugely.

Of course, is the smug response of the Lancaster researchers. A level results have improved massively since the 1960s and the pool of talent has, therefore, widened. The article I read on their research said nothing about the methodology they had employed. I do not know whether they had studied the intellectual rigour of question papers over the years, or had read examiners' reports, or what. I do know, from work I commissioned when I was Chief Inspector, that standards over time in GCSE and A level examinations have gone dramatically downhill. This truth was resisted for years but is now pretty well universally acknowledged – except, it seems, by researchers at Lancaster.

It is in the interests, of course, of the higher education industry to defend the improved statistics and to celebrate any study which refutes any suggestion of malpractice, deliberate or systemic. This week's school league tables show the positive impact of Mr Gove's reforms on the school sector. It is perhaps time that the Government focused more rigorously on higher education. We have a situation where more and more students are going to university. The number achieving good degrees increases every year. The truth is that many of the courses they study have neither academic rigour nor vocational relevance. The Vice Chancellors sit there slapping themselves on the back. It is a situation which cannot go on forever. Can it?

***

The evidence in this report does not support the headlines

March 2014

We all want bright young people from disadvantaged homes who have had the misfortune to attend schools with low expectation and no academic grit to have the chance to fulfil their potential at university. Most of us, it seems, want this so much that we are prepared to pounce on every scrap of inadequate evidence in order to promote the cause of positive discrimination.

Last week, the Higher Education Funding Council (HEFC) published research purporting to show that students from state schools are more likely to achieve a top degree than students from independent schools.

Seventy per cent of state school students who achieved three B grades and who graduated in 2011 achieved a 2:1 or a first class degree compared to 61 per cent of students who had been privately educated. The percentages for ABB students are 76 to 69 respectively. Note, though, that when it comes to straight A students the percentages (88 per cent) are identical.

I stress this last point because, as Barnaby Lenon, the spokesman for the Independent Schools Council, has pointed out, the majority of students who go to independent schools achieve A and A* grades at A level. It is also worth adding, as Lenon noted, that independent schools admit a good number of students on bursaries who might otherwise have gone to a state school.

It is also worth considering the actual numbers we are talking about. 130,000 students graduated in 2011. 67.8 per cent of these students achieved a 2:1 or a first class degree. 32.2 per cent, or roughly 43,000 were awarded a 2:2 or a third class degree. The percentages quoted by the HEFC might seem significant, but when the actual numbers are low, percentages always do seem significant. Remember, too, that the difference between a 2:1 and a 2:2 degree might well only be two marks and that the business of awarding degrees is far from an exact science. The unreliability and, indeed, uselessness of A levels as evidence for university admissions is a further problem.

The world and his wife have jumped on the HEFC 'findings' because the drive to smash the elitist stranglehold independent schools are said to have on higher education has become unstoppable.

It is 'potential' that is now meant to matter, not actual achievement. How, one might ask, does one assess potential? How does one respond to the fact that maths tutors in top universities are already having to lay on remedial classes so that their students can cope with the demands of the syllabus? Potential is fine in principle, but in practice it helps, given that a degree only lasts three years, if students in their first year are properly prepared for the material they are to study.

But the killer sentence from the report has been ignored by virtually everybody. The HEFC comments: 'We found that those from the most disadvantaged areas have consistently lower higher-education degree outcomes than those with the same prior educational attainment from other areas'.

Is anyone surprised that young people from grammar schools and comprehensive schools serving leafy suburbs do much the same at university as their peers from private schools? The great problem, as everyone acknowledges, is how we identify and nurture the academically gifted who go to failing schools. This report tells us that we have not begun to tackle this problem.

Instead, it has inspired a wholly predictable cry for more positive discrimination in favour of state school pupils generally. We are never going to help the bright child from an impoverished home who has gone to an impoverished school until we stop meddling with entry grades and begin to work seriously to identify and support the primary school children who could, given the right education, win scholarships to Oxford and Cambridge.

***

University education should not need to have an immediate practical relevance

October 2014 *[Abridged]*

A speech given last week by Professor Andrew Hamilton, the Vice Chancellor of Oxford University, attracted a fair bit of media attention. Most commentators focused on his statement that the Government's visa system was preventing top students from abroad coming to UK universities. Towards the end of his speech, he made what was an even more important remark. Oxford, he said, 'reserved the right to investigate subjects of no practical use whatsoever'.

Bravo, I thought. We live in an age where not only politicians, but most vice chancellors, reduce the whole purpose of a university education to utilitarian ends. The assumption is that 18 year olds study for a degree in order to secure a decent job that will pay them good money. We need universities, the politicians tell us, because the UK has to survive in an ever more competitive global economy, and our competitive success depends upon a workforce which has the necessary 'higher order skills'.

We seem to have completely forgotten the fact that the intellectual and emotional benefits conferred by a liberal university education which has no immediate practical relevance are essential to the healthy functioning of a democracy.

Writing on de Tocqueville's *Democracy in America*, in his classic book on higher education, *The Closing of the American Mind*, Allan Bloom remarked that 'the great democratic danger .... is enslavement to public opinion'. Every man in a democracy is free to come to his own conclusions, and every man's conclusions are as valid as every other man's. This would be fine if men were capable of coming to independent judgements. The truth is that 'some kind of authority', as Bloom puts it, 'is often necessary for most men and is necessary, at least sometimes, for all men'.

Access to the traditional wisdom embodied in 'subjects of no practical use whatsoever' offers, paradoxically, the likelihood of greater independence of thought, because without it men will be dependent upon fashionable orthodoxies and the 'tyranny' of public opinion. Every man's decision might in principle be as important as every other man's, but political and social life demands consensus, which means that in most situations the will of the majority prevails. This, Bloom argues, is the most dangerous form of tyranny, 'not the kind that actively persecutes minorities, but the kind that breaks the inner will to resist because there is no qualified source of non conforming principle and no sense of superior right'.

Americans, de Tocqueville observed, talk constantly about individual rights, but only rarely display independence of mind. He might have been writing about 21ˢᵗ century England.

Now the majority of schools, state and independent, have succumbed to the tyranny of a curriculum inspired by notions of relevance and accessibility. The same rot has undermined university education. Anyone who dares to question this orthodoxy is dismissed with a snarl of withering opprobrium as an 'elitist'.

Three cheers for Oxford and its vice chancellor.

Education and Politics

From his weekly blogs for *The Sunday Times*

Could I have played it differently?

June 2011

It must have been a couple of months before, within three weeks of each other, they both died. I was sitting with my parents in the front room of the flat they had on the seafront at Deal. My father looked at me and said that I would never be awarded an honour. I can remember his exact words. 'You've upset too many people', he said, 'why did you have to court so much controversy and irritate everybody?' I looked out of the window at a depressingly brown English Channel and sighed before answering. This was a sensitive issue. They both would have loved me to have had some recognition and my father had never understood why, in his view, I had not been able to keep my head down, do what was expected of me and, duly rewarded, retire gracefully when the time came.

He is not the only one, of course, who has asked me this question. I have asked it, countless times, of myself. In part, I have to admit that what my father was implying is true. There is a streak in me that likes confrontation. Rationally, I know that it sometimes makes sense to back off, even when you think you are in the right. It is important to win friends and influence people and you can only fight so many battles at once. Would I have played things differently as Chief Inspector if I had my time again? Perhaps, if I had had the intelligence and strength of will to overcome these personality defects.

On the other hand, the old adage is true. You can't make an omelette without breaking the eggs. When I became Chief Inspector in 1994 it was quite clear to me, as it was to so many thousands of parents and so many people in the world of business, that there were massive problems in state education. What most people outside the world of education do not realise is how firmly the educational established is entrenched and how utterly determined it is to protect its territory. The late Ron Dearing, who was parachuted in to mastermind the reforms of the National Curriculum when I was Chief Executive of the School Curriculum and Assessment

Authority, once said to me that he had never worked in an industry or an area of public service where there was so much resentment, bitterness and personal spite. He was right.

I could have tried harder. I could have bitten my lip in debates with the likes of Tim Brighouse and the late Ted Wragg. I could have found, on occasion, more diplomatic language. Would any of this have made any real difference? I do not, in the end, think so. The problems were too serious and too widespread and the personalities involved, not just my own, were too huge. What would have been the point of spending six years as Chief Inspector if I had not taken every opportunity to speak out about the ways in which the system was failing so many of our children?

Nothing would have given me greater pleasure than to have told my parents that I had been awarded a knighthood. When the letter informing me of the award arrived I was not so much excited as saddened by the fact that, for them, it had come seven years too late. For their sake, I wish things could have been different. I know, however, that I could not have accepted an award that had been given to me simply because I had been Chief Inspector and I had played the expected political game. My independence mattered and still matters to me. I upset Labour politicians and, while supporting the basic thrust of Michael Gove's reforms, I have criticised him time and time again for not mounting a more radical attack on the forces that still obstruct the progress we all want for our children. My father could be pretty bloody-minded, too. His father was impossible. I like to think that they are up there smiling quietly to themselves.

***

Organisations should realise they can learn from complaints

June 2012

Personally, I am not very good at complaining. I don't mind sending a badly cooked meal back in a restaurant. 'No problem', the waitress said recently, as she took my plate of half frozen chips back to the kitchen with a flounce of sublime indifference. But, when it comes to confronting any bureaucracy, my determination crumbles as swiftly as my patience ebbs. I only have to listen to the recorded music and the start of the menu options and I know that I am going to decide that life is too short.

So, I am full of admiration for *Sunday Times* reader, Joseph Reynolds, who for the last twelve months has been waging war on every conceivable government bureaucracy to try and get somebody to agree that the GCSE media texts his daughter, using the word loosely, 'studies' for her English examination are a complete waste of everybody's time. He simply refuses to give up.

You will find an example of his latest effort in my 'Answer the Question' column in the main paper. This time, it is the head of the 'Communications and Engagement' team at Ofqual, the body which is meant to regulate exam standards, who has given him the brush-off. Yes, I wondered, too, about what on earth the term 'engagement' is meant to signify. Who is this person meant to 'engage'? And is the engagement intended to be military, as in 'to engage the enemy', or does it have a personal and perhaps amatory significance, as in 'to get engaged'?

Who knows, and who really cares? These government bureaucracies spawn new teams with new labels all the time. What does interest me is the inability of those in charge to understand that they can learn from the complaints their organisation receives. Sure, there are those written in green ink, which need a quick despatch, but I have always felt that a good number raise issues which deserve senior management consideration.

Take the rudest letter I received as Chief Inspector of Schools. It was from a man called Peter Ireland, who was then headteacher of The Nelson Thomlinson School in Wigton. He had been visited by two inspectors and was furious at their condescension and rudeness. I knew the inspectors involved, and I felt that it might be interesting to find out more.

Two minutes after Peter had sat me down in his office, I knew that my long trip from London to Cumbria was justified. He was telling me things about the inspectorate that I did not want to hear but that I needed to know. More than that, he was, clearly, an outstanding headteacher who had a great deal to teach me about the business of school leadership.

Peter Ireland is now Dean of Education at the University of Buckingham, responsible for a teacher training course which, next year, will have nearly 300 students and the most exciting and practical Masters programme for heads and aspirant heads I have ever seen.

If I hadn't taken Peter's initial complaint seriously, I would never have had the good fortune to meet this remarkable man. The chief executives of government bodies obviously need some sort of complaints mechanism, but when it comes to the real 'engagement' that can benefit their organisation, they should realise that there is no substitute for their own, personal attention.

***

Idiosyncrasy or banality?

June 2012

It is not often that I find myself nodding in agreement with anything that emanates from the teacher unions. Last week, however, the Head of Research at the National Association of Headteachers (NAHT), Lesley Gannon, responding to the news that the inspection reports on two different schools contained identical sentences, said: 'Inspectors just cut and paste, regurgitating wording from the evaluation schedule. Therefore the reports are more similar than they are individual'.

She is right. They are. They always were. It is a problem which worried me deeply when I was Chief Inspector. On the one hand, teachers, understandably, expect consistency from one inspection team to another; on the other, equally understandably, they question the meaningfulness of inspection reports which time and time again focus on the same issues and all too often use pretty well identical language.

In an ideal world, this is a circle which could be squared. We would have enough inspectors who were able to make individual judgements on a school. They would engage with the particular ethos and the specific strengths and weaknesses of the school and they would come to their own disciplined and professional, but personal conclusions. But we do not have enough such inspectors. Ofsted has always struggled to recruit the outstanding educationalists it needs. Successive chief inspectors have, therefore, had to rely on frameworks and guidance that help to deliver a common approach, but which, as a consequence, reduce the process of inspection to something mechanistic and banal.

There is a deeper problem, too. To an extent, schools differ one from another, but their achievements and their failures are, inevitably, very similar. Their pupils learn to read, or they do not learn to read; teachers mark books, or they do not mark books; children benefit from a wide range of extracurricular activities, or they do not benefit. There are only so many words which can be found to describe these common features.

One of the reasons why I resigned as Chief Inspector was because I could not face drafting another annual report on the state of the nation's schools. I had written six, and I knew that I had run out of new things to say. If I were still in post today, twelve years on, I would still be writing the phrases and the sentences I wrote all those years ago.

Lesley Gannon wants 'the best inspectors to freestyle a little more'. I would use different language, but I agree with her. I predict, though, that if Sir Michael Wilshaw were to grant her wish, within a month or two he would find that letters were piling up on his desk, full of complaints about inspectors writing idiosyncratic reports.

I am glad that it is Sir Michael and not me who is now wrestling with this problem.

***

We should not fall for the cosy and comforting clichés

June 2012

Monetary greed, a lust for power, a hunger for fame: most of the baser human instincts have motivated me, at one point or another, during my professional life. On the plus side, as the years went by and I understood more and more about what actually happens in so many schools, I became more and more determined to do what I could to drag problems out into the open and to try and find solutions.

The usual mess, then, of human imperfection. I need to add, though, something else to the pot. I blame Kenneth Richards, the man who taught me English in the sixth form at Wallington Grammar School in the 1960s. He made me start thinking about language. We would spend hours discussing why these words had been written in this order, what difference it would make if another word had been chosen, whether the paragraph or the poem hung together as an emotionally and intellectually meaningful statement.

'The limits of my language mean the limits of my world', as Wittgenstein famously said. In adult life, engaged in the never ending debate about the education we offer our children, I have been infuriated by the threadbare rhetoric which so often passes for thought. I said in my first annual lecture when I was Chief Inspector: 'If the thinking is woolly, simplistic and intellectually corrupt, then the subsequent action, whatever the level of investment, will achieve nothing'.

It still goes on. Nick Clegg's response to Michael Gove's proposal to reintroduce O levels was a classic example. 'What you want is an exam system which is fit for the future, doesn't turn the clock back to the past … … so it works for the many and not just for the few'.

Does anybody ever unpack the assumption that the way in which we did things in the past is necessarily an anachronism when it comes to the future? Does anybody ever stop to think that the many may not be able to benefit from an education and an exam system which challenges the few?

The failure of GCSE examinations is undeniable. It should have been clear to Sir Keith Joseph back in the 1980s, when he decided to abandon O levels and CSEs, that no one examination could possibly stretch the most able and, simultaneously, engage the many. But the evidence, however incontrovertible, is irrelevant to the Nick Cleggs of this world, who trumpet their cosy and comforting clichés.

Martin Amis once wrote a book called *The War Against Cliché*. It should be compulsory reading for any politician who wants to contribute to the educational debate. We will never have the education our children deserve until our politicians and our educationalists start to think.

***

In this case money is not the answer

September 2012

If any one thing confirms the froth of the Government's supposed commitment to curb public expenditure, it is the Department for Education's determination to spend £1.25 billion of taxpayers' money on the so-called 'pupil premium'.

Introduced in April last year, this premium was designed to give schools an extra £600 for every pupil from a disadvantaged background they had on roll. Last week, an Ofsted report revealed that the initiative is having a significant impact in only one in ten schools. Most appear to be spending the money on equipment or school uniforms or educational trips – anything, in fact, other than the support of children whose educational potential is deemed to be disadvantaged by their background.

I can't say I am surprised by the Ofsted findings. The sum of £1.25 billion is an awful lot of money. £600 per pupil is not. What would I do if I were a headteacher deciding how to use this extra resource? I haven't the faintest idea.

But the underlying problem is deeper. It isn't just that nobody thought seriously about whether the money could actually make a difference. Or how it could be allocated to best ensure that it might. It is the continuing assumption in a time of intense economic gloom that if we spend more we will solve the problems the nation faces.

Schools do not need more money to educate disadvantaged children better. They need to improve the quality of teaching they provide and, at secondary level, to re-think the nature of the curriculum they offer. Above all, primary schools need to teach their children to read. There is absolutely no reason why any child who does not have a serious intellectual impairment should not be able to read by the age of 11. The affluence or the poverty of their home background is a complete irrelevance.

There is a more fundamental problem still. This is the utopian belief, rampant in Liberal Democrat circles, and now shared, it seems, by all too many compassionate Conservatives, that political action can transform the world.

Better teaching can certainly touch individual lives. That was my belief when I was Chief Inspector, and I have done everything in my power throughout my career to try to improve the quality of teaching. Is Nick Clegg really surprised, however, by the much quoted statistic that one in five students from the poorest one fifth of families achieve five A* to C GCSE grades including English and maths, compared to over three quarters of young people from the richest fifth? You can emphasise the influence of nature or the impact, positive or negative, of nurture. The balance between the two doesn't much matter. The fact is that the child whose mother is a doctor and whose father a lawyer and who has books scattered round their home is more likely to achieve good exam results than the child who comes from a home where the parents have never worked and nobody talks to anybody very much.

This is not to say that schools should not do everything in their power to help the student from the impoverished background. It is simply to question the self-indulgent romanticism of utopian politics. At the best of times, such romanticism is unlikely to achieve anything real. When the country is languishing in a double dip recession, it is a major reason why the economic gloom is likely to intensify.

***

The restrictions on a teacher's daily duties should never have been agreed

April 2013

Which was the silliest of the many silly decisions Labour education ministers took between 1997 and 2010? It is a hard question, worthy of Michael Gove's tough new GCSE examinations.

Was it Education Action Zones, an early initiative intended to bring teachers, parents and employers together to develop 'innovative' strategies to reform failing secondary schools? Was it Ed Balls' decision to introduce a cobbled together diploma which was meant to 'bridge the academic vocational divide' and become, in his words, the 'qualification of choice' which would replace A levels? In the event, virtually nobody signed up for this new course and it was left to Gove to put the whole failed plan out of its misery soon after he took office. Was it Sir Jim Rose's progressive new approach to the primary National Curriculum that would have seen traditional subjects buried in a complex of cross-curricular themes and skills if it had ever been implemented? Was it the new approach to teacher pay which Mr Blair trumpeted at the time as a radical piece of modernisation that would reward excellence and transform the teaching profession? No, not really, not when the rules of the game ensured that virtually every teacher who applied for the pay increase was successful. So much for the introduction of a genuine performance incentive.

There are many other worthy candidates. I think, myself, though, that the agreement made with the teacher unions in 2003 which made it possible for teachers to refuse to do any routine administrative or practical tasks, such as photocopying and stapling or collecting money for school trips, which enabled them to opt out of key professional responsibilities such as the keeping of records and the analysis of test and examination results, and, most important of all, gave them the right to refuse to cover for absent colleagues, is probably the crassest example of the whole flawed approach which characterised this damaging decade in which state education went backwards.

Now, Michael Gove is planning to remove these ludicrous restrictions on a teacher's daily duties. Predictably, the unions are furious. Chris Keates, the General Secretary of the NASUWT, complained last week that Gove was 'determined to remove any provisions which support teachers in working effectively to raise standards'. Really? So she thinks that it is better for a teaching assistant than a teacher to stand in front of a class when a teacher is absent? She doesn't think that teachers should be scrutinising test results in order to determine the progress their pupils are making? Her absurd lamentations underline the absolute sense of what the Secretary of State is proposing.

In 2000 there were 79,000 teaching assistants. Two years ago there were 220,000. The total cost to the taxpayer is estimated at around £2 billion. Teaching assistants can make a very important contribution, particularly when they work with children who have learning difficulties. But this massive expansion has meant that more and more children are being taught by unqualified adults. Some, no doubt, are excellent practitioners despite the fact that they have no formal training. I know, however, from my *Sunday Times* postbag that more and more parents are becoming more and more concerned at the ludicrousness of a situation where teachers are given time off teaching to prepare lessons which are then taught by non teachers.

Mr Gove is standing up for these parents. This is one more example of how he is doing everything in his power to reverse the damage inflicted on state education by his predecessors. Everyone who cares about what happens in our schools should be supporting him in his fight with the teacher unions and his political opponents.

***

Hearings should be private so that employers are not held to ransom

May 2013

A recent edition of the *Times Educational Supplement*, the trade journal for teachers, announced that the 'introduction of performance pay in schools risks a surge in fraud as teachers falsify data to secure a pay rise'. Various lawyers have apparently predicted 'an administrative nightmare', with many more claims for sex and racial discrimination.

As I read the article, I could not stop myself visualising the lawyers smiling to themselves as they rub their hands discreetly under the table, contemplating the delicious prospect of the fees rolling in.

I have no doubt that Mr Gove's proposals for a new performance pay system for teachers will result in an increase in legal claims. This is the culture in which we live. Any headteacher who has attempted to remove an incompetent teacher will have spent hours negotiating with union representatives and, quite possibly, answering solicitors' letters. I know from my own experience that the most hopeless of teachers can and will take refuge behind every employment right the government has granted them.

The real absurdity is the fact that schools, like all other employers, are fearful of the time, expense and negative publicity involved if a case goes to an employment tribunal. It is the latter which is often the most significant factor in leading to cases being settled out of court with the claimant receiving large sums of money they do not deserve. I have never understood why these cases have to be played out in the glare of media attention. The most wild and unfounded allegations are inevitably seized upon by journalists desperate for a good story. By the time the defence has quashed this kind of nonsense, the damage has been done. If the employer is found to be in the wrong, then, of course, their guilt should be made public. But why can the hearings not be held in private so that the employer is not always held to ransom?

Performance pay in education is long overdue. The current arrangement sees a teacher's salary increase every year irrespective of the impact they have on their pupils. There is no incentive for a poor teacher to improve and there is no way in which a good teacher can be rewarded.

Vexatious complaints may be inevitable, but their number will be minimised if schools ensure that the criteria used for the award of performance pay, which should be rooted in the regular appraisal of a teacher's classroom performance, are crystal clear and understood by appraiser and appraisee alike. Despite protestations to the contrary, it is not difficult to define the characteristics of good teaching. Neither is it impossible to train middle and senior management in the skills of lesson observation and appraisal discussion. If these two conditions are met and there is a proper appeals process then the lawyers' glee at the prospect of a surge in profits might just be premature.

***

The education budget could be used to much better effect

May 2013 *[Abridged]*

His surname was O'Hara, and his Christian name was (I think) Eddie. He was the Labour MP for somewhere like Knowsley, and a member of the Education Select Committee. Every time I appeared before that committee to be quizzed about my misdeeds as Chief Inspector he would ask me the same question. 'Do you think', he would say, 'that things would be better in our schools if the Government was prepared to spend more money on education?'

Needless to say, since it was a Conservative administration at the time, this was a party political attempt to embarrass the Government. I always told him that I did not, and he always told me that that's what all chief inspectors replied whilst they were in office. It was a different story, he would add, once they had retired.

I was, of course, conscious of the political implications, but my answer was in fact honest. I did not and I do not think that the quality of the education our children receive is determined by the amount of money the Government is prepared to invest in schools. So I was not surprised to read last week that the think tank, Reform, believes that the education budget could be reduced by almost one fifth with no significant impact on standards.

Anybody who has worked in Whitehall knows that millions of pounds are wasted every year on consultancies and committees and awaydays and travel expenses and unnecessary meetings and the rest of it. Mr Gove has done many excellent things since he was appointed Minister for Education, but he has yet to cull quangos like the National College for School Leadership and the office of the Children's Commissioner. He could and should look at the number of officials in his own department, which continues to be far too high. There is a great deal of fat at the national level when it comes to educational expenditure.

Reform was looking at the efficiency with which individual schools deploy resources rather than waste at the top. Their report reaffirms some of the conclusions I reached twenty years ago. Take, for example, the issue of class size. The smaller the class, the more teachers a school needs to employ. Is there a correlation between small class sizes and improved pupil performance? Contrary to popular belief, the evidence we analysed when I was Chief Inspector suggested that, with the exception of the youngest children in infant classes, the answer was no. What matters is not the size of the class but the quality of the teacher.

The current Chief Inspector, Sir Michael Wilshaw, has picked up this point, arguing that schools should not be afraid to pay good teachers more, even if this means that class sizes have to rise. It is obvious, really, isn't it? A child in a class of ten taught by an incompetent teacher is going to make less progress than a child in a class of twenty taught by a teacher with excellent subject knowledge, high expectations and a mastery of the craft of the classroom.

Similarly radical questions need to be asked about the millions of pounds that are spent by schools on 'professional development' for their teachers. They may invite consultants (at £1,000 or more a day) to visit the school to talk to staff. They may send their teachers on external conferences. The underpinning belief is that more training automatically results in better teaching. The professional development industry grinds on and the opportunity costs involved in taking teachers out of their classrooms are even more serious than the actual costs of the consultant or trainer.

We can argue about whether the total education budget could be reduced and, if so, by how much, but there is absolutely no doubt in my mind that, nationally and locally, the money that we, the taxpayer, gives to pay for our schools could be used to much better effect.

***

This is a battle for the soul of education

October 2013 *[Abridged]*

Reading last week's letter to *The Times* criticising the Government's education reforms, you would think that Michael Gove, the minister responsible, was some latter-day Herod, presiding over the slaughter of 21st century innocents.

Poet Laureate, Carol Ann Duffy, and the couple of hundred academics and writers who signed the letter are 'gravely concerned'. They deplore the 'incessant testing and labelling' to which children are supposedly subjected. They think that 'the new national policies around curriculum, assessment and accountability are taking enormous risks with the quality of children's lives and learning'. They predict 'devastating consequences for children's mental health'.

Gosh, is all I can say. Or, possibly, tosh. I don't deny these dignitaries their democratic right to express their views, but really.

Take testing. There is a simple reading test for 6 year olds, national curriculum tests in English and maths for 7 year olds and tests in English, maths and science for 11 year olds. There are GCSE examinations for 16 year olds and A level examinations for 18 year olds. This hardly amounts to an 'incessant' programme of testing. Gove, moreover, has taken steps to end the modular assessments which resulted in GCSE students sitting interim tests throughout the two years of their course, he is doing his best to cut back the burden of coursework, and he is abolishing the AS examination which blighted the first year of sixth form study with an unnecessary assessment.

More fundamentally, no education minister in recent times has cared more about education and children. Gove knows that our collective failure over the last fifty years to expect enough of young people and to teach them enough about the magic and the mystery of the world in which they live has had 'devastating consequences' for millions. He wants children to be taught what they need to know if they are to lead fulfilled lives. He wants them to be challenged and inspired. The Blob hates him for having such unacceptable ambitions.

The Blob has been writing apocalyptic letters to newspapers for decades. In the early 1990s, when we were re-drafting the National Curriculum for English and had the temerity to suggest that every school child should have the opportunity to read some of the great classics of English literature, five hundred academics sneered that in these post modernist days there was no such thing as a 'classic'. Gove himself has been subjected to a barrage of criticism, most recently from a group of 'experts' on 'early childhood', who apparently believe that young children should spend their entire lives playing in a sand pit.

Shapeless and inert, the Blob sits heavy on schools and teacher training institutions alike, squashing the oxygen of thought out of the profession. I have been prodding leading figures within the Blob for the last twenty-five years, and the litany of complaint is always the same. The National Curriculum should be abolished so that teachers can teach whatever they like however they like. There should be no tests, no examinations until students reach the age of 18, and, of course, no Ofsted. Teachers should be facilitators and mentors who release the innate creativity of the young. It is like talking to a member of an extreme religious sect, whose default setting is the robotic repetition of a received wisdom and who cannot contemplate the possibility of somebody else ever having anything sensible to say, particularly if that somebody is a Conservative Secretary of State for Education.

It is no coincidence, of course, that the academics and trade unionists who constitute the Blob have been making so much noise recently. Gove's reforms to teacher remuneration give schools the freedom to make their own decisions on how much they pay their teachers, and strike, therefore, a blow at the heart of union power. His determination to move teacher training out of universities and into schools threatens the jobs of hundreds of academics working in education departments.

What is surprising is how the anguish of the Blob has spread into the world of independent education. There was a conference last week at Wellington College called the 'Positive Education Summit'. Its aim was to emphasise the importance of happiness, well-being and character building, and the subtext was to deplore the myopia of those, like Michael Gove, who focus too exclusively on the academic. Tim Hands, the Headmaster of Magdalen College School and the new chairman of the Headmasters Conference, spent most of his speech at the HMC autumn gathering lambasting Gove and the Government for its supposed obsession with examination results and league tables.

The battle for the soul of education is, it seems, far from won. What kind of education do we want as a country for our children? Are we prepared, teachers and parents alike, to stand shoulder to shoulder with the Secretary of State or are we going to allow the anguished criticisms of the Blob to drag our schools backwards into a culture of low expectation and underachievement?

***

The reasons for thirty years of no real progress

January 2014

Those who believe in the myth of progress envisage, I presume, a heaven on earth when reason has cut through folly and eradicated wickedness. I wish I could share their optimism. Experience tells me that life is not like this. Two steps forward and one back is the reality, if we are lucky. We might make progress of a kind, but it will not be sustained without vigilance and effort and possibly not even then.

I am nonetheless depressed by the failure over the last thirty years to make any real progress in the reform of state education. Why is it that so little has been achieved when so many have tried so hard and so much money has been spent? Here are six explanations.

The first and most fundamental problem is that we no longer think that education is an enterprise in which the young should be initiated into their cultural inheritance. This initiation demands a willingness to engage with what appears irrelevant and which is often difficult. We want instant gratification. We think that the young must be fed gobbets of this and that which connect with their immediate personal experience of the world. We encourage them to think that it is their opinion that matters rather than their ability to submit to a body of knowledge which dwarfs their egotism and ignorance. There is no hope of progress in education when the thinking which informs the enterprise of reform is so fundamentally wrong.

Second, we have the schools we deserve. The society our schools serve is grossly materialistic. When politicians and many educationalists talk about education they do so in utilitarian terms. What matters is the contribution the curriculum makes to the competitiveness of UK plc in the global economy. Vice Chancellors talk more often of how their universities foster a spirit of enterprise and entrepreneurialism than they do of the virtues of disinterested scholarship. If this is true of universities, what hope is there for schools?

Third, Secretaries of State for Education come and go. I have taken a keen interest in education over the last four decades, but I would be hard pressed to tell you the names of half the men and women who have sat behind their big desk in the Department for Education. Michael Gove is the first Secretary of State in my professional lifetime who has a real personal understanding of what the educational enterprise must involve. Again, it is hardly surprising that the efforts of reform go nowhere when the politician in charge has no grasp of what needs to be done.

Fourth, even when we have a minister like Gove, progress is difficult because the odds are stacked so hugely against him. There are 24,000 state schools in the country and there are precious few levers a politician can pull. Look at the way the National Curriculum has been subverted in so many schools. How can any minister, however intelligent and determined, ensure that the ministerial edict actually has any impact on what happens in classrooms?

Fifth, and connected to this, there is the resistance of the educational establishment. Politicians need educationalists to translate their ambitions into detailed policy. Gove has a Chief Inspector of Schools, Sir Michael Wilshaw, who, for the most part, clearly shares his thinking. He has precious few other people upon whom he can rely. Ideas he abhors are pursued in the quangos and academy trusts and free schools which are meant to be the agents of his reforms. This is a huge problem.

Sixth, and finally, we are more interested in equality of opportunity than we are in education. We persist in thinking that all students have the same intellectual abilities and aspirations and we quake nervously when anyone, like, for example, Dominic Cummings, Michael Gove's current special adviser, dares to raise the truth that intelligence is to a very significant extent inherited. The rose-tinted spectacles through which we view the potential of the young make it very difficult for anyone to develop the policies and practice which will allow students who have different kinds of ability to fulfil their potential.

It is a depressing list. I wish, as the New Year begins, that I could offer some answers.

***

Leadership involves the determination to do what is needed

September 2014

It is true that anyone attempting to reform an organisation or business needs to do what they can to ensure that those involved in the reforms understand and, hopefully, agree with the changes which are being made. It is also true that nobody can keep everybody happy all of the time, that omelettes involve breaking eggs, and that, if your main aim is to 'reach out' and feel the pain of each and every 'stakeholder', then you are unlikely to make much progress.

Some years ago, when Tony Blair set up the National College for School Leadership, I interviewed its first chief executive, Heather du Quesnay. I asked her the quality she thought most important in a school leader. She replied 'empathy'. Empathy, not, note, a firm grip on what constitutes the educational good, or the ability to analyse the particular issues in the individual school, or the relentless determination to make things happen, whatever the obstinacy of the opposition. None of these things seemed actually to matter anywhere near as much to her as the 'emotional intelligence' of the man or the woman in charge. It helps, of course, if a leader is able to understand why somebody is behaving in the way they are behaving. You can then, as Machiavelli might have argued, select the best possible response. But, empathy in the sense of 'I feel your pain', this is something else.

We live in an age of conciliation. When Nicky Morgan was appointed to take over as Secretary of State for Education from Michael Gove, the move was spun as the onset of the new dawn. She was going to 'reach out' and establish better relations with the teaching profession. The theme now was going to be conciliation.

But what does conciliation mean? Is it to make substantive concessions in the light of the opponent's demands? Or is it to smile sweetly and be nice in the hope that those who are being patronised are gullible enough to drink it all in?

Time will tell as far as Ms Morgan goes. The history of thirty years of educational reform is, though, clear. I was asked in an interview recently what progress I thought had been made in education in the last few decades. My answer was pretty negative. There are those who used to argue, when Gove was king, that his reforms had changed everything. I am a great admirer of what he tried to do, but this assertion was, I am afraid, a triumph of naive hopefulness over the reality of what continues to happen in the classrooms of our schools.

What ultimately matters in education, as in every other human activity, are the beliefs which guide everyday action. Gove wanted, rightly, in my view, to replace a set of beliefs which emphasised concepts of relevance and accessibility over a commitment to the disciplined study of a body of knowledge which should never be reduced to the personalised whim of the individual student. If anything, more teachers are more enthusiastic than was the case a few years ago about the development of learning skills, the encouragement of children to voice opinions about topics they know nothing about, and the role of the teacher as a facilitator rather than an authority in their subject.

Gove's National Curriculum and examination reforms have the potential to change the intellectual climate. The potential: there is a long, long way to go before his ambitious programme is translated into reality. You either believe that education is the initiation of the young into bodies of important knowledge or you think that it is a utilitarian business in which the only thing that matters is the development of the skills employers think they need. You either see it as a quasi religious enterprise which involves humility and patience or you bang the drum for the importance of a curriculum which connects with the pupil's immediate experience as painlessly as possible.

Nicky Morgan can pretend to be nice. She can be nice. But, if she wants to carry on the reforms her predecessor started she cannot conciliate in the substantive sense of making concessions. Leadership involves the determination to do what is needed, however vocal and intransigent the opposition.

***

A disproportionate response

November 2014

'Proportionate' is one of those weasely words, like 'appropriate' and 'fair', which means whatever you want it to mean. That is why it is so popular. An awful lot of people in public life do not want what they say to mean anything. Sometimes, though, something happens which is so blatantly 'disproportionate' that no amount of linguistic slipperiness can cover the nonsense of what is going on.

Last week we learned that Sir John Cass School in Tower Hamlets has been failed by Ofsted because of its failure to monitor the activities of an Islamic society set up by some of its sixth formers.

I do not, for one moment, think that we should take the radicalisation of young Muslims lightly. But I have always thought that the way to avoid radicalisation is to offer the disadvantaged a way out of poverty and hopelessness and alienation. This is where education comes in. In the 1990s, Sir John Cass was a failing school. Its current Head, supported by a strong governing body, confronted the institution's many problems and for many years this secondary school has been a beacon of excellence in an extremely disadvantaged community.

Ofsted inspectors have twice recognised this excellence and given the school the top grade of Outstanding. Now, because a snap inspection revealed one problem, it is deemed to be an unsafe environment for its students and, therefore, a failing school.

What, other than the demoralisation of the school community, is this reversal of fortune going to achieve? Why could the inspectors not have pointed the problem out and relied on the exceptional management team to deal with it? The answer is that Ofsted, encouraged, no doubt, by the Department for Education, has become a key player in the war against terror and, more generally, the campaign to ensure that every school across the land is promoting the cause of British values.

So, a primary school in rural Lincolnshire has been told that, while its educational provision is generally excellent, it could not be judged Outstanding because it does not have enough non-white pupils and has not done enough to broaden its children's experience and understanding of the multicultural diversity of 21st century England.

Faith schools of all persuasions are being criticised because they do not promote the values which politicians deem to be essential to our society. There seems to be no room for flexibility, no recognition of the fact that schools which serve different communities and faith groups might very legitimately believe that they should reflect, to some extent at least, the particular values of that community. It is an intolerant and inflexible approach, which is, quite rightly, causing a great deal of concern in many schools and parent groups.

Ofsted has always had to inspect schools against the legislation. The best inspectors in the past, however, have exercised some discretion and professional judgement when they have identified some aspect of a school's provision which in some way contravenes the law. Their response has been proportionate.

***

At least this time we are being spared the utopian dreams ….

April 2015

In the run up to the 1997 election, Tony Blair positioned education centre stage. He told us that, if he were to be elected, the life chances of our children would be transformed through a radical reform of state education.

It did not happen, of course, and I suspect that his decision to focus on education had more to do with the fact that Bill Clinton had played a similar card in his journey to the White House than it did with any deep belief or interest in the subject of educational reform. But, like most of us, Blair no doubt did believe that schools can make a real difference to individual lives.

Can they? I have no doubt from my own experience that the answer is yes. The grammar school that I attended opened my eyes to areas of intellectual interest that have been of huge importance throughout my life. More prosaically, without a degree I would never have become a teacher and I might well not have gone to university if it had not been for my teachers at this grammar school.

But this answer has to be qualified. I have just re-read Anthony Powell's novel, *A Dance to the Music of Time*. He begins by introducing us to four boys who are contemporaries at a school which is obviously Eton: Kenneth Widmerpool, Charles Stringham, Peter Templar, and the narrator, Nicholas Jenkins. It then follows their lives through the decades which follow.

Widmerpool, overweight, socially gauche and teased at school, becomes a successful businessman, a colonel during the Second World War, a Labour MP, a member of the House of Lords and, finally, the Chancellor of a new university. On the face of it, he has a successful life, but the reality is he remains a ludicrous figure throughout. Stringham, for all his family wealth, descends into alcoholism and dies at the hands of the Japanese during the war. Templar, a happy, self-confident boy at the beginning of the book, slides into a depression which ends with his throat being cut in Cairo. Jenkins marries happily and lives an apparently contented life in the country as a minor intellectual and novelist, but his is a life which avoids disasters rather than one which accumulates triumphs.

It is an intelligent, sensitive, deeply humane, and, at times, very amusing book. It is also a deeply depressing book. Did their privileged education at Eton define the adult life of these four boys? Of course it did not. Education never does. It can open doors, but whether one walks through and what one does with the opportunity that opens up is a matter of character, and no school, not even Eton, despite the reams of nonsense that are written at the moment about the importance of schools training character, can in fact have much impact upon the personalities, for better or for worse, which are forged during our earliest years and inherited from our parents.

Our lives are a matter of character and destiny. Doors open and doors close. We can, like Widmerpool, do everything in our power to ensure that we are in the right place at the right time, but in the end what we achieve is a matter of luck and of our ability to seize the moment.

I wish education were higher up the political agenda during this election and I still hope that, as 7 May approaches, one of the parties might say something interesting about how standards may be improved in our schools. I am glad, though, that we are not being subjected to the utopian dreams of politicians who want us to believe that they really have the power to bestow a happy and contented life upon our children.

***

… but it is the culture, not the policies, that matters

May 2015

Does it really matter that there has been very little discussion of education in the run up to next week's election? Does it matter that none of the political parties has had anything radical and exciting to say about raising standards in the nation's schools?

I don't think it does. It is not government policies which determine how teachers teach and how much, therefore, pupils learn. The ideas which teachers pick up through their initial and in-service training matter much more. Let me give you two examples which have caught my eye as I have browsed through recent press cuttings.

The first concerned the marking of pupils' work. Dr Rebecca Allen, who is the Reader in Economics of Education at the UCL Institute of Education, believes, apparently, that we need to explore the possibility of teachers reducing their workload through the outsourcing of marking overseas. She has told a conference that outsourced marking has been proved to be extremely reliable and that it would only cost £2 to £3 an hour.

It is hard to think of a more ridiculous idea. Marking is one of the teacher's core responsibilities, and for obvious reasons. Pupils need to know that their written work is being read and taken seriously. They need to have their mistakes pointed out and their achievements praised. They need to know that this is being done by the teacher who teaches them because the relationship between teacher and pupil is crucial to the progress the pupil makes. Teachers, for their part, need to see for themselves how their pupils are thinking and the problems they are having in their understanding so that they can plan new lessons and offer extra support to those who are having difficulty.

This is so obvious that it should not need to be said. But we have an academic occupying a senior post at a prestigious educational institution who does not, it seems, have the faintest idea about the realities of teaching.

The second news item I noticed was a story about how Mark Dawe, the Chief Executive of the OCR Examination Board, thinks that students sitting examinations should be allowed to use search tools like Google. He believes that this would help examiners assess the ability of students to apply knowledge. It is not, he is suggesting, the knowledge pupils have mastered that matters so much as the use that they can make of it and the opinions they have about it.

Beyond the fact that he is suggesting a major change to how examinations are conducted, there is nothing particularly new about his argument. For the last twenty to thirty years, many educationalists have suggested that nobody really needs to know anything about anything. We can look up what we do not know on the Internet and it is thinking and learning skills upon which teachers should focus so that the young can find out things for themselves and become ever more proficient at problem solving. The truth, of course, is that if you don't know much about the subject you are trying to research on the Internet you are likely to drown in a sea of often irrelevant information. More fundamentally, the discovery of a solution to a particular problem or the expression of an opinion which has any credibility or meaning depends upon the knowledge you have about the subject under consideration.

What relevance does this have to the importance of the policies politicians promote? It is, and the history of education in the UK over the last forty years shows this very clearly, that political initiatives come and go. They are frighteningly ephemeral. What is frighteningly resistant to change is the intellectual and ideological climate within the world of education. This climate has been created by people like Rebecca Allen and Mark Dawe, educationalists who promote a particular and pernicious view of what the educational enterprise should involve. The climate or culture within which teachers teach eats political initiatives for breakfast.

Assisted Dying

Assisted Dying

First published in *The Sunday Times*, October 2009

Ten minutes ago I sat down at the computer to think through my reaction to the advice on assisted suicide that Keir Starmer, the Director of Public Prosecutions (DPP), published last week. Seeking inspiration, I managed, just, to pour myself a glass of wine which, with infinite caution, I struggled to raise to my mouth. Halfway up, my arms refused to function. They froze. My hands began to shake and the glass fell into my lap. I am now contemplating the red stain across my trouser legs.

Motor Neurone Disease (MND) is not much fun. I was diagnosed three years ago. At the time I could walk up the hills around our house in Snowdonia and was still managing the odd rock climb. I went to the doctor because I sensed my muscles were weakening, but I did not believe anything was seriously wrong. I am now more or less wheelchair-bound and basic activities such as cutting up a steak or, indeed, drinking a glass of wine, have become increasingly difficult. Getting up the stairs each night is more of an adventure than most of the climbs I once enjoyed.

I am, nonetheless, one of the lucky ones. Some MND patients are diagnosed in their twenties. Some die within weeks of diagnosis. I am 62 and have had my best years. I am not complaining and I am still glad to be here.

Indeed, there are positives to being terminally ill. This afternoon we drove down the Aberglaslyn Pass. The trees were beginning to turn and a dappled light lit up the hillside. I have known this valley for fifty years, and, my appreciation sharpened by the knowledge that next year I might not be here to see them, the mountains and lake have never seemed more beautiful. So, too, with poems and paintings, music and, above all, friendships: in a curious way, I am grateful for the intensity of the experiences MND has given me.

That said, like every MND patient, I know that each day life gets a bit more difficult. In my case it was my left ankle that weakened first. Then the left leg. The right leg followed. My right arm packed up slightly faster

243

than the left. Now two fingers on my left hand feel increasingly numb. Cramps lock fingers on both hands into a claw-like paralysis. Sooner or later my breathing and swallowing muscles will be affected and I will die.

Death does not bother me. The manner of my dying does. I want to be in control as much as I can for as long as I can. I don't want to become an irascible, self-pitying burden. The prospect of palliative care in a hospice, however humane, fills me with fear and despair. I want to know that I have a way out.

If you can walk to the clifftop or swallow the pills unaided, you are in control of your destiny. If you can't, you are dependent on your nearest and dearest. The question for anyone with a degenerative disease is: do you go before you are ready, while you still can, or do you risk the prosecution of those you love?

Does Starmer's guidance mean those of us in this situation can delay a decision to kill ourselves, in the knowledge that anybody who helps us when we are unable to act independently will be immune from prosecution? No, of course not. It is a fudge. The person most likely to help anyone take his or her life is the person most likely to benefit from the will. That person may have been 'wholly motivated by compassion', but they stand to gain financially and will, therefore, given the DPP's advice, be under suspicion and could, theoretically, spend fourteen years in jail.

Predictably enough, groups from the Law Society to Dignity in Dying are arguing that the DPP's advice amounts to a change in the law and that the question of assisted suicide must be decided by Parliament. Personally, my heart sinks. I understand why Debbie Purdy, the MS sufferer whose campaign prompted the DPP's guidance, has sought to clarify the law, but I wish she had not.

As Chief Inspector of Schools, I believed it was possible to define what constituted good teaching and to use these criteria to inform the inspection process in a sensitive and professional manner. What we now have is a damaging bureaucracy that militates against creative teaching. It is better, I have concluded, to leave some things unsaid and to rely on the humanity and wisdom of those responsible for inspection.

As an MND patient, I feel much the same about the clamour to clarify the law on assisted suicide. I dread the pompous pronouncements from the great and the good who have no personal understanding of what it is to die a protracted death or to watch anyone they love die such a death. I have no faith the resulting law will make things clearer or better. Once, doctors made their own decisions. Some, bravely, still do. The greater the public clamour, the more definitive the law, the less likely it will be that any doctor will have the courage to exercise individual judgement and do what he thinks right for the patient in his care.

***

First published in *The Sunday Times,* December 2011

My father stirred suddenly on the sofa. 'Why can't we lie down together', he said, 'hold hands, and die?' My mother nodded quietly in agreement. I had thought they were both asleep and had been wondering when to go and make a cup of tea. As it was, I sat there, not knowing what to say, tears filling my eyes.

What is there to say when you have watched your parents decline physically and mentally to the point where they cannot cope? When they have sunk so deep into their individual desperation that they have begun to blame each other for the pain of their situation? When they know, and you know, that things are only going to get worse?

A couple of months later, it became impossible to look after my father at home and he went into the local cottage hospital. Every time I visited, a man in the bed opposite, who had, as a clergyman, spent his life comforting the sick in such places, would call out to me. 'There isn't a God, is there? No God would allow us to suffer like this, would He?'

I would go and sit with him, hold his hand, try to reassure him that his God was still with him. Then I would move across the ward to my father. He never said much. He hated being there and wanted more than anything in the world to go home. I had to tell him that he could not, and I think he began to hate me, too.

The night he died, I sat until 10 o'clock, listening to his erratic breathing, and wondered what to do. My mother was at home and she could not cope properly on her own. I bent over, whispered 'goodnight' and told him, though I knew I would not, that I would see him in the morning. The phone went in the early hours and a nurse told me he had died. When my mother woke I wondered how she would take the news. She did not break down in tears. She didn't do anything for several minutes. Then she turned her poor face, twisted since the last stroke, to me and said 'Well, he's got what he wanted, hasn't he? I wonder how long I will have to wait'.

She died three weeks later. I was in Wales and had called to see how she was. We had talked about how, when the weather got better, I was going to bring her up to stay with me. Then, half an hour later, the phone went again. It was her carer, who told me that my mother had said she didn't feel well and, twenty seconds later, had collapsed in her chair.

Christine and I walked round Llyn Gwynant that afternoon. The winter sun lit up the black waters of the lake. I felt an enormous sense of relief. For her and for me. The anguish of the last few years was over. They did not have to suffer any more. I did not have to know that, whatever I did, it was not enough.

Eight years on, it is I who cannot cope. I was diagnosed with Motor Neurone Disease in 2006. My days of walking and mountain biking in the Welsh hills are over. It is a wheelchair, now, for me, and the most important object in my life is the slide board which makes it possible for Christine to lift me in and out of it.

Nobody understands anything about MND. Something goes wrong in the brain or the nervous system and messages are no longer sent to your muscles. As a result, you lose the ability to move. My legs went first, and then my arms. I am waiting for the next stage, when you can no longer swallow or breathe. I spend quite a lot of time thinking about what I ought to do.

There is no cure for MND. The best they can do is prescribe a drug which is meant to prolong life by a couple of months. Fifty per cent of patients die within fourteen months of the diagnosis; ninety per cent are dead within five years. Professor Stephen Hawking, who celebrates his 70th birthday this week, has had the disease for the best part of fifty years.

Anything seems possible when MND decides in its mysterious and insidious way that it is going to take over your life.

I am into my sixth year, and I am certain that I had the illness for several years before I finally bothered to visit the doctor. So, in a sense, I am one of the lucky ones. That does not mean I am going to escape. You think, for a month or two, that the decline has stopped, and then suddenly you know it hasn't. You know that something else has given up.

Last night was not good. I have only myself to blame for the indigestion that followed a takeaway curry. I can live with indigestion. What kept me awake was my fingers. They have begun to twist themselves over into a fixed claw shape. My toes, actually, are doing the same, but they are not making so much fuss about it. When my fingers lock over they cramp up, and it is painful. I lay in bed trying to straighten them and managed to mesh my hands together as though I were praying. This helped to relax them, but I then found I could not unmesh them.

I lay there in the dark, trying to resist a rising feeling of panic. I could have woken Christine, of course, who would have rescued me as she always does. But she was fast asleep and she is at my beck and call throughout the day. So I forced myself to lie there and wait for the cramps to unlock and dawn to come. I lay there thinking about the fact that my parents had left it too late. What, I asked myself, over and over again, was I going to do?

When you have MND there are only three options. You kill yourself while you still have the physical ability to do it. You hang on for as long as you can and you end up in a hospice. Or you and your loved ones decide that you are going to find a way out, whatever the law might say, when the time is right.

If I had been on my own, I would have killed myself three years ago. I cannot remember the exact date, but the moment when I realised that time was running out for me as an independent human being is crystal clear.

A couple of steps lead down from the back garden into the courtyard of our house in Wales. I suddenly found myself flat on my face in that courtyard. I lay there for a moment or two, turned myself over and contemplated the canopy of trees above me. I remembered my father saying to me on his last visit that he was frightened of falling down those very steps. I had said to him: 'Don't worry, Dad. You're not going to go anywhere'. Now, it was me that was frightened. I knew exactly where I was going to go.

But I was not on my own. I had my wife to look after me and to think about. I had my daughter and grandchildren. I had my conviction that, if you are thinking of killing yourself, you need to think very hard. My basic attitude has always been that one should soldier on, stoic and insouciant in the face of life's tribulations. I have not always managed to live up to this precept, but I have tried. Too often, suicide is at best a selfish and at worst an aggressive act. I did not and I do not want my suicide, if it comes to that, to be selfish or aggressive.

What, though, do you do? Do you all sit down round the kitchen table and discuss whether the time is right? How can anyone expect one's wife or daughter to tell them that the moment has come? You cannot, of course. It is a nonsense. But decisions do not always have to be made explicit. I believe that when the time is right there will be a tacit understanding which will not need to be talked through in some farcical family conference.

I am glad that I did not tuck the hosepipe into the exhaust and start the engine. As I dictate this and Christine types, a purple, yellowish bruise has spread across the sky. There are good things as well as bad when you know that you are living on borrowed time, and the beauty of the world becomes ever more poignant.

So, too, do the trivial occurrences of daily domestic life. 'Let's have a cup of tea', she says. I manage to drink it without spilling most of it down me. I push a chocolate finger biscuit round my mouth without dislodging my dodgy bridge. There is fish and chips for dinner and a couple of episodes of *Sons of Anarchy* to watch afterwards. What more can a man want?

In my case the answer to this question is simple. I want our noble Parliamentarians, our bishops and archbishops, the great and the good of the medical profession, to shut up. I want them to stop poking their vainglorious fingers into something they cannot possibly understand. I want the right to die at a time of my choice, assisted, if necessary, by those who love me enough to help.

Let's park the argument that any change to the assisted dying law is going to expose hundreds and thousands of vulnerable people to the wicked machinations of relatives who want to bump them off. Let's stick with me. I have MND. I do not want to die before I am ready, but, equally, I do not want to end up in the living hell that was my parents' last years.

Some members of the National Union of Teachers might possibly disagree, but I think I am in possession of my mental faculties. I am happy to appear before any panel of psychiatrists or to be quizzed by any lawyer. The fact that I have a terminal illness, which will, sooner or later, make it impossible for me to swallow or breathe, is public knowledge. Why should the law dictate the timing and circumstance of my death? What possible damage to the public good could that death do?

I will ignore the puerile response some readers may be tempted to make to this question. The obvious truth is that it would do no harm at all. It is what, when the time is right, I want. In the last years of their lives it was what my parents wanted for themselves. It is what, I suspect, thousands of people want this Sunday and millions more will want when they, too, find themselves facing the questions I am facing.

Imagine. Just for a moment. Stop what you are doing. Shut your eyes and pretend you are in a wheelchair. You want to clean your teeth. Your husband or wife has given you the toothbrush. They are trying to help you raise the brush to your mouth. Your hands cramp round the handle and the brush misses its target. You let it go. You try again. The same thing happens. On the third or fourth go you manage, sort of, to clean your teeth. Then the toothpaste has to be mopped up off your clothes. That was this morning's indignity.

If you had asked me five years ago whether I would be able to put up with such nonsense, I would have laughed. My impatience was legendary. Now, every day I amaze myself. My inability to turn the pages of a book, or to answer an email, frustrates me enormously. There is the odd expletive, of course, but I have come to accept the tightening constraints of my everyday experience. The one thing that continues really to try my patience is the grandstanding of those who oppose any form of assisted suicide.

It cannot be beyond the bounds of human ingenuity to construct a system in which somebody suffering from a terminal illness, who wants to die, but who is unable to kill themselves unaided, could apply to the state for permission. Independent medical and legal expertise could be brought to bear, and a judgement reached. As a thoroughgoing libertarian, the whole idea makes me snort, but, if people are worried about the potential abuse of any change in the law then I could accept the checks and balances which might allow common sense to prevail.

If there are no practical impediments, then it boils down to one group of people imposing their values on another. I can respect the religious conviction of the churchman who believes that life is God given and must be endured until God decides otherwise. Indeed, I have considerable sympathy with this position. Taking one's own life should, in my opinion, be, in every possible sense of the phrase, an act of last resort. But, if I have come to the point where that act is what I want, I do not think that anybody else's convictions should stop me doing what I have decided to do.

Neither do I think that somebody who is terminally ill should have to dig deep into their savings and travel to Switzerland. You have, in fact, to be able to swallow the glass of sodium pentobarbital unaided, and I have probably passed that point. I can still swallow, but, unless I am lying down, the odds against me being able to raise the glass and hold it to my lips are now too high. In any case, even if I had the physical capacity, I do not want to travel to a foreign country to have a poison ministered to me by strangers. I want to die in my own home.

I went through a phase when I thought that I should campaign to get the assisted dying laws changed. I decided against. The sad truth is that today's politicians do not have the courage to confront an issue that is this contentious. I do not think my decision about my death has anything to do with any Member of Parliament. I know, moreover, that the publicity which would surround any such campaign would make it even more difficult for doctors to exercise their professional judgement when they are caring for the terminally ill.

Prior to Shipman, one GP said to me recently, doctors would do what was necessary to minimise suffering. Now, the prospect of an enquiry into the circumstances surrounding any death makes most reluctant to do anything other than prolong life. It may not be what the patient wants. It may not be what the doctor wants either. But that is where we are and because I would rather rely upon the professional discretion of my GP than the pusillanimity of a Parliament fearful of rocking the media boat, I do not think that a campaign is going to do anybody in my position any good.

Actually, I am hopeful. 'Beam us up, Asrael', as my friend, Geoffrey Hill, once, rather pithily, put it. Come the day, I am confident that Asrael, assisted, perhaps, by a couple of my friends, will beam me up to everybody's satisfaction. The debate about the ethics and dangers of assisted dying will no doubt rage on, long after I have disappeared. Good luck to them all, I say. Samuel Smiles had it right. I have a copy of *Self-Help* by my bedside table.

PS: To maintain domestic harmony, I should point out that the Woodhead household does not live on takeaways alone.

***

First published in *The Sunday Times,* June 2014

It is not yet 9 o'clock, but the sun is already warm on my face. There is that Mediterranean certainty of real heat to come. When I shut my eyes I can dream that I am standing on the rim of the Verdon Gorge in Haute Provence, wondering whether to spend the day spread-eagled on the tendon-popping verticality of the white limestone cliffs or swimming in the blue-green water of the river 2,000 feet below.

In fact, I am sitting in my wheelchair in what used to be a Herefordshire farmyard.

A red kite hangs motionless in the sky. There is a commotion in the open barn opposite me as swallows slice through the air to confront a magpie which has had the audacity to strut, backwards and forwards, arrogant and indifferent, on the floor beneath their nests. A poppy has appeared from nowhere, the pinkish red of its petals complementing perfectly the creamy yellow stamens. Teasels and daisies march in their profusion on our front door. Somewhere, in the distance, a cockerel crows.

The poppy in our courtyard.

There is an occasional whiff from the septic tank. A wasp circles my head malevolently. It is not Provence, and it is not Paradise. But there is nowhere I would rather be. It is as close to Eden as a quadriplegic is likely to get.

When, eight years ago, I was diagnosed with Motor Neurone Disease, I didn't think I would still be around in 2014. I remember my consultant saying that if there was anything I particularly wanted to do, it might be an idea to get on with it fairly quickly. Fifty per cent of people with MND die within fourteen months of the diagnosis; ninety per cent are dead within five years.

I don't, incidentally, think that my survival has anything to do with, in the words beloved of obituarists, my 'courageous struggle' with the illness.

It has been, like so much else in life, a matter of luck. Someone has decided that I deserve a little longer in the sun, or, depending on how you look at it, that the misery should be prolonged.

The historian, Tony Judt, who died of MND in 2010, compared his experience of the illness to being locked in a prison cell that shrank by an inch or two every week. It is a good analogy. But, actually, over the last couple of years, my physical condition has not changed very much.

I am more twisted in my wheelchair, and my head falls a little more grotesquely to one side. The hotel we use in London has mirrors in the lift: I make sure I keep my eyes tightly closed. I can no longer move the cursor about on the computer screen, but that's about it. The bad news for me came last autumn, when I was taken into the local hospital with a high temperature, to be told that I had colon cancer and, for good measure, some rather large stones in my left kidney.

When my eldest granddaughter came to visit me, she looked at me rather solemnly and remarked that I was in the wars and that it wasn't fair. Deep down I agreed with her. MND ought to be enough for one lifetime. But life isn't fair and it doesn't help to indulge in infantile fantasies that it should be. I have survived more scrapes than I care to remember in the mountains, and I walked away pretty well unscathed from a serious car crash. You can't be lucky all the time.

The main problem, it seemed, with the cancer and the kidney stones was whether I would survive the general anaesthetic. As far as I was concerned, there really wasn't a decision to make. I did not want to drag out the time I had left feeling as wretched as I was. If I recovered from the operations, then I would presumably feel better; if I didn't, then they could switch off the life support machine. I had a battery of tests and the doctors came to the conclusion that the risks were worth taking.

So the operations went ahead. They cut the cancer out and, mercifully, it hadn't spread. A month later, the kidney stones were despatched and, though that precipitated a few feverish days as infection flooded through me, all is for now well on that front too. Lady Luck had, once again, turned her kindly face upon me.

On 18 July, Lord Falconer's Assisted Dying Bill will have its second reading in Parliament. This Bill proposes that anyone who has a terminal illness, who is judged by two doctors to have less than six months to live, and who is mentally competent to determine the timing of their own death can be given life-ending medication to be self administered.

Falconer argues, rightly, that, because his Bill focuses so categorically on the terminally ill, it would not legalise assisted suicide. The elderly and the disabled, for example, are not included in his proposals. Neither would it legalise voluntary euthanasia, because the individual would have to self administer the medication. In other words, this is a small, very cautious attempt to clarify an area of the law which is currently opaque and which would give anyone in my situation a peace of mind which we do not at present have.

The latest survey conducted by the campaigning group, Dignity in Dying, shows that 80 per cent of the public believe that the law should be clarified in the way Falconer wants. Does this mean his Bill will be passed on the nod? No, far from it. There are those in both Houses of Parliament who believe that they have a moral duty to prolong my suffering to its perhaps imperfect palliative end.

What irritates me is the presumption. We all know intellectually that we are going to die. When the consultant sitting across the table has told you that in all probability you have not long to live, that your muscles will waste away and that breathing and swallowing may well become progressively more difficult, then the reality of that death has an emotional impact which nobody in good health can understand.

One opponent of the Bill has said that there is no need for the law to be changed because if the terminally ill wish to die more quickly than nature intends then they can starve and dehydrate themselves to death. I was told by a doctor that if I was to choose this way out then no medical assistance to alleviate my suffering would be offered to me.

It is an option that at some point I may have to choose to take. It is an option I considered last winter. I would prefer a swifter and more comfortable end. Who wouldn't? Why does anyone think they have the right to deny those who are terminally ill a peaceful and dignified exit? Or, what is equally important, the reassurance of knowing that there is a way out if the suffering becomes too great?

The argument, of course, is that the slope is slippery. The truth is that in Oregon, where an assisted death is legal, fewer than 80 people out of the 30,000 who died in 2013 asked a doctor to assist their end. I simply do not believe that people in the UK are more wicked than people in Oregon. I do not see how the safeguards that Falconer's Bill proposes could be easily overcome by anybody who wished to persuade a terminally ill person that they should die.

My suffering is not too great. The sun is still shining and the septic tank has stopped whiffing. The frame of my wheelchair is digging into my left shoulder blade and an insect has decided to crawl into my right ear. In other words, I'm struggling with life's usual little irritations. But I could be on the tube, or stuck at Heathrow, gazing morosely at the departures board, or, heaven forbid, making yet another appearance before the Education Select Committee.

I would love to climb once more in the Verdon Gorge and to eat again in the square at Castellane, the little town that nestles under a huge rock at the entrance to the gorge. But I can't. I never will. Instead, I have a mind well stocked with memories and the infinite beauty of my present surroundings.

I am neither depressed nor angry. I am not emotional in any way. I simply want reason to prevail when Lord Falconer's Bill has its second reading.

The swallows have returned. They are gathered in the sky and are swooping in and out of the barn. If birds can be angry, they are. Mr Magpie must be strutting his stuff.

***

Blog for *The Sunday Times*, a few weeks before his death in June 2015

Last Wednesday, *The Times* ran a leader, prompted by the death of Jeffrey Spector at the Dignitas Clinic in Switzerland, which argued that no change should be made to the law governing assisted dying.

Judging from the comments made on this leader, the majority of readers disagreed. I did, too. This sentence, in particular, stuck out for me: 'The risk of legalising assisted suicide is that it plants suicide as an option in the minds of more vulnerable people when it might not otherwise have existed'.

I wonder what evidence there is for this categoric assertion. More fundamentally, I wonder at the assumption that this 'risk', if it exists at all, should be enough to deny those who could benefit from a change to the law the opportunity to choose when they die.

A humane society does everything in its power to protect the vulnerable. But this imperative should not be absolute. I remember a conversation in 2009 with a senior Conservative politician. I suggested that it would be a good idea if a future Conservative government were to bring in a system of educational vouchers in which every parent had access to a sum of money equivalent to the cost of educating their child in a state school. They should, I argued, have the freedom to spend that money in a state or a private school, and, if the latter charged fees that exceeded the value of the voucher, they should be able to top up the voucher with their own money. The politician disagreed. He did not think that it was right to offer an opportunity to some parents which others, less concerned about the education their children received, might not take up.

It is the same argument as that used by the *Times* leader writer, and it does not seem to me to be very different from the old socialist belief that if everybody cannot have it nobody should have it.

I continue to think that the introduction of a voucher scheme would stimulate the supply side in education, thus encouraging competition amongst schools. Competition, in turn, would result in schools offering a better standard of education.

Given the state of my health, I am more interested these days in the assisted dying debate. It seems to me obvious that, if the law were to be changed along the lines Lord Falconer is proposing, sufficient safeguards could be built in to protect the vulnerable. Equally, I cannot see how anybody can really believe that the state should decide the timing of my death. But we live and we die in a society which has elevated its proper concern for the weak and the disadvantaged to a position where the needs and the rights of those who could benefit from a change in the law are brushed to one side.

Conclusion

Conclusion

Written in February 2015 and published in The Sunday Times *following his death in June 2015*

The day had dawned fine, but by the time Phil and I had started walking up the hill the sky was clouding over. We were heading for Clogwyn du'r Arddu, the great black cliff near the summit of Snowdon. I did not know it, but this was to be my last rock climb.

We left the tourist path, crossed the ridge and dropped down into the cwm, threading our way through the boulders until we reached the lake that lies at the foot of the cliff.

Over on the skyline, a seemingly endless troop of walkers were wending their way up the railway track to the Snowdon summit. Here in the cwm, there was nobody. We sat by the lake for a while, and then scrambled up the slope towards the start of the climb.

It was then that I started to worry. Phil, agile as ever, had gone on ahead. I found myself stuck on a greasy little slab of rock, worrying about whether my foot would slide off the hold and precipitate me back down the slope. 'Bloody hell', I thought, 'we haven't even reached the climb proper and I'm in trouble'. Phil chucked an end of the rope down and, secure in the knowledge that I wouldn't go anywhere, I swung up to the start of the first real climbing.

I won't dwell on the detail of what followed. This was a climb I had done four or five times already. That day, physically and psychologically, it was a nightmare. I lurched from hold to hold, desperate to try to make height before I ran out of strength. Rarely have I been so relieved to get to the top of a rock climb.

Scrambling down an easy route back to the lake, I couldn't see how to climb down an awkward ten foot wall of rock. I let myself drop onto the ledge beneath. My knees buckled, and I nearly went over the edge.

I should have thought, shouldn't I, that something was obviously not right? That something was that I had Motor Neurone Disease, and was about to start a long slide into more or less complete paralysis. But we human beings like to kid ourselves, don't we? The thought that something was seriously wrong didn't even cross my mind.

The penny began to drop a couple of months later. We were walking in Knoydart, that magical, inaccessible stretch of land that sticks out from mainland Scotland towards the Isle of Skye. Walking on defined paths was not too bad, but once we struck off through the heather, it was hopeless. Every five minutes I would lose my balance and fall over. I began to wonder.

Nine years on, I am still wondering. A week before Christine and I were to be married in Gwydir Castle in north Wales, my consultant told me that I had MND. She hedged the message with all sorts of caveats about more tests having to be done and not jumping to conclusions, but it was obvious what she thought. 'If there's anything you really want to do', she said in a low key matter-of-fact way, 'it might be a good idea to do it soon'.

Fifty per cent of MND patients die within fourteen months of diagnosis. Ninety per cent die within five years. I am lucky. My decline has been slow. It took a year or two before I had to use a stick. It was another year before I managed to topple backwards and smash my head on our slate floor. Then it was a manual wheelchair, with Christine hauling my not inconsiderable weight up hill and down dale. Now the wheelchair is motorised and zooms up and down to facilitate an often inglorious slide in and out of bed. We have survived thus far, and as far as the MND goes, if I can continue to cope with the frustrations of everyday living, there is a good chance that I will continue to survive, God willing, for a while yet.

It staggers me to say this, but actually the frustrations of everyday living are not any more the real issue. At first, as my body gave up on me and I lost the ability to feed myself or to clean my own teeth, to turn the pages of a book or, a recent development, to move the cursor about on the computer screen, I would find myself seething internally. What preoccupies me now is something more fundamental.

In the last months of his life, the painter, Roger Hilton, became obsessed with *King Lear*. He would lie on his dishevelled bed in his cottage at Botallack, near to Land's End, surrounded by overflowing ashtrays, half empty bottles of whisky and, as he once complained, empty jam jars of paint water which his neglectful wife had allowed the cats to drink. Through the long hours of sleepless nights he turned the pages of Shakespeare's play. I have not yet allowed a donkey into my bedroom to eat my cigarette ends, but I think I know what intrigued him.

Act III, scene IV: The mad Lear is braving the storm on the heath, accompanied by his loyal manservant, Kent, and Edgar disguised as poor Tom. 'Is man no more than this?' Lear asks. 'Thou art the thing itself', he tells the wretched Tom. 'Unaccommodated man is no more but such a poor, bare, forked animal as thou art'.

It is fifty-three years since I first read these lines. Sitting looking out over the school playing fields, I nodded sagely as we discussed their import and congratulated myself on my insight into the profundities of human existence.

Today, towards the end of my life, I wonder at the profundity of my ignorance, then and now.

What are we when the layers of the onion are peeled back? Why do we spend our lives in the pursuit of material gain? Why is the fog of self delusion so all encompassing? I try, these days, to avoid looking in the mirror. When I do, I see the 'poor, bare, forked animal'. A crumpled, twisted figure in a wheelchair, gazing dumbly at the floor because my neck will not hold up my head.

Does this mean that my life has been reduced to something contemptible and meaningless? Or, has the illness which has ravaged my body served me well in stripping away the irrelevance and pretension of my earlier life in order to allow some possibility of contemplating what is truly worthwhile? And, if the latter, what is this insight which glimmers out there in the dark?

Who knows? I am well aware that these questions are (how shall I put it?) barely pubescent. I do not have the answers, and neither, I suspect, does Stephen Hawking, or anybody else who, for whatever reason, has been reduced to my state. We do not know whether Lear died in a state of bliss, or from the shock of realising that Cordelia had been killed. Either way, his experiences on the heath had not led him to any cosmic insight into the nature of human existence. There are no answers. All we can do, as our greatest twentieth playwright put it, is 'fail again', and 'fail better'.

Hilton suffered from peripheral neuritis, and, propped up in bed on his left elbow, painted with his right hand until the pressure on the inflamed joint forced him to learn to paint with his left. He nonetheless continued to draw and paint until the stroke which killed him. He continued to poke and probe at the psychological weaknesses of the friends who came to visit him and he communicated with his wife through a series of nocturnal messages and drawings, which have been collected in the magnificent *Night Letters*. In private, in the small hours of the night, he no doubt experienced times of bleak depression, but the man who emerges from *Night Letters* has a volcanic energy and a driving, acerbic wit that is a lesson to us all in the triumph of human will over physical adversity.

I am back home now, after a trip to London earlier this week to see the latest in my long line of consultants. In late 2013, I was diagnosed with colon cancer, and, as a special treat for good behaviour, kidney stones. Two operations in the spring of last year went well. The kidney stones were excised and the tumour removed from my colon. I sat in the garden last summer feeling quite smug. That sense of having survived the storm disappeared when a routine scan revealed that the cancer had spread to my liver.

The disabled cab we had booked to take us from the hotel to the London hospital was late. I felt my frustration rising. Christine was instructed to phone the firm and reprimand them for their inefficiency. We were told that the cab was just four minutes away. Five, six, ten minutes passed. I was about to explode when a voice in my head told me not to be such a prat. Here I was, about to be examined by a specialist in his field and in a top hospital. Why, when so many other people in this world have to make do with inadequate or non existent health care, could I not appreciate my good luck, rather than rage about the petty nonsense of a late taxi?

We made it. I can't say that I enjoyed looking at the images of my liver with the tumours sitting there, blankly and malevolently cocking a snook. The upshot, though, was good. I would need to finish off the cycle of chemotherapy I have been having since the autumn and undergo some tests, but an operation might well be possible. There was still hope.

I fell half asleep on the motorway coming back, only to wake with a start when we pulled into the Warwick services. I had been dreaming about Ladhar Bheinn, a mountain in Knoydart which looks out towards the Cuillin Ridge on Skye, thinking of my many efforts to climb it. Rain, hail, wind and cloud had conspired on several occasions to drive us back down to Barrisdale and a boat which would ferry us across the black waters of Loch Hourne to the civilised delights of the Glenelg Inn. Then, one day, everything went right, and I shall never forget walking along the summit ridge to the trigpoint. We gazed out over the panorama which had opened in front of us, transfixed by the sparkling sea and the jagged irregularity of the Cuillin Mountains.

Hell, I thought, if I had my life again, I would live it differently. But then, we all think that, don't we? Youth, as they say, is wasted on the young. The truth is that memories like these are a blessed talisman to guide us through the blackness of the occasional dark night.

Maybe, to push the bounds of incredulity, some of my articles and speeches may have made a difference to the world of education. Maybe, even, some of the interminable hours I wasted in the Department for Education might have had a little impact on the development of national policy. Anyway, the past is the past and there is no point in wishing it to have been any different.

The light was fading as Christine manoeuvred the van down the lane which leads to our home. Clusters of snowdrops in the hedge winked at me, welcoming me back.

Biographical Details

20 Oct 1946	Born in Cockfosters, London
1952 to 1957	Attended Selsdon Primary School
1957 to 1964	Attended Wallington Boys' Grammar School
1965 to 1968	Studied English Literature at Bristol University
1968 to 1969	PGCE at Bristol University
1969 to 1972	First teaching post at Priory Boys' School, Shrewsbury
April 1970	First marriage – Cathy Woodhead (dissolved 1976)
1972 to 1974	Second teaching post at Newent School, Gloucestershire
1974	MA at Keele University
1974 to 1976	Third teaching post at Gordano School, Bristol
April 1975	Birth of daughter, Tamsin Lucy Woodhead
1976 to 1982	Lecturer in English and Education at Dept of Education, Oxford University
1982 to 1988	English Adviser, then Chief Adviser, Shropshire
1988 to 1990	Deputy Chief Education Officer in Devon, then Cornwall
1990 to 1993	Deputy, then Chief Executive, National Curriculum Council
1993 to 1994	Chief Executive, School Curriculum and Assessment Authority

1994 to 2000	Her Majesty's Chief Inspector of Schools in England
2000	Began career as education journalist, first with *The Sunday Telegraph*, then regular column with *The Sunday Times*
2004	Became founding Chairman of Cognita Schools Ltd.
2003	Established Education Department and began professorship at Buckingham University
Oct 2006	Second marriage – Christine Woodhead
2011	Received knighthood
2011	Received Hon Doctorate from University of Buckingham
2015	Died 23 June

Publications

1981	*Writing and Responding: a course for English Language examinations* (with Anne Miller and Pat O'Shea), OUP
1984	*Nineteenth and Twentieth Century Verse*, OUP
1992	*Curriculum Organisation and Classroom Practice in Primary Schools: A Discussion Paper* (written with R Alexander and J Rose)
2002	*Class War*, Little Brown
2009	*A Desolation of Learning*, Pencil-Sharp

[Other publications include annual lectures as HMCI and pamphlets for Politeia and the Centre for Policy Studies]